THE BOOK OF
SHAKESPEARIAN
USELESS
INFORMATION

M000166714

Bruce Montague trained at the RADA and, after seasons at Birmingham and Colchester reps, joined the Old Vic directed by Robert Helpmann. He appeared in several plays with Vivien Leigh, including *Twelfth Night*, in which he played Orsino to her Viola, and he supported her in *La Contessa*, her final English appearance. He is credited with nearly 300 TV shows and films, ranging from guest appearances in *The Saint* to *New Tricks*. He is best remembered for the BBC sitcom *Butterflies*, in which, as Leonard, he wooed Wendy Craig's Ria relentlessly for five years. In the satirical TV series *Whoops Apocalypse!* he portrayed the hapless Shah of Iran, and he has recently been a guest villain in several episodes of *Hollyoaks*. He played in Jerome Robbins's production of *Fiddler on the Roof* with Topol at the London Palladium, where he remained for a further three years to play Mr Brownlow in Sam Mendes's production of *Oliver!* He was the Manager, M. Firmin, for two years in *Phantom of the Opera* at Her Majesty's Theatre for Hal Prince. He starred in *Last of the Red-Hot Lovers* at the Strand Theatre, and more recently toured *42nd Street* for two years, directed by Mark Bramble. For Sir Peter Hall he was Juliet Mills's husband in *Bedroom Farce*. He spent 2016 at the Savoy Theatre playing Flo Ziegfeld in Harvey Fierstein's revision of the musical *Funny Girl*. He is the TV face of Stannah Stairlifts until 2020. As a writer, his latest books are *Wedding Bells and Chimney Sweeps* and *Birds, Bees and Educated Fleas*. *The Book of Shakespearian Useless Information* is published on 3 March 2016 to commemorate the quatercentenary of Shakespeare's death. Bruce has been married to the actress Barbara Latham for fifty-four years; they have two children and live in Brighton.

THE BOOK OF

SHAKESPEARIAN
USELESS
INFORMATION

WITH A FOREWORD BY TIM RICE

metro

Published by Metro Publishing,
an imprint of John Blake Publishing Ltd
3 Bramber Court, 2 Bramber Road,
London W14 9PB, England

www.johnblakebooks.com

www.facebook.com/johnblakebooks ⬛
twitter.com/jblakebooks ⬛

First published in hardback in 2016.

ISBN: 978-1-78418-990-7

British Library Cataloguing-in-Publication Data:

A catalogue record for this book is available from the British Library.

Design by www.envydesign.co.uk Printed in Great Britain by CPI Group (UK) Ltd

1 3 5 7 9 10 8 6 4 2

Papers used by John Blake Publishing are natural, recyclable products made
from wood grown in sustainable forests. The manufacturing processes conform
to the environmental regulations of the country of origin.

Every attempt has been made to contact the relevant copyright-holders, but some
were unobtainable. We would be grateful if the appropriate people could contact us.

FOR BARBARA

AND

FELLOW ACTORS

AND

ALL THEATRICAL NUTS

Contents

Brief Glossary

Latin abbreviations for money; Roman numerals

Money:
li = pound sterling (from Latin *libra*)
s = shilling (*solidus*)
d = pence (*denarius*)

Roman numerals:
i = 1 (ii = 2, iii = 3 etc.)
iv = 4 (i.e. 1 subtracted from 5)
v = 5
vi = 6 (vii = 7 etc.)
ix = 9 (i.e. 1 subtracted from 10)
x = 10
xi = 11 (xii = 12 etc.)
l = 50

xl = 40 (i.e. 10 subtracted from 50)

c = 100

These numerals may be repeated more than once, meaning a multiple of the amount: hence iii means 3. And a smaller figure before a larger means you subtract the lesser from the greater, meaning ix = 9.

Foreword

I am amazed that any man of the theatre, even one as distinguished
and experienced as Bruce Montague, could compile a book of
over 400 pages of vital information about William Shakespeare, let
alone one of useless information. But this is what the indefatigable Mr
Montague claims to have done.

On closer inspection it is quickly apparent that the information
contained within these tasteful covers is not really useless at all. I
suppose fans of the Bard have got by for over four centuries without
having access to all or even most of the facts herein, but 'useless' is
not the adjective that springs to mind when they are all so lovingly
assembled in one place.

I have myself ventured into the allegedly useless information
field when I co-authored a succession of books that were little more
than lists of hit records. These books were extremely successful,
not just because a lot of people like pop music, but because a lot

of people like lists. In a way Bruce's book is an upmarket list as fact after fact tumbles from the page, but so diverse and wide-ranging are they, that any feeling that this is a cold reference book is instantly dismissed.

Mr Montague demonstrates that facts need not be cold — that fact in itself is something that too many teachers of today ignore. I am so glad that I learned the dates of kings and queens, of wars, discoveries and inventions at an early age — the perfect framework for later appreciation of why or how people acted as they did. This work provides such a framework to our greatest literary figure for our better understanding of his life and work and times. And of course the final fifth of this sturdy tome consists of irresistible facts and figures of posthumous Bardolatry.

Almost as gripping as the Shakespeare info is Bruce's Epilogue, which tells of the foundation (accidental) of the Useless Information Society in the 1960s, whose chief inspiration was the late Keith Waterhouse. In an age when we are bombarded day and night by information, warnings, guidelines and (mainly half-witted) opinions, with the sole intention of bossing us around, it is a blessed relief to know that the spirit of technically inessential yet indisputably illuminating intelligence lives on, nowhere better than within these pages.

TIM RICE

Actus Primus

Scena Prima
Prologue

This book commemorates the 400th anniversary of William Shakespeare's death on 23 April 1616.

In 1966, on the 350th anniversary of Shakespeare's death, I was at the Theatre Royal, Windsor, under contract to the legendary producer, John Counsell. On learning that the Poetry Society occasionally paid me for contributions, Mr Counsell asked me to write a piece for his in-house magazine called *Curtain Up*. My effort resulted in a short, tongue-in-cheek obituary with the title 'All Swans are White (except the black ones)'. It meant something to me at the time. The article, demonstrating how, half a century ago, we pictured Shakespeare, is reproduced at the end of this book in Appendix H.

Since the days of Plato, formal debate normally opened with an incontestable premise. 'All swans are white' was one such hypothesis. Then, ten years before Shakespeare died, Willem Janzoon stumbled across Australia and discovered black swans!

Ah! Lackaday! Following this, all philosophical conclusions had to be reconsidered.

William was baptised on 26 April 1564 but his actual date of birth is unknown. The twenty-third is arbitrarily accepted because it conveniently coincides with St George's Day. Supposing William Shakespeare did have a party to celebrate his fifty-second birthday after which he became mortally ill, would he have perished on the same day? By 25 April he had been buried in the chancel of Holy Trinity Church, Stratford.

In the archives of the Folger Shakespeare Library, Washington DC, there is a diary written by John Ward – vicar of Stratford-upon-Avon from 1662 to 1681. Ward made notes of references passed on to him by people who knew Shakespeare. He mentions that William Shakespeare held his fifty-second birthday party at New Place in Stratford-upon-Avon and that '... Shakespeare, Drayton and Ben Jonson had a merry meeting, and it seems, drank too hard, for Shakespeare died of a feavour there contracted.'

Rev John Ward wrote on page 140 of his diary: 'I have heard that Mr Shakespeare was a natural wit, without any art at all; hee frequented the plays all his younger time, but in his elder days lived at Stratford, and supplied the stage with two plays every year and for itt had an allowance so large, that hee spent att the rate of 1,000 l [£]a year, as I have heard.' Written half a century after Shakespeare's death, anecdotes such as this seem to be the result of Chinese whispers. As recently as the 1950s, an income of one thousand pounds per year exceeded the aspirations of most working people in the UK. So are

any of the titbits handed down to us about Shakespeare worth the
paper they're written on?

There are over 14,000 books devoted to aspects of Shakespeare
in the British Library catalogue. The *Shakespeare Quarterly* logs around
4,000 new works every year, from monographs to tomes. Fresh books
continually arrive – largely conjectural.

Ralph Richardson wrote the preface for Marchette Chute's book,
Shakespeare of London, 1951: '...Do we want another book about
Shakespeare, in London or anywhere else? The lifeline of the master is very
faint indeed; we know it all by heart. Why trace it once again?' Two
paragraphs later, Sir Ralph added, 'One always makes a mistake when one
thinks that one knows all about everything, even when it comes to the few
simple facts that we think we know about the life of Shakespeare.'

In *All The World's A Stage* Ronald Harwood stated, 'There is no
point in trying to derive a playwright's views and personality from the
playwright's work.'

Historian A.L. Rowse, who strove to read Shakespeare's
character from his plays, made the following points: '... the historical
sense is important and chronological order essential. How could one
appreciate the work of Beethoven if one thought the last quartets
came before the early piano sonatas? ... Much of the nonsense that
has been written about William Shakespeare... comes from ignorance
of the Elizabethan age and its conditions.' (from A.L. Rowse,
Shakespeare the Man, 1973).

5

In New York, one of the bartenders who ministered to the needs of the writer O. Henry (1862–1910) was called John Hunter. Mr Hunter returned to England and, years later, became Poet Laureate under his real name of John Masefield. In one of his books entitled *William Shakespeare* he wrote: '... New Place, the house where Shakespeare died, was pulled down in the middle of the eighteenth century. For one museum the less let us be duly thankful.'

Twelve pages later he added: 'Legends are a stupid man's excuse for his want of understanding. They are not evidence. Setting aside the legends, the lies, the surmises and the imputations, several uninteresting things are certainly known about him.'

This book attempts to assemble some of the legends, the lies, the imputations and a lot of uncommon facts from the late Tudor and early Jacobean period, arranged in loose chronological order to establish William Shakespeare in his milieu. Your chronicler presumes that anyone bothering to pick up this tome shares with him – to quote George Bernard Shaw – 'a love of Bardolatry'.

BRUCE MONTAGUE, 2016

Scena Secunda

The Way
Things Were

The Internet provides 160 million pages referring to Shakespeare, and the number is growing. This book tries to avoid most of them.

In the fourteen years leading up to the birth of William Shakespeare in 1564, England managed to get through five monarchs.

First, tipping the scales at over 280 pounds (20 stone) was Henry VIII. Two weeks after he expired, his lead coffin exploded outside the chapel in Windsor and 'all the pavement of the church was with the fat and the corrupt and putrefied blood foully imbued.'

Jane Seymour died shortly after giving birth to Henry VIII's son. At the age of nine, Edward VI acceded to the throne. Having no mother to influence him, he was a chip off the old block and took on the task of heading the Church of England with enthusiasm. A sickly lad, Edward was careful to nominate his successor before meeting his maker at the age of fifteen. Lady Jane Grey was his choice because she was a Protestant as well as being his first cousin once removed. Unfortunately, she was soon removed permanently.

There were ructions in high places. Mary Tudor was the sole survivor of the union of Henry VIII and his first wife, Catherine of Aragon, whose other five babies (including three sons) all died within weeks of their births. Therefore, Mary had a far stronger claim to the throne than Jane. On the other hand, Mary was old school – a staunch Catholic.

The people of England were confused, particularly in Ipswich where both Lady Jane Grey and Mary Tudor were proclaimed to be queen within an hour of each other.

Lady Jane Grey edged into the lead and held on to the top job for nine days.

Mary Tudor marched into London and confined Jane Grey to the Tower of London. Seven months later, Lady Jane and her husband, Lord Guildford Dudley, were beheaded. Jane was just seventeen.

For the next five years Mary Tudor tried to steer England back to the Church of Rome, although her approach lacked subtlety. She signed orders sending over 280 religious dissenters to the execution block, earning her the sobriquet 'Bloody Mary'.

Mary Tudor (1516–58) (Bloody Mary) is sometimes confused with Mary Stuart (1542–87) (Mary, Queen of Scots). Mary Stuart's paternal grandmother was Henry VIII's sister, Margaret. This meant that Mary Stuart was somewhat low in the order of precedence, being merely a great-niece of Henry VIII. She was also nine years younger than Elizabeth Tudor who was waiting in the wings.

The marriage between Mary Tudor and Philip of Spain was not made in heaven and after nine months he returned to his mistress in Madrid. Mary was prone to phantom pregnancies. Five years later, still childless, she died of unknown causes.

In 1558 the crown was placed on the head of Elizabeth, the twenty-five-year-old daughter of Ann Boleyn. Following in her father's footsteps, Elizabeth forced the country back to Protestantism. Though widely referred to as 'the Virgin Queen', it was privately alleged that Robert Dudley was better informed.

Throughout Elizabeth's reign Catholics were looked upon as potential assassins and indeed, they were still plotting when she died forty-five years later. The Gunpowder Plot to blow up Parliament brought these anti-Protestant feelings to a head after James I ascended to the throne.

From 1581, failure to attend church on Sundays became a crime called 'recusancy'. Under the Act of Uniformity, the penalty was £20 per month – a fortune in those days. William's father, John Shakespeare, was fined on at least two occasions and was eventually pressured into paying up.

9

In the year of the Spanish Armada (1588) £45,000 was raised from recusants' fines to help subsidise Drake's sailors, who were not just hard pressed but many of whom were literally 'pressed' into service, by unscrupulous 'press gangs', who kidnapped them.

The Shakespeares were Catholics and when William came to man's estate (meaning when he reached manhood) he married into a Catholic family. Whether he ever embraced the new religion is a moot point. He avoided making an issue of it. For the first four decades of his life, he lived as a loyal subject of the Tudors.

How did the monarchic dynasty acquire the name of 'Tudor'? Following the death of Henry V, his widow Queen Catherine married a Welshman called Owain ap Maredudd ap Tewdwr. This was too much of a mouthful for the average Englishman to pronounce so it was anglicised to 'Tudor'.

Scena Tertia

A Green and Unpleasant Land

📖 The Romans founded London between AD 43 and 50.

📖 In AD 200 the Romans constructed a Great Wall round London, not so much to keep marauders out as to keep the inhabitants in. [See Appendix A]

📖 By the time of the Tudors, the Privy Council had control over everything that took place within the boundary of the city walls. The Mayor of London imposed hefty restrictions on theatre companies in the parts of London under his control. Outside the walls it was harder for central government to enforce the law.

📖 When Henry VIII dissolved the monasteries, their lands came under the control of the crown and were called 'Liberties'. James Burbage – carpenter, actor and the first theatrical entrepreneur –

chose a site just beyond the mayor's authority in 'the liberty of Holywell' of Finsbury Fields, the site of an abandoned monastery, on which to build the first permanent playhouse.

Elizabeth had direct authority over her Privy Council, the membership of which she personally appointed. During her forty-five years of rule there were only thirteen sessions of Parliament. The privileged aristocracy was at the apex of England's social structure, and continues to be so today.

Queen Elizabeth's coronation cost approximately £16,800. Today that would convert to several million.

Elizabeth was illegitimate in the eyes of Catholics, for they believed that Mary Stuart Queen of Scots, as the senior descendant of Henry VIII's elder sister, was the rightful queen. Throughout the early years of Elizabeth's reign, Catholics plotted to give the English crown to the Queen of the Scots, Mary Stuart.

When wind of Mary, Queen of Scots's scheme came to the ears of Queen Elizabeth she was less than pleased. On 1 February 1587, Mary Stuart's death warrant was signed and sealed.

A law was passed in 1547 to ensure that vagabonds were branded and imprisoned for two years. Escape was punishable by death or life enslavement. This draconian attitude to homelessness softened over time but even fifty years later no begging was permitted without a permit.

Travelling players were banned during Edward VI's short reign. It was not until 1559 that Elizabeth I granted permission for the revival of touring acting companies.

The word 'drama' comes from the Greek meaning 'action'.

The 1563 Act – known as the Statute of Artificers – gave the medieval guilds and their successors total control over young people apprenticed to a trade. A prospective apprentice needed to come from a family owning an estate with an income of at least forty shillings.

Acting companies were not organised as guilds and therefore did not require apprenticeships. However, boy actors could be indentured to those members of the company who happened to be attached to outside guilds.

Able-bodied workers ineligible for apprenticeships were expected to work in agriculture. Hence the word 'yokel' – someone tied to the yoke or a plough, as opposed to someone who practised a trade. Yokel means 'an ignorant rustic'.

The first time that the name of 'Shakespeare' (or its near approximation) appeared in English records was in 1248. The fellow referred to was William Sakspeer of the village of Clopton, which is little more than a mile north of Stratford-upon-Avon.

Scholars are uncertain as to the identity of William Shakespeare's great-grandfather. The choice has been narrowed to either Adam Shakespere of Baddsley Clinton or John Shakeschaffte of Balsall.

🕮 During Queen Elizabeth's reign, no more than four million people inhabited the British Isles.

🕮 At the time of Shakespeare's birth, London, with a population of about 170,000 people, was the biggest city in Europe.

🕮 In the year preceding Shakespeare's birth, one quarter of London's inhabitants died of the plague. Even so, forty years later, at the turn of the century, London's population had climbed to 200,000.

🕮 By the year 1600, 20,000 people visited the playhouses every week.

🕮 The second biggest town in England was Norwich, with a population of 15,000.

🕮 Nine hundred people lived in the small fishing village of Liverpool, which had Norwegian trade connections. The local dish was known as lobscouse stew – a precursor to Irish stew – made from beef and fish and onions. 'Lobscouse' became truncated to 'scouse' and the locals were known as 'scousers'.

🕮 In the Domesday Book, commissioned by William the Conqueror, Stratford was noted for having twenty-one 'villeins' (peasants, subjects to a lord of the manor) and 7 'bordarii' (the lowest rank of villeins, who were virtual slaves belonging to the local 'lord of the manor').

By the time Shakespeare was born, Stratford-upon-Avon had fewer than 2,000 inhabitants. There was still a lord of the manor. It was recorded that there were two-hundred-and-seventeen houses, four inns and well over a thousand elm trees. Owls were plentiful.

The word Avon is from the Celtic – *afon* – meaning river. Stratford is an elision of the Roman words for 'street' and 'crossing'. Stratford-upon-Avon means 'a street crossing over a river'.

To the north of Stratford there was the Forest of Arden. Shakespeare's mother was Mary Arden. The name 'Arden' derives from a Celtic word meaning wooded valley. In Europe, the word for The Ardennes – a region of extensive forests, rough terrain, rolling hills and ridges – stems from the same root.

To build the average house in those days, sixty to eighty trees had to be felled.

The ten main streets of Stratford were cobbled and barely wide enough to allow two wagons to pass each other.

Stratford possessed a gaol called 'the cage'. It also boasted a pillory, a ducking-stool, stocks and a whipping post.

The distance from Henley Street, Stratford-upon-Avon, to the Globe playhouse on the South Bank of London is 92.9 miles. It takes approximately thirty-one hours to walk this distance.

The royal palaces of Whitehall, Westminster Hall, Parliament House and Westminster Abbey (then known as the Abbey Church of St Peter) were two miles to the west of London – outside the city walls.

Queen Elizabeth's grandfather, Sir Geoffrey Boleyn (1406–63), originally a hatter, was buried in the church of St Lawrence Jewry in the Yard of the Guildhall, London. He had been a merchant and Lord Mayor. Elizabeth's popularity with Londoners stemmed to some extent from the fact that she came from the same common stock as the rest of them. It was declared that she was 'descended from citizens'.

In her later years, Elizabeth tended to leave her bosom uncovered, causing shocked comments among flustered foreign ambassadors. Other ladies, under the illusion that it would be bad form not to copy royal etiquette, developed dresses that allowed for a wide expanse of décolletage.

Elizabeth considered herself a paragon of cleanliness. Most people washed only occasionally because it was feared the plague might be carried in water. However, the queen is alleged to have declared that she bathed every three months, 'whether I need to or no.'

Water was brought to the City of London from springs in Islington and Bloomsbury. Wooden pipes were developed for the purpose. They were filthy and inefficient. Water carriers were commandeered from as far away as Hampstead in times of drought.

During Shakespeare's lifetime, England continued to use the old Julian calendar, resulting in the New Year beginning on Lady Day – 25 March. Many other continental countries switched to the Gregorian calendar in October 1582, but it was not introduced into England until 1752, when eleven days had to be erased in order to fit in with the rest of Europe.

The terms 'Mister' and 'Missus' were unknown. 'Mr' and 'Mrs' were the shortened versions of Master and Mistress. The next rank up on the ladder of gentility was 'gentleman' or 'gentlewoman'. Obtaining a coat of arms ensured this elevation. Shakespeare was determined to attain this status.

As a schoolboy, Shakespeare rose at dawn. Prayers were said before breakfast. Nuncheon (a light mid-morning snack) was taken at noon, followed by an hour's siesta. Work finished at 7.00 p.m. Nuncheon typically consisted of bread, cheese and beer. (The word derived from *noon* and *shench*, meaning cupful.)

Churches exerted great influence. Holidays were still 'holy days'.

The main London quays in the sixteenth century were at Queenshithe (near Blackfriars) and Billingsgate (east of London Bridge). The Thames was crammed with boats, dead animals and sewage. By all accounts, the smell was appalling.

Bubonic plague was sometimes referred to as the Black Death, due to discoloured 'buboes' in the groin and the skin of the victims turning black. Plague was an agonising killer causing vomiting, swollen tongue and excruciating headaches. In times of an outbreak, corpses littered the streets because there was nobody left to bury them. In winter time the disease disappeared when the fleas that spread the illness became dormant.

The cause of the plague was not pinpointed until 1897, when a Japanese researcher, Masanori Ogata, identified the bacterium *Yersinia pestis* carried in the blood of fleas. Rats, as hosts to fleas, were blamed for the outbreaks of plague. Fresh research 118 years later revealed further information.

After analysing nearly 8,000 outbreaks of plague, it was established that the creature responsible for hosting the fleas was actually the great gerbil, *Rhombomys opimus*. (Published in a paper as 'Proceedings of the National Academy of Sciences' – 2015.) Sustained periods of hot weather in Central Asia triggered growth in the population of these rabbit-sized gerbils. They migrated westward along the silk route from China. Warm, wet weather in the Far East led to outbreaks of plague in Europe at approximately fifteen-year intervals.

Constant visitations of the plague demoralised the population. They sought mutual comfort and consequently sexual promiscuity increased. Syphilis was rife. The cause of half the premature deaths in the towns was venereal disease.

It was alleged that most people did not disrobe to engage in sexual intercourse.

Everybody suffered from lice, both of the head and of the pubic variety. The population accepted this as a normal condition, as lice had been with them for centuries.

At the coronation of Henry IV in October 1399, Thomas Arundel, the archbishop, was about to lower the crown onto Henry's head when he became aware of the king's scalp heaving with lice. Arundel was so startled that he backed off in shock and dropped the symbolic gold coin, which rolled away into the aisle of Westminster Abbey. It has never been found.

Ditches were used as sewers. Houndsditch was so called because dead dogs were thrown into it. Horse manure, beggars and cut-throats littered the roughly-gravelled streets. London stank.

Kentish Town takes its name from a tributary of the River Caen that was used as a ditch. The words 'Caen Ditch' became corrupted over the years to 'Kentish'. The gypsy village that grew beside it was sardonically called a town.

'Wyk' is the Old English name for market. Aldwych is where the old market used to be before Covent Garden became established.

In 1393 King Richard II compelled landlords to erect signs outside their premises. The legislation stated: 'Whosoever shall brew ale in the town with intention of selling it must hang out a sign, otherwise he shall forfeit his ale.'

The purpose was to make alehouses easily visible to passing

inspectors – borough ale tasters – who would decide whether the quality of the ale was up to standard. John Shakespeare, William's father, became an official ale taster in 1556.

In Stratford-upon-Avon there was considerable trade in malt and farm produce. Traditional English ale was made solely from fermented malt. The practice of adding hops to produce beer, although introduced from the Netherlands in the early fifteenth century, was not to everybody's taste, causing an early 'Campaign for Real Malt'.

Malting is the process of converting barley or other cereal grains into malt for use in brewing, and takes place in a 'maltings', sometimes called a malthouse. Barley is the most commonly malted grain, in part because of its high enzyme content, though wheat, rye and oats are also used. On several occasions, Shakespeare's father was accused of hoarding malt.

Water was treated with suspicion. It carried something that induced amoebic dysentery. The staple drink of the populace was ale (a cloudy beer), or wine made from grapes, pressed by human feet (literally!). Hygiene was non-existent.

Aboard naval ships, rum and ale were eventually substituted for water. The regulations demanded that in hot weather seamen should drink eight pints per day. This resulted in a Catch-22 situation. They were in trouble if they drank less, but if they glugged 'one over the eight' they were deemed unfit for duty and due for a good flogging.

Even in more recent times, it was sometimes dangerous to drink water. In order to demonstrate that tap water in Paris was safe, the novelist Arnold Bennett (1867–1931) drank a glassful, despite the admonition of the garçon who served him. Within a week of returning to his London home, Bennett died of typhus.

The price of sugar rose from one shilling and fourpence per pound in 1586 to two shillings and twopence per pound by 1612.

The substance used to clean teeth consisted of a formula that had changed little since the age of the ancient Egyptians. Rock salt was crushed with pepper. Mint and dried iris flowers were added to this and mixed together to create a rough substance that people proceeded to rub over their teeth with rags or 'chew-sticks' (twigs with frayed ends). This process exacerbated bleeding gums.

The common people sweetened their food with honey because sugar was a scarce commodity, brought from the Far East. With the discovery of the Caribbean islands, sugar became more readily available but still too expensive for most of the population. Queen Elizabeth adored sweet food. She also enjoyed the recently imported tobacco, with the result that her teeth and those of her courtiers turned black. Despite the advice of Bishop Aylmer in 1578, she refused to have any teeth extracted. Lacking toothbrushes or viable toothpastes, the middle classes began painting their teeth black too, so that the possession of black teeth became fashionable as a sign of wealth. Everyone tried to keep up with the evil-smelling inner circle of the royal court.

🕱 Dye was expensive. To display their affluence, richer people wore black clothes when sitting for portraits.

🕱 The average wage of the 'working man' was one penny per hour. By the time Shakespeare died, this had risen to twelve pence per day.

🕱 It was considered essential for any respectable Elizabethan to wear gloves and a hat, and it was an absolute insult not to wear gloves in the royal presence.

🕱 John Shakespeare would have sold a fair, or good quality, pair of gloves for fourpence.

🕱 It was customary for men to carry daggers or rapiers. Apprentices carried knives. Ladies carried bodkins or long 'farthingale' pins for self-defence. It was *de rigueur* for a 'gentleman' to wear a sword. Once he secured his family's coat of arms in 1596, Shakespeare wore a sword as a matter of course.

🕱 The majority of people, being poor, considered acorns a delicacy. Pork from pigs fattened with acorns was considered to give a much better flavour (and still is).

🕱 By the time Shakespeare was born, houses were being built with chimneys, meaning that smoke no longer had to escape through a hole in the roof. Carpets were replacing reeds as floor coverings. Wooden platters were giving way to pewter dishes. In richer homes, glass was used for windows, mostly the sort of thick 'bottle' glass (incorporating circular textural shapes) that you could hardly see through, but it kept the draughts out and let some light in. Glass was an expensive luxury and, in the early stages of development, was produced by French '*gentilhommes verriers*', the only ones who knew the secret of making it.

Glass was so expensive that if you moved house, you took your lattice windows with you – these were also known as 'leaded light' windows, or 'lights', and were panels made up of small pieces of glass (it wasn't then possible to make large sheets) joined together by thin lengths of lead 'cames', which had an H-shaped cross section, in order to accommodate the glass edges. The majority of people could not afford glass windows and made do with strips of linen soaked in oil.

Regulations demanded that the wooden timber uprights of the ground floor walls of a Tudor house were placed nine inches apart. This was considered sufficiently narrow to prevent burglars from squeezing between the intervening filling of wattle-and-daub.

In 1578, Walter Raleigh introduced the virgin queen to the first 'Virginia' tobacco, referring to it as 'tobah'. He demonstrated how to smoke it using a pipe, the stem of which was more than six feet in length. Raleigh spread the rumour that tobacco acted as a deterrent to the plague, after which its popularity grew rapidly.

Because of the growing belief in the benefits of tobacco, there came a time when smoking was compulsory at Eton College, and boys were flogged if they failed to indulge.

In order to finance further expeditions to America, Walter Raleigh made a wager with Queen Elizabeth that he could calculate the weight of smoke. He placed two identical cigars on opposite sides of a pair of scales, lighting only one and making sure no ash fell. After the cigar had burnt itself out the difference in weight was declared to be the weight of the smoke given off. The queen financed Raleigh's next American adventure.

Potatoes were discovered by the Spanish in 1537 and arrived in England from Peru in 1588, introduced by one of Sir Walter Raleigh's navigators – Thomas Harriot. Potatoes were regarded with suspicion because the leaves of the potato plant resemble deadly nightshade, to which it is distantly related. Tomatoes continued to be thought of as poisonous until as late as the nineteenth century.

Parsnips made an appearance at that time, but at first they aroused suspicion, since it was rumoured that they could only be grown in excrement.

Queen Elizabeth took a liking to the newly discovered artichokes and ordered her master cook, Daniel Clarke, to grow them in a garden farm near Albany Street. This enterprise did not meet with much success. Today a pub called The Queen's Head and Artichoke stands near the original site.

In the sixteenth century, a person who survived into his or her fifties was considered old.

There are, on average, 2,671 lines in a Shakespearian play. Plays ran for less than two-and-a-half hours and were acted without intervals, so it is calculated that actors spoke considerably faster than they do now. Elizabethans were more attuned to the spoken word than the audiences of today.

Until about 1585, a horse and cart was the usual mode of transport. Packhorses and asses were ubiquitous.

Coaches were unknown in England until late in the sixteenth century. Roads built by the Romans, left unrepaired for a thousand years, had become too rough for coaches to traverse them. Even by the seventeenth century when 'Flying Coaches' were introduced, the journey from Edinburgh to London took ten days.

When Queen Elizabeth died in 1603 at Richmond Palace, a courier was dispatched to Edinburgh to inform King James of this. Changing horses every twenty miles, it took three days for the courier to reach his destination. Edinburgh is 400 miles from Richmond.

The word 'coach' is derived from the English pronunciation of the Hungarian town of Kocs, from whence coaches originated. Henry FitzAlan, nineteenth Earl of Arundel, had spent time on the Continent as an emissary of Henry VIII, and brought a coach back with him to England.

The journey from London to Stratford took four days on foot or two days on horseback. A convenient stopover was The Crown Tavern at No 3 Cornmarket Street, Oxford, owned by John and Jennet Davenant. This became a favourite overnight stop for William Shakespeare at the turn of the century. In years to come, the Davenants were to feature prominently in Shakespeare's life.

In 1548, *The Union of the Two Noble and Illustre Families of Lancaster and York* by the lawyer Edward Hall (1497–1547) was published posthumously. Shakespeare used this as a principle source for his plays that were based on history.

In Rome, until AD 500, the Colosseum amphitheatre staged battles between gladiators in front of 35,000 people. By contrast, the original London Globe playhouse had a capacity of 3,000.

Abutting the north-west walls of the Fleet prison – on the north of Ludgate Hill – stood a tavern called The Bell, founded in 1420. One of its landlords was called Savage, and by 1580 it became known as the Bel Savage Inn. It provided entertainment in the forms of fencing, 'interludes' and bear-baiting. In particular, it became notable as one of the first London tour-venues for theatrical companies.

Church bells did more than mark the hours. The 'little bell' summoned the boys to school in the morning. The 'great bell' tolled the knell of passing day to mark the curfew. (No-one under the age of twenty-three was allowed on the streets after dark.) It cost ninepence for the bells to ring at a funeral. The great tolling bells in London were far more expensive.

There were over one hundred churches in the City of London.

It was common practice for urban houses to open their upstairs windows and chuck the contents of chamber pots into the street, preceded by the shouted warning – if you were lucky – of *'regardez l'eau'* corrupted over time to *'gardez loo'*. It was not a good age to be deaf. This is the derivation of today's term 'loo' meaning a WC. In the middle of the streets ran 'kennels' – open drains along which sluiced the detritus of chamber pots, animal droppings and all manner of dead creatures.

Until 1604 'Sumptuary Laws' were in place. These laid down the law as to the amount and type of clothing a person was permitted to wear according to their rank or annual income. The reason for these laws was to restrict the amount of imported fabrics, the idea being to bolster and support home production of these. Knights of the Garter and their peers were the only class permitted to wear blue or crimson velvet. Persons with annual incomes of less than £20 were not allowed to wear gowns made of satin, although a blind eye was turned when a satin doublet was worn.

Serious crimes were punishable by death. Citizens from the lower social orders were hanged. The privilege of being beheaded was reserved for the wealthy.

Tudor children played with wooden dolls called 'Bartholomew babies', so named because they were sold at St Bartholomew's Fair in London.

On page 50 of her book *Shakespeare of London*, Marchette Chute writes, 'There were no printing presses at Stratford. There were none anywhere in England, except the fifty-three in London and one each, carefully licensed, at Oxford and Cambridge.'

A 'noble' was a gold coin that was originally worth the equivalent of six shillings and eight pence. Later, when its value rose to eight shillings and four pence, yet another coin was introduced to replace it. This new coin was called the 'angel' with, confusingly, a value of six shillings and eight pence. Someone thought it would be a good idea to have ten-shilling coins too, which were called 'royals'. Shakespeare sometimes used coins in a punning way. For example, in *Henry IV Pt 1*, Prince Hal says, 'Give him as much as will make him a Royal man, and send him back to my mother.' The audiences had to be quick on the uptake to appreciate this type of humour.

Sometimes there were as few as six actors in a touring company. By the 1590s the numbers increased to fourteen or fifteen yet there was always a requirement for doubling. Actors were accustomed to play several parts.

By the end of the sixteenth century, the producer Phillip Henslowe hired jobbing actors (outside of the permanent company) for ten shillings a week in London. However, on tour he paid only five shillings per week. (Proportionally, little has changed in four hundred years.)

To differentiate between characters, actors frequently changed their stage hats. This had the added advantage of concealing the string bow on top of the head that tied on the quick changes of beard. Spirit gum was not invented for theatrical use until the middle of the nineteenth century.

Before the London playhouses were erected, acting companies on tour round the country nearly always set up their stages in the courtyards of local inns. In Stratford, during Shakespeare's youth, there were four inns large enough to stage shows.

London was just another town on the theatrical touring circuit until 1577, when the playhouse called 'The Theatre' was erected. Performances always took place in daylight hours.

To confuse things, open-air theatres were called 'playhouses' and indoor theatres were called 'theatres'. Indoor theatres with adult performers did not materialise until the turn of the century (circa 1600).

Many words have changed their meaning over the years. 'The stands' or 'standings' usually described theatre galleries. 'A scaffold' could mean either the stage itself or the gallery above. 'Degrees' referred to tiered-seating.

Elizabethan plays evolved out of Bible stories and were expected to continue presenting moral maxims – in particular, the triumph of good over evil. 'Miracle' or 'Mystery' plays went out of fashion at the start of the Protestant Reformation in 1532. The 'Chester plays'

29

survived a little longer; these were tolerated because they lacked specific Catholic sentiment, however even these productions petered out after 1575.

Anyone travelling around England without credentials was designated 'a Vagabond' and subject to imprisonment. To avoid falling into this trap, acting companies licensed their personnel according to the appropriate Act of Parliament. To be doubly safe, the companies sought the patronage of titled people. Theatrical troupes then called themselves 'The Earl of Leicester's Men', or 'The Earl of Warwick's Men', or 'The Earl of Worcester's Men', and so on.

Beverages such as tea, coffee and chocolate had been heard of but did not reach the shores of England during Shakespeare's lifetime. (See Appendix F.)

Astrologers were consulted on anything considered important: for example, to ascertain the best day to open a theatre or when to set off on a journey. The three witches in the play *Macbeth*, divining the future, would not have been considered particularly weird. James 1 believed in witchcraft and wrote books on the subject.

Tudor women did not wear knickers. Sometimes they wore men's breeches under their dresses. Most people changed clothes only when the dirt or the smell became intolerable.

The chief object of alchemy was the transformation of base metals into gold. Throughout her reign, Queen Elizabeth gave alchemy serious consideration. She believed the philosopher's stone (which could reputedly do the above) would be discovered and that the occult arts could extend the human lifespan and uncover a universal cure for disease.

Traditionally, it was believed there were four basic elements: earth, fire, water and air. Each was considered to represent a different quality of the universe: dry, hot, moist, cold. Humans possessed these qualities in varying degrees, lending him or her a disposition in proportion to the percentage of each element. Hence Jonson's play, *Every Man in His Humour*.

The word 'humour' was used many times by Shakespeare in relation to character. It did not develop its modern association with 'fun and laughter' until the late seventeenth century. In Sonnet 91 he wrote:

Every humour hath his adjunct pleasure,
Wherein it finds a joy above the rest.

A rush of blood to the head created a sanguine temperament, yellow bile produced an irascible quality, phlegm was indicative of a phlegmatic temperament and black bile signified melancholy. Shakespeare's writings are infused with such theories, for instance: melancholy controlled by Saturn, a 'phlegmatic state' controlled by the moon, a 'choleric temperament' controlled by Mars and sanguinity being under the influence of Jupiter.

In *The Taming of the Shrew*, Petruchio says, 'I'll curb her mad and headstrong humor.'
And:

I tell thee, Kate, 'twas burnt and dried away,

And I expressly am forbid to touch it;

For it engenders choler, planteth anger,

And 'twere better that both of us did fast,

Since of ourselves, ourselves are choleric,

Than feed it with such overroasted flesh.

In *Henry VI, Part 2*:
'What, what, my lord? are you so choleric/With Eleanor, for telling but her dream?'

In *Hamlet*, Ophelia is overwhelmed by her isolation at court, her overbearing father and Hamlet's dismissiveness. She displays the classic symptoms of melancholy.

In *Love's Labour's Lost*: 'So it is, besieged with sable-coloured/ Melancholy, I did commend the black oppressing humour/To the most wholesome physic of thy health...' (Ferdinand – Act 1 Sc 1)

In *The Comedy of Errors*: 'When I am dull with care and melancholy,/ Lightens my humour with his merry jests.' (Antipholus of Syracuse – Act 1 Sc 2)

Prince Hal in *Henry IV, Part 1*: 'I know you all and will awhile uphold/The unyoked humour of your idleness.'

A final example from *The Taming of The Shrew*: 'Heaven cease this idle humour in your honour!'(The Lord – Scene 2 of Induction)

Tudor beams were rarely stained black in the manner to which we are today accustomed. Beams were either maintained in their original wooden timbre or whitewashed. Wooden posts in playhouses were often painted to resemble Italian marble.

In his plays, Shakespeare made reference to at least one hundred and eight garden plants and over sixty species of bird. He named eight varieties of rose and six varieties of apple.

The word 'donkey' was pronounced to rhyme with monkey, the donkey being 'dun' coloured.

Many words were pronounced differently in Tudor times, for example, 'July' rhymed with 'duly' (July being a shortened version of Julius).

There were no rules for spelling in written English. People wrote language as they heard it or as they imagined it should be heard.

Philip Henslowe, father-in-law of the actor Edward Alleyn, used no punctuation at all.

In Shakespeare's youth, the names of several Welshmen appeared in Stratford's records: Ap Roberts, Ap Rice, Ap Williams, Ap Edwards, Hugh ap Shon, Howel ap Howell, Evans Rice, Evans Meredith, and others: 'Ap' means 'son of' in Welsh.

'Dad', the Welsh word for father, was used only once by Shakespeare.

The Elizabethans' idea of fashionable couture was a smooth, unbroken fit with the clothes curved with whalebone or padded with buckram. Both sexes strove for narrow waists, flaring hips and broad shoulders. Men often wore corsets to achieve the desired effect. Women's costumes were complicated because of the use of pins. Various sections of costume were detachable so that different colour combinations could be displayed. The pins were called 'great farthingale pins', 'middle farthingale pins' and so on according to the area of costume to be held together. Hooks and eyes were available but costumiers relied heavily on pins, costing a penny per hundred.

The farthingale was a hoop skirt originally stiffened with the bones of the subtropical giant crane bird. The word derives from the Spanish *vertugardo*. It became popular in French court circles and was introduced into England in the late 1570s. The Great farthingale; 'low before and high behind', came into vogue in the 1590s.

Ruffs began to grow in size towards the end of the sixteenth century. The bigger the ruff, the bigger the social standing of the wearer. In Shakespeare's plays even prostitutes wouldn't be seen without a ruff. The larger the ruff the more underpinning was needed, requiring wire and pasteboard. A contemporary remarked 'every day worser and worser.'

All women wore hats. The poorest women wore a linen hat called a coif. Rich women wore ostrich feathers in their bonnets.

Playhouses spent lavishly on silk flags to fly from the roofs. Accounts note flags costing upwards of thirty shillings. To announce the imminent start of an afternoon's entertainment, the playhouse would hoist its flags while a trumpet would be blown on three separate occasions. An echo of this can still be heard in theatres to this day. A bell is usually rung three minutes before 'curtain up'. A minute later, it is rung again. Finally, there comes the one-minute warning, the last bell to summon patrons to their seats.

Each playhouse had its individual logo. For example, the Globe displayed a big sign depicting Atlas weighed down with the world on his shoulders.

Beyond the city wall to the eastern bank of the River Fleet was a stretch of pasturage known as Smoothe Field. As its name suggests, the flat ground made it an ideal spot for jousting and duels. Between the horsepond and Turnmill Brook was a grove of elm trees where public executions took place until Henry IV's reign, when death sentences started to be carried out at Tyburn (now Marble Arch). Smoothe Field became corrupted to the name we use today: Smithfield.

Scena Quarta

Kith and Kin

🕮 1417

The name of Shakespeare was first recorded in Wroxhall, fourteen miles north of Stratford. Some academics suggest the origin of the name 'Shakespeare' was formed from Sigisbert, or from Jacques Pierre.

🕮 1490

William Shakespeare's grandfather, Richard Shakespeare, was a husbandman farmer. He leased farms in Snitterfield, seven miles north of Stratford-upon-Avon, from Robert Arden, the father of Mary Arden, who was to be the great poet's mother. Richard lived to the age of seventy-one and died in 1561. He left an estate valued at £38.17s (shillings; £38.85 in today's money) at a time when a house could be bought for £40.

In the 1520s, Richard Shakespeare took on the lease of another 80-acre plot of land on the corner of Bell Lane that bordered Snitterfield Brook.

1522

Mary Boleyn began an affair with the king. Twelve days before the recorded birth of Henry Carey, Henry VIII made a royal grant of land, including the borough of Buckingham, to Mary Boleyn's husband, William Carey 'in tail male' (meaning it could subsequently be inherited through the male ancestral line).

1526

4 March: Mary Boleyn gave birth to a male child said to be the king's son (he was named Henry Carey, and became Lord Hunsdon).

The Sub-Prioress of the nunnery at Wroxhall was called Jane Shakespeare.

1529–30

John Shakespeare (William's father) was born at about this time.

A tod of wool weighed 28 pounds and cost fourteen shillings. A glover bought fleeces, using the hides for their leather and in theory, he handed back the wool to the farmer. It was not in the glover's remit to sell wool. If he had wool to spare and he did sell it on, strictly speaking this was against the law.

1534

Parliament passed the Act of Supremacy, making Henry VIII supreme head of the Church of England and Wales, while Ireland was still a foreign state.

1535

20 April: The vicar of Isleworth, John Hale, stated to the council that he had seen the nine-year-old Henry Carey, and identified him as the king's son.

4 May: John Hale was executed at Tyburn 'for denying the King's supremacy,' (meaning for belittling the king by suggesting he had fathered an illegitimate child).

1536–40

Henry VIII ordered that 625 monasteries, priories, convents and friaries in England, Wales and the English colony in Ireland should be disbanded. Following the Dissolution, Catholics either had to renounce the Papacy and comply with the new religion or risk being arrested for treason, with its inevitable death sentence.

1540

Shakespeare's mother, Mary Arden, was born. She was the daughter of Robert Arden and Mary Webb – the second daughter of Sir John Alexander Webb who had died in 1516. Mary Arden was the youngest of eight daughters. On his death, Robert Arden's inventory included eight oxen, two bullocks and seven cows.

1544

At the age of fourteen, John Shakespeare, William's father, moved to the nearby town of Stratford, where he was indentured for seven years to Thomas Dixon and apprenticed to become a glover. He was to specialise in using white leather to make these items. Such specialists were known as 'whittawers'. The Glovers, Whittawers and Collar Makers Company required the protection of a guild.

Tom Dixon's wife came from Snitterfield. As well as being a master glover, Dixon was the innkeeper of The Swan at the bottom of Bridge Street. Stratford still has an inn, The White Swan, known affectionately to thirsty thespians as The Dirty Duck.

Nearby there were two other inns, The Bear and The Angel.

John's brother, Henry Shakespeare, remained in Snitterfield as a farmer. Uncle Henry had a hard nose for business and a reputation for barely managing to keep one step ahead of the law. He survived into his eighties, a grand age for those times.

1547

29 September: Miguel de Cervantes was born in Madrid, Spain. Cervantes became famous for his creation, *Don Quixote*. In 1612, the first part of this book was translated into English and printed. In what was to be his last work before he retired, Shakespeare had a hand in adapting *Don Quixote* for the stage, calling the play *Cardenio*. Sadly, the manuscript has been lost.

Two houses away from Shakespeare's Henley Street cottage, the blacksmith, Richard Hornby, set up his forge by the stream.

Opposite the Shakespeares lived two families of shepherds: the Coxes and the Davieses.

By 1550, the Portuguese and Dutch colonists established over 3,000 sugar mills in Brazil, Surinam and the islands of the West Indies. Trading posts on the Pomeroon River in the north of South America exported demerara sugar cane to Europe in unprecedented quantities. This did not bode well for people's teeth.

1548

In February the Bishop of Worcester ordered the removal of all images from the walls of the Holy Trinity Church, Stratford, in accordance with the anti-Catholic drive. The response was distinctly sluggish.

1552

Having served his apprenticeship, John Shakespeare was officially registered as one of twenty-three glovers in Stratford-upon-Avon. He traded illegally in wool and also made malt. Wool was a valuable commodity. There were by-laws to promote the sale of woollen goods. To boost the wool industry, woollen caps had to be worn on Sundays. Corpses had to be wrapped in woollen shrouds.

There were sixty-seven brewing households in Stratford.

As a glover, John was obliged to hang a sign outside his Henley Street house, part of which he converted into a shop. The appropriate symbol was a pair of glover's compasses.

The Guild of the Worshipful Company of Glovers of London was formed in 1349. At its inception an ordinance was issued forbidding the sale of gloves at night because 'folks cannot have such good knowledge by candle-light as by day-light, whether the wares are made of good leather or of bad, or whether they are well and lawfully or falsely made, on pain of forfeiting to the use of the Chamber the wares so sold by candle-light.'

John Shakespeare is first mentioned in the records for 'making a muckhill at chamber's door.' He was fined twelve pence for establishing a refuse heap near the houses rather than at the end of the street. This was the equivalent of two days' wages to a manual labourer. Stratford-upon-Avon had four or five official dumping grounds.

1553

Stratford Town Trust initially derived its income from the properties and funds of two charities, the Guild and College estates. Both institutions were suppressed at the Reformation and their property confiscated by the Crown. This ended the 'welfare provision' and caused a breakdown in local government.

The townspeople of Stratford petitioned for a charter so that they could exercise a measure of local government control. Edward VI granted the Royal Charter on 25 June, just nine days before his death at the age of sixteen.

The Royal Charter established the first Stratford Corporation and transferred to it much of the property of the former Guild and College with specific responsibilities to provide a school, maintain the almshouses and pay the vicar.

The school was known as the new King's Grammar School, the king being the late Edward VI. The schoolmaster was entitled to £20 per year, out of which he had to provide an usher for the lower grammar school – that is for the 'petite' children under seven years of age (known as the petty school).

The fourteen officers on Stratford Council now called themselves Aldermen. The ruling body of the local church was replaced by two chamberlains and four constables. The new statutes laid down that there was to be an annual election of a 'bailiff (e.g. mayor), serjeants at the mace, constables and such other officers as might prove necessary.'

Although Stratford was granted a corporate charter, there was an anomaly in this part of Warwickshire because it retained a few features of an ancient manorial borough, meaning it had a 'Lord of the Manor'. By the turn of the century, this was Sir Edward Greville, a grasping and aggressive man whose 'heavies' made themselves known both in London and in Stratford. It will become clear later that Shakespeare's younger brother seems to have conspired with them at one point. However, at an even later stage, when Greville tried to 'enclose' the common land, Shakespeare himself threw his weight against him.

No householder was allowed to accommodate a lodger in his home without permission of the bailiff.

There was a nine p.m. curfew for anyone under the age of twenty-three.

The penalty for slander or disobeying a local by-law was three days and nights in the stocks.

The punishment for a woman found guilty of murdering her husband was death at the stake, although it was common practice for the executioner to strangle the woman before burning her. The penalty for a man who murdered his wife was hanging.

1554

John Lyly was born in Kent and educated at Oxford. He became an MP and coined the expression, 'All is fair in love and war'. His witty and mannered literary style acquired the name – euphuism, after his books: *Euphues: The Anatomy of Wit* and *Euphues and His England*. His ambition was to take over as Master of the Revels from Mr Tilney, but this never came to pass. As a dramatist and poet, he was one of Shakespeare's rivals. His grandfather was William Lyly, who wrote the Latin textbook studied by Shakespeare at school. John Lyly died in 1606.

1555

Watermen or wherrymen used a small boat called a wherry or skiff to ferry passengers along and across the rivers. With bad rural roads the Thames was the most convenient highway in London. Until the middle of the eighteenth century London Bridge was the only one below Kingston. (Kingston is so called because the sacred stone on which the early kings of England were crowned happened to be there).

An Act of Parliament formalised the wherry trade by setting up a company with jurisdiction over all watermen plying between Windsor (in Berkshire) and Gravesend (in Kent). The act empowered the London mayor and aldermen to make and enforce regulations. A seven-year apprenticeship was compulsory to gain an encyclopaedic knowledge of the complex currents and tides on the Thames. Wherrymen had to pay quarterly contributions to the Guild of Watermen and Lightermen, causing constant grievance with company rulers who were frequently accused of taking bribes to 'free' apprentice watermen.

Most wherrymen were retired sailors. By all accounts, their language was 'fruity'.

1556

Shakespeare's maternal grandfather, Robert Arden died. His daughter, Mary Arden, was one of her father's executors.

25 July: birth of George Peele, an English dramatist, with a reputation for dissipation. Being a product of Oxford University he resented Shakespeare's success, because the latter only attended a grammar school. He died in 1596.

It is generally agreed that this was the year in which Anne Hathaway was born at Hewlands Farm in the village of Shottery near Stratford. Her name was actually Agnes but in those days the 'g' was silent. Her birthplace can be visited today. It is known as 'Anne Hathaway's Cottage'.

Full-size replicas of Anne Hathaway's cottage have been built in Bedfordale, Western Australia, and Victoria, British Columbia, at Odessa College, Texas and at Staunton, Virginia.

William Shakespeare's uncle and auntie, Edmund and Joan Lambert, lived in Barton-on-the-Heath.

2 October: John Shakespeare bought the adjacent property to his home in Henley Street from Edward West and knocked the two houses into one. The ground rent was sixpence per year, paid to the Earl of Warwick who at the time was the ultimate Lord of the Manor of Stratford. The eastern wing of the house is traditionally referred to as the birthplace of William Shakespeare.

3 October: John Shakespeare was sworn in as one of the two chamberlains in charge of borough property and finances. His duties included being the official ale taster. It was a tough life but somebody had to do it.

Late October: John went on to purchase a tenement, including its garden, in neighbouring Greenhill Street.

John Shakespeare and his wife Mary both owned signet rings, used to press into a wax seal on documents or letters to produce a designed impression, as a way of identifying themselves, which was an alternative to writing a signature using a pen. John's impression bore his initials. Mary's was of a cantering horse.

December: Mary Arden's father died. She inherited the family's farm, which survives to this day in Wilmcote, Warwickshire. It is called Mary Arden's House. The Ardens traced their ancestry back to before the Norman Conquest. Mary gave birth to eight children, five of whom survived childhood. On his mother's side, William Shakespeare was descended from an ancient, well-to-do lineage.

1557

December: Mary Tudor ('Bloody Mary') was the reigning monarch. Therefore, John Shakespeare married Mary Arden in a Catholic ceremony. She was the daughter of his father's former landlord in Snitterfield. John was twenty-six and Mary was seventeen. She had six older sisters, later to become William's aunts. Mary's father possessed over one hundred-and-fifty acres of farmland in Wilmcote, three miles from Stratford. In fact, he was the largest landowner in the district.

1558

At the age of twenty-nine, John Shakespeare was appointed as one of four constables supervising the night watch in Stratford whilst retaining the day job: ale tasting.

11 July: The baptism of Robert Greene in Norwich. His academic results at St John's College, Cambridge were underwhelming. He became an industrious writer and lived a dissolute life in London. Aged thirty-four, following a lavish banquet where the diners included Thomas Nashe, he fell sick 'of a surfeit of pickle herringe and Rennish wine' and died on 3 September 1592. Overindulgence appears to have been an occupational hazard amongst the writing fraternity.

15 September: The first child of John and Mary Shakespeare was baptised and named Joan but she survived only two months and died in November.

6 November: Thomas Kyd was born in London. He was a grammar-school boy and remained a confirmed bachelor like his friend, Christopher Marlowe. He wrote a successful play called *The Spanish Tragedy*, and it has been suggested that Kyd wrote the first version of *Hamlet*. At the age of thirty-five, he was imprisoned by the Queen's Privy Council following a search of his lodgings that revealed: 'vile heretical conceits denying the eternal deity of Jesus Christ found amongst the papers of Thos. Kydd, prisoner, which he affirmeth he had from C. Marley' (meaning Marlowe). It is believed that Kyd was tortured to obtain this information. He died on 15 August 1594.

17 November: Queen Mary, popularly known as 'Bloody Mary', died.

Elizabeth I became queen and religion in England reverted to Protestantism. Up and down the country, churches and their congregations wrapped up their candlesticks and tucked them into hidey-holes.

1559

16 January: A Sunday. Coronation day. Catholics declared Elizabeth I to be illegitimate, as she was the daughter of Anne Boleyn. Elizabeth was a staunch Protestant, and the twenty-fifth sovereign of England, Wales and Ireland, although her authority in the Emerald Isle extended

only as far as 'The Pale' – a staked fence stretching from Dalkey, south of Dublin, to Dundalk.

The expression 'beyond the pale' meant you had strayed beyond the boundaries of the kingdom and therefore beyond protection.

The Earl of Worcester, a Catholic, carried the third sword in the coronation ceremony. He was patron of a company of actors that played at Stratford when Shakespeare's father was bailiff.

On the accession of Elizabeth, her first cousin (and probably, in fact, half-brother) Henry Carey was created Baron Hunsdon of Hunsdon, in the county of Hertfordshire. There was no other Lord Carey so the fact that he was not created Baron Carey, as would be expected, was unusual and highly suggestive. This was as near as an official acknowledgement that Henry Carey, Lord Hunsdon, was indeed the illegitimate son of Henry VIII.

Church attendance was made compulsory under the Act of Uniformity. The penalty for non-compliance was a fine of up to £20 per month – an astronomical sum at the time.

All public figures had to kneel and swear an oath of allegiance to Elizabeth I.

George Chapman was born in Hitchin (Hertfordshire). Without benefit of a university education, he was bright enough to be selected as an assistant to one of the English commissioners, Rt. Hon. Sir Rafe Sadler – the other commissioners were the Duke of Norfolk and the Earl of Sussex. Their commission was to guard and examine Mary

Queen of Scots. Chapman did not advance in this appointment and instead he became a dramatist, working for Philip Henslowe. Forty-five years later, in collaboration with Ben Jonson, he wrote *Eastward Ho!* (1605), a play that scoffed at the influx of inebriated Scotsmen flocking into London with the accession of James I. This production failed to amuse the court and resulted in a jail sentence for the authors.

Among George Chapman's successes were two plays called *The Fatal Love* and *A Yorkshire Gentlewoman and her Son*. No copies exist because of a tragic story that took place in 1720 when John Warburton was the Somerset Herald in the College of Arms. He collected old manuscripts and happened to be a heavy drinker. One day, he went into the kitchen for a dram and left a pile of dramas on the table. On his departure, his cook, Betsy Baker, assumed that the papers had been left behind for her to light the stove. Weeks later, when Warburton recollected where he had left the manuscripts, he revisited the kitchen to discover that Betsy had burnt at least fifty unique works, including the George Chapman plays and at least three other unpublished plays by Shakespeare [see the Year 1720 for more detail].

John Shakespeare was appointed by the courts as 'affeeror', who was a person who decided what fines should be paid for minor misdemeanours. No doubt he took on this onerous task trusting it would not interfere with his other job of ale-tasting.

1560

13 October: Anthony Munday was baptised. He became such a successful playwright that Ben Jonson gave him the accolade, 'poet to the city'. At the age of twenty-six, Munday dedicated a work to the

patron, Edward de Vere, seventeenth Earl of Oxford, and because of this it is assumed that Munday was one of his actors. He also wrote the play *Fidele and Fortunatus* in which Robin Hood and his Merry Men feature. Success did not last. He ended up as a draper and died on 10 August 1633.

William Perrott owned the King's House Inn in Stratford-upon-Avon. For 'the Oak Room' he commissioned a mural with a moral: the story of Tobias and the Angel. Eventually it was painted over. Only in the last hundred years has it been revealed again. The tavern is now called The White Swan.

1561

John Shakespeare was elected Chamberlain of the Borough of Stratford, which put him in charge of the revenues of the Stratford Corporation.

Church archives reveal that five stained-glass windows were removed from Holy Trinity Church, Stratford and images were 'hacked' but fulfilment of the order to remove Catholic embellishments was delayed until 1563.

1562

Construction of the new schoolroom above the old guildhall took place between 1562 and 1563, which John Shakespeare, as a Chamberlain, oversaw.

2 December: John and Mary Shakespeare had another daughter. Margaret Shakespeare was baptised, but survived for only five months.

1563

In January, John Shakespeare – still Chamberlain – noted in his accounts that two shillings were 'paid for defacing images in the Chapel, Rood loft taken down.' In fact, John ensured that the religious murals on the walls were only concealed with whitewash. He was four years late in carrying out this edict. The chancel was partitioned off and the pictures within it were left intact. *The Dance of Death* on the North Wall was untouched. Stone altars commemorating ancient Catholic hierarchy were removed.

30 April: Little Margaret Shakespeare was buried.

Michael Drayton was born at Hartshill (Warwickshire). He was educated at Oxford University and became a notable playwright. His *Heroical Epistles*, published in 1596, drew on the same material used by Shakespeare in *Chronicles of England, Scotland and Ireland* by Raphael Holinshead (1577).

Philip Henslowe, in his diaries, credited Michael Drayton with collaborating in twenty-three plays. Drayton died on 23 December 1631.

Actus Secundus

Scena Prima
1564–80

1564

This was the year when the coachbuilder, Walter Rippon, designed the original State Coach for Queen Elizabeth. It had 'doors on either side that could be opened and closed at pleasure ... so that all her subjects could behold her, which most gladly they desired' (on a state visit to Warwick – from *Travel and Roads in England* by Virginia A. LaMar).

The lack of roads made coach travel outside of cities impractical. Wherever possible people preferred to transport goods by water. Anyone needing to make a journey rode a horse or went on foot. Shakespeare would have travelled back and forth to Stratford on horseback.

💀 15 February: Beating Shakespeare to the cradle by little more than two months was Galileo. The astronomer and scientist was born in Pisa, Italy. Forty-four years later, his telescope – the first practical one of its kind – caused a sensation. During Shakespeare's lifetime, Galileo's revelations regarding the sun and the planets, Venus, Saturn and Neptune were the subject of common gossip.

💀 26 February: Christopher Marlowe was born in Canterbury, son of a shoemaker. Marlowe burst on the literary scene like a fireball and died out almost as quickly. Had he survived longer, Shakespeare might have remained in his shadow without attaining literary primacy.

💀 23 April (St George's Day): By common consent this is the accepted date of William Shakespeare's birth in Henley Street. He was John and Mary Shakespeare's third child and the first to survive.

💀 26 April: Shakespeare was baptised at Holy Trinity Church, Stratford-upon-Avon. It was a Sunday in the Julian calendar but a Thursday in the Gregorian calendar. Consequently there has often been confusion regarding dates. In England, the Gregorian calendar did not come into use until September 1752.

💀 The entry in the register of Holy Trinity Church reads: '*Gulielmus filius Johannes Shakespeare*' (William, son of John Shakespeare). His godfather was Alderman William Smith, a haberdasher who also resided in Henley Street. The vicar was John Bretchgirdle, a humanist with Catholic sympathies. After giving birth, a woman was considered 'unclean' and as a result it was not the custom for a mother to be present at the baptism (see below).

The registration of the baptism was discovered in record books tucked away in Worcester's archives. Later, a minister called Richard Bifield added his signature as a witness to the certificate and also marked three heavy Xs next to Shakespeare's name. The reason for this is a mystery because Bifield did not become vicar until 1597, thirty-three years after the event.

Somehow, many of the official records from Warwickshire and Shropshire have ended up in the county of Kent.

Godparents were known as godsips or gossips. Apostle spoons were gifted to the baby. Heads of saints were represented on the spoon handles. The duty of a godparent was to encourage the child to learn the Christian creed and the Lord's Prayer.

One third of babies born in England died in their first year. The average life expectancy of an adult male was forty-seven.

25 May: Mary Arden, Shakespeare's mother, held a 'churching feast' on the occasion of her being 'churched' at Holy Trinity in Stratford. As mentioned above, for a month following parturition, mothers were considered to be 'unclean' and not allowed into church. That is why godparents stood in for them. Once the 'churching feast' was over, festivities were held to which other women would be invited. It was a sort of hen party giving rise to the expression 'Many women: many words'.

THE BOOK OF SHAKESPEARIAN USELESS INFORMATION

🕱 11 July: Eleven weeks after Shakespeare's baptism, there was a sad note in the parish register next to the name Oliver Gunne. The vicar's entry noted: *Hic incipit pestis*. (Here the plague has begun.) During the next six months, 237 Stratford residents died.

🕱 The Arden family, from which Shakespeare descended on his mother's side, were well known Warwickshire Catholics. The head of the clan, Sir Edward Arden, was executed for treason in 1583. His last words claimed that his 'real crime was profession of the Catholic faith.'

🕱 During Edward VI's brief reign, the extra revenues from the acquisition of the monasteries and chantries were used to endow a national network of free schools. Most scholars concede that Shakespeare attended the King Edward VI (grammar) School in Stratford.

🕱 29 September: Shakespeare was five months old when Robert Dudley, Knight of the Garter and Master of the Horse to the Queen's Majesty, was created Earl of Leicester. Though he was a married man, he had a liaison with Queen Elizabeth that was warmly reciprocated. One Sunday, her husband being out, Amy Robsart, who was Lady Dudley, gave her servants the day off to attend a country fair while she remained alone in the house. That evening, when the staff returned they were greeted by the appalling sight of their mistress with a broken neck, lying at the foot of the staircase in the main hall. The suspicion that Queen Elizabeth and Dudley had something to do with Amy's death blighted their romance. After that, all hopes for it to blossom further were dashed.

Leicester was instrumental in founding the official Oxford University Press and his interest in the theatre was manifold. In 1559, he formed his own Company of Players and in 1574 he obtained for them the first royal patent ever issued to actors, so that they could tour the country unmolested by local authorities.

Leicester's patronage had a political purpose: the actors could spread the word of Protestantism. Plays were meant to proclaim a sense of pride in Englishness.

A treatise on sexually transmitted disease (*Omnia quae adhuc extant opera*) was published by the anatomist Gabriele Falloppio, who gave his name to the fallopian tube. He was the first to advocate condoms to avoid catching syphilis. He claimed he had tested his invention of linen sheaths on a thousand men with 100 per cent success.

Venus was the goddess of love. Mercury was the only known cure for syphilis. Hence the expression, 'a night with Venus and a lifetime with Mercury,' which was coined by Richard Wiseman in 1676.

1565
In January the River Thames froze over.

In Stratford, John Shakespeare was appointed one of fourteen aldermen.

While William was still a child, his father as a councillor, paid nine shillings out of the town's funds to a touring theatre company 'to play in the Gild Hall', enabling councillors to watch the opening performance for nothing. This would have occurred several times during William's youth.

Stratford was a centre of the gloving industry that was once widespread throughout the whole district to the west of the town. The Gild Register mentions eight glovers – inhabitants of Stratford – in the early sixteenth century. The heyday of the trade was in the reigns of Elizabeth and James I. On market and fair days, John Shakespeare and his fellow glovers occupied the most important position in the town, at the High Cross, where they set out their stalls. So proprietory did they become that eventually the glovers were made responsible for paving the street.

Conrad Gesner, the Swiss naturalist, helped to popularise the pencil – the word derives from the Latin root '*pincellus*' meaning penis. Near the village of Seathwaite in Cumbria, England, a large deposit of graphite was discovered that could easily be sawn into thin sticks. This was the first and only discovery of such a solid deposit of graphite. At first it was thought to be a form of lead and therefore called plumbago. To this day we refer to 'a lead pencil' although the element lead has never been part of a pencil. Shakespeare may have used pencils.

1566

1 September: Edward Alleyn was born. He was the younger son of a Bishopsgate innkeeper and became a star actor thriving on the roles created for him by Christopher Marlowe. He worked mainly for the Admiral's Men. Known as Ned to his contemporaries, he

was two years younger than Shakespeare and became the Tudor equivalent of a millionaire. He founded Dulwich College in 1619 and died in 1626.

13 October: Gilbert Shakespeare, brother of William, was baptised in Stratford. He was probably named after Gilbert Bradley, another glover who lived on Henley Street. Gilbert Shakespeare became a haberdasher in the parish of St Bride's in London, supplying needles and thread. He signed his name in a neat Italianate hand, and appears to have returned to Stratford by the turn of the century, when he helped his brother with his land purchases. He died at the age of forty-five.

1567

John Brayne built the first purpose-built venue for entertainment to be erected in London, at an estimated cost of £15. He hired two carpenters to construct a space for an open-air playhouse in the yard of a farmhouse situated outside the city wall of Aldgate, near Mile End. The building was converted into a tavern called The Red Lion. The playhouse's stage was forty feet wide and thirty feet deep, with a trapdoor from which devils and witches could spring. An '18 foot turret of Tymber' was erected at the back of the stage.

November: Thomas Nashe was born in Lowestoft, Suffolk, the son of a curate. He was educated at St John's College, Cambridge and went to London in 1589. Nashe found fame as a satirist and gained notoriety with some obscene stories, one of which became known as *Nashe's Dildo*. He wrote the play *The Isle of Dogs* with Ben Jonson, but it was never published because of its 'seditious and slanderous manner'. Nashe joined forces with Robert Greene in an exchange of barbed insults with the writers Richard and Gabriel Harvey. He died in 1601.

John Shakespeare was appointed Justice of the Peace but declined the post of Bailiff of Stratford. The current incumbent had defaulted and it is thought John felt he was nominated as a second-best choice. Perhaps he didn't want to give up the day job: sampling the local ale took up much valuable time. However, this was a task he manfully upheld for ten years.

This was an age when most people could not read. Morals and ethics had to be explained by way of the spoken word, so the Protestant Reformation made the sermon the focal point of a church service. These monologues tended to go on for a long time. Consequently, pews started to be introduced into the churches so that worshippers could take the weight off their knees while listening to the preachers.

1568

In Stratford, John Shakespeare had earlier turned down the post of High Bailiff (the equivalent of Mayor) but now he consented to take on the position. It entitled him to be addressed as *Master* John Shakespeare. It also gave him a ceremonial gown of scarlet that he could wear when he took his seat on the front pew of the church of the Holy Trinity. He continued to serve as Justice of the Peace issuing warrants and negotiating with the lord of the manor on behalf of the corporation. It is thought probable that he persevered with his ale-tasting duties in a purely private capacity.

1 November: Jane Sheppard was baptised at St Margaret's, Westminster, London. She called herself Jennet. Her father, William Sheppard, held an office in the 'Catery' procuring foodstuffs for the royal household. Jennet was destined to be intimately associated with William Shakespeare. When she married, her name became Davenant.

Jennet Davenant's brothers – Thomas and Richard – were glovers and became professional embroiderers and perfumers working for both Elizabeth I and, upon his accession, for James I.

1569

15 April: Joan Shakespeare, William's sister, was baptised. Joan would marry a hatter, William Hart, (destined to die within a week of his brother-in-law). Joan's descendants continue to the present day.

It was common practice for children at the age of five to start 'petty school' (from the French *petit*, small), where they would spend two years learning their 'abecedarius' (an alphabet book, which used successive letters of the Hebrew alphabet as the first letter of each stanza) and the catechism.

Although it has not been proven, on the balance of probability William Shakespeare attended the new King's Grammar School. His father's position on the town council would have ensured that tuition was free.

The schoolroom still exists and can be reached after climbing a stone staircase. It is a long and narrow room with a high ceiling and oak-beams. Shakespeare, on leaving his home in Henley Street would creep like a 'snail with his satchel and shining morning face' for two blocks, then turn at the Market Cross to enter the old 'Gild Hall' above which was the classroom, divided into two parts: petty and senior.

School started with prayers followed by lessons from 7.00 a.m. to 12.00 midday and from 2.00 p.m. until 5.00 p.m. In the summer, school started an hour earlier. It was customary to go home early on Thursdays and Saturdays. Sunday was the day of rest.

Every morning each of the forty boys was expected to take to his class a supply of ink, a quill and twelve pieces of paper.

William Lyly (1468–1522), the first headmaster of St Paul's School, London, wrote the standard books used to teach English and Latin in grammar schools. Edward VI gave a royal proclamation to *The Short Introduction to Grammar* and it became the set text. Apart from learning to read and write, the children of that time would have studied Ovid in the original Latin, although Shakespeare's mature writing betrays his reliance on translations. William Lyly's grandson, John, became a writer contemporaneous with Shakespeare.

According to Stanley Wells in *Shakespeare: Sex and Love* (2010) there is only one clear record (of a court witness, Joyce Cowden) to prove that formal education of girls was available in Stratford. He adds, 'it was probably only at the level of petty, or dame's school.'

Dame schools were usually taught by women and were often located in the home of the teacher.

Some scholars surmise that when Shakespeare finished his schooling he became an assistant schoolteacher, possibly in Lancashire. The connections are tenuous but they do exist. Here is an attempt to follow the often-mooted path.

On the assumption that Shakespeare went to Stratford Grammar School, his first teacher was Walter Roche, who retired to a local rectory soon after Shakespeare's arrival at the age of seven.

Simon Hunt came next. He was a closet Papist. When Shakespeare was eleven, Simon went on a pilgrimage to Rome in order to become a Catholic priest and a missionary.

The next teacher was Thomas Jenkins, whose tutors at Oxford included Edmund Campion – Catholic saint and martyr. Jenkins remained in Stratford until 1579, by which time Shakespeare was fifteen.

Shakespeare's formative years were influenced by the leanings of his Catholic-minded teachers.

Thomas Jenkins was succeeded by John Cottam (aka Cotton and Cotham). Cottam paid £6 to Jenkins to take his place as teacher.

John Cottam's younger brother, Thomas, was a Jesuit priest in Rome. When he returned to England he was accused of performing exorcism on vulnerable young women. To persuade him to confess, he was tortured and removed on 4 December 1580 to the Tower of London, where he endured the rack and the 'scavenger's daughter' (a torturing device described in detail in this book at the close of the year 1581). On 30 May 1582 Cottam was executed at Tyburn with three other priests. John Cottam's term at Stratford ended on almost precisely the date of his brother's execution.

Cottam's ancestral seat was in Lancashire, seven miles northeast of Preston. His father, Lawrence, was a man of substance. Immediately adjacent to the Cottam estate was Alston, the country-seat of Alexander Houghton, a gentleman of wide cultural interests who owned a collection of musical instruments. In particular, he retained a troupe of players.

John Cottam's father, Lawrence, was financially involved in a land deal in 1558 with Alexander Houghton's brother, Thomas, who, on being identified as a recusant, fled to Flanders. The Houghtons' inheritance consisted of property not only in Alston, but also in the parish of Dilworth itself, where the Cottams had their family home.

It has been mooted that 'nine out of the twenty-one Catholic schoolmasters who were executed under Elizabeth I were Lancastrians.'

In 1582, Shakespeare's friend Alexander Aspinall was appointed as schoolmaster in Stratford. Shakespeare was eighteen, but he became friendly with the older man, and legend has it that Shakespeare fashioned a bouquet to accompany the gift of a pair of gloves when Alexander courted Anne Shaw, mother of Shakespeare's friend, Julius Shaw. Lancashire-born Aspinall is reputed to be the model for those pedantic and ludicrous schoolmasters in *Love's Labor's Lost*, *Anthony and Cleopatra*, and *Two Noble Kinsmen*. Be this as it may, Shakespeare would have left school a couple of years before Aspinall arrived, but they may have known each other in Lancashire.

21 October: Meanwhile, back at Stratford, James Langrake of Whittlebury, a government informant, reported that 'Shappere alias Shakespeare' had loaned £80 to John Musshem of Walton D'Eiville, Warwickshire, to be repaid on the feast of St Andrew (30 November) with £20 interest. John Shakespeare was accused of lending money at an interest rate above 10 per cent in breach of the 1552 statute, making him guilty of usury. The matter came to a head in the following year. (See 3 February, 1570).

The first state lottery was held in England. Queen Elizabeth's attitude was that her subjects would gamble whether or not there were laws against it. So why forbid it?

1570

23 January: The first recorded assassination using a firearm took place. The Scottish regent, James Stewart, first Earl of Moray was killed by James Hamilton, sparking off a civil war in Scotland.

3 February: John Shakespeare came to court before the barons of the exchequer to hear the perjury charge brought against him the previous October by James Langrake. He pleaded not guilty. The attorney general asked for a trial by jury. In order to avoid further expenses, John Shakespeare requested that he be allowed to pay a reasonable fine. The barons accepted his proposal and fined John Shakespeare forty shillings.

February: Queen Elizabeth persuaded Parliament to pass the Reformation Bill defining Holy Communion in terms of Reformed Protestant theology, as opposed to the transubstantiation of the Roman Catholic mass. It ordered that ministers should not wear the surplice or other Roman Catholic vestments, and it permitted abuse of the Pope in the Litany. It allowed priests to marry, banned images from churches, and confirmed Elizabeth as Supreme Governor of the Church of England.

Pope Pius V was extremely displeased. He declared Queen Elizabeth was a heretic and excommunicated her, declaring: 'Elizabeth, the pretended Queen of England and the servant of crime.'

A coat of arms would entitle John Shakespeare to be called 'Gentleman' on a permanent basis so he applied for one from the Herald's office in London. His request was rejected.

1571

On the expiration of his term of office as a justice of the peace, John Shakespeare was appointed High Alderman. However, he was having credibility issues in his social world. According to court records, he was accused of acquiring 300 tods (8,400 pounds) of wool with the promise of returning it later plus interest. This was considered another usurious act.

28 September: Ann Shakespeare was baptised. She was John and Mary's sixth child and another sister for William. She died before her eighth birthday.

28 September: In London the House of Commons introduced the first pro forma bill symbolising its own authority over its affairs.

Modelled on the Bourse in Antwerp, Thomas Gresham founded the Royal Exchange in London, in order to stimulate international trade.

1572

3 January: The company of Lord Leicester's Men wrote to their patron requesting that the actors be appointed 'not merely the Earl's liveried retainers' but also his 'household servants' — a distinction that enabled them to come and go in London without restriction. The letter goes on to assure their patron that the actors would not expect 'any further stipend or benefit,' from the earl. All they asked for was to enjoy his legal protection while operating as an independent theatre company. The signatories were: James Burbage, John Perkin, John Laneham, William Johnson, Robert Wilson, and Thomas Clarke. These were the first five men to be listed on the royal patent of 10 May 1574.

John Shakespeare's nemesis, the government informer, James Langrake, again went to the authorities and claimed that soon after 26 February 1571, John 'Shaxspere' of 'Stretford super Haven' and John Lockeley had illegally bought 200 tods (5,600 pounds) of wool at fourteen shillings per tod from Walter Newsam and others. John was accused of being a 'brogger', meaning an unlicensed, illegal, wool dealer. (He'd been dealing in wool being moved from Nottingham to Wiltshire).

February: Harrow School was founded under a royal charter.

In the spring, John Shakespeare and Adrian Quiney journeyed to London to represent Stratford at Westminster law courts.

It became law that vagabonds had to be licensed. The second Vagrancy Act of Parliament described Vagabonds as 'all fencers, bear-wards, common players in interludes, & minstrels, not belonging to any Baron of the realm or towards any other patronage of greater degree.' Unless an actor could prove he was under such patronage, he was subject to a sliding scale of penalties:

First offence: 'to be grievously whipped and burnt through the gristle of the right ear with a hot iron of the compass of an inch about.'

Second offence: 'to be deemed in all respects a felon.'

Third offence: 'Death.'

11 June: Ben Jonson was born. He was educated at Westminster School, apprenticed to a bricklayer (his stepfather) before becoming a soldier, then an actor and dramatist, and enjoying an enduring friendship with William Shakespeare. On 28 July 1597, when he was an

actor at a South Bank playhouse, Philip Henslowe noted in his diaries that he loaned Jonson £4. Shakespeare appeared as an actor – as the elder Knowell – in Jonson's play, *Every Man in His Humour* (1598). Jonson was made an M.A. of Oxford in 1619. He was the first (unofficial) poet laureate and happened to be present at the fateful birthday party in 1616 at which William is alleged to have overindulged and died. Jonson was buried in Westminster Abbey at the age of sixty-five on 6 August 1637.

5 July: Inigo Jones, best known as an accomplished architect, was born in Smithfield, London. His father was a Welsh cloth worker. Inigo started as an apprentice joiner in St Paul's Churchyard. He served at the Court of King Christian IV of Denmark and on his return to England, between 1605 and 1640, he is credited with staging over 500 performances. He introduced movable scenery and the proscenium arch to the English theatre.

24 August: St Bartholomew's Day: The day of the 'blood-red wedding', a phrase allegedly coined by the young king, Charles IX, in his subsequent nightmares. Between 5,000 and 30,000 people were killed in Paris. This was referred to as the St Bartholomew's Day Massacre, the slaughter of Huguenots (French Protestants) organised by the mother of King Charles IX. It was a horrific and cynical attempt to prevent the marriage of the king's sister to a Protestant. [For a fuller account, see my book *Wedding Bells and Chimney Sweeps*, page 135.]

Thomas Dekker was born in London. He was educated at a grammar school. He was associated with forty plays according to Henslowe's diaries. Ben Jonson considered him a 'bumbling hack' implying that Dekker was what we call today a 'play doctor', revising and updating old material. He was perpetually in debt and went to prison in Poultry Compter. He died in Clerkenwell on 25 August 1632.

By Michaelmas term, John Shakespeare's difficulties were getting worse. James Langrake again submitted accusations against him, claiming that on or after 1 September 1571 at Snitterfield, John Shakespeare had bought from Edward and Richard Graunte one hundred tods of wool at fourteen shillings per tod. Because this case was dropped, it is suggested that John Shakespeare paid off Langrake. This may be true, because in 1574 Langrake was given a year in the Fleet prison for taking bribes. John Shakespeare habitually broke the restriction imposed by the 1552 statute limiting wool buying to manufacturers or certified wool merchants.

1574

11 March: The baptism of Richard Shakespeare, William's younger brother by ten years. He remained in Stratford and died, unmarried, on 4 February 1613. Nothing much is known about him.

23 April: William Shakespeare's tenth birthday.

Simon Hunt became schoolmaster at King's New School, Stratford, where he remained until 1577. These schoolmasters were exceptionally well paid – allegedly more than masters at Eton. Simon left to train at the seminary in Douai, France, as a Jesuit missionary. In essence, this establishment was a 'Catholic University of Oxford in exile'.

For the acting company that he had assembled in 1559, Robert Dudley, first Earl of Leicester obtained the first royal patent ever issued to actors. As mentioned earlier, this enabled them to tour the country unmolested by local authorities because they were safely under court patronage. Previously, rogues and vagabonds (including itinerant actors, or 'players' as they had been called) were subject to detention or a day in the stocks for practising unlicensed begging, or far worse punishments (see year 1572).

10 May: James Burbage, John Perkin, John Laneham, William Johnson, Robert Wilson, and Thomas Clarke were the first five men to be listed on the royal patent to legalise an acting company.

Under the royal patent, censorship and approval of themes could be made only by the Lord Chamberlain and his Master of the Revels. Once the players had the Master's approval for their plays, they could act them anywhere in England without local interference. This remained in force for the rest of Elizabeth's reign.

Thomas Heywood was born in Lincolnshire, and educated at Peterhouse, Cambridge. He worked for the Admiral's Men in London. In October 1596, he was mentioned in Philip Henslowe's diaries as a player and a playwright. In 1633, Heywood claimed to have had a hand in at least two hundred-and-twenty plays. The essayist, Charles Lamb (1775–1834), described him as 'a prose

73

Shakespeare'. He was buried in St James's Church, Clerkenwell on 16 August 1641.

1575

John Shakespeare paid £40 to purchase two houses with orchards in Stratford.

25 January: Queen Elizabeth granted a monopoly on producing printed sheet music to Thomas Tallis and William Byrd.

John Shakespeare's name appeared in sixth place on the council list of thirty-eight freeholders.

9 July: Queen Elizabeth visited Kenilworth Castle, twelve miles from Stratford. While the Earl of Leicester's Players entertained, the Earl himself (Robert Dudley) was wooing the virgin queen with avidity.

Shakespeare gave the following lines to Oberon in *A Midsummer Night's Dream*:

My gentle Pucke come hither; thou remembrest
Since once I sat upon a promontory,
And heard a Meare-maide on a Dolphin's backe,
Uttering such dulcet and harmonious breath,
That the rude sea grew civill at her song,
And certaine starres shot madly from their Spheares,
To heare the Sea-maids musicke.
   [From the First Folio 1623.]

Some scholars speculate that these lines were conceived by Shakespeare when he was eleven. Their theory is that he may have been taken to Kenilworth to see a pageant presented by the Earl of Leicester to entertain Queen Elizabeth. The water devices included a dolphin and a mermaid. In reality, the mermaid was constructed out of an eighteen-foot long canoe, and a twenty-four-foot long boat was mocked up as a dolphin. Your chronicler considers the connection contentious.

Thomas Jenkins, the Stratford schoolmaster, found his own replacement in John Cottam, who resigned shortly into his tenure when his younger brother, Thomas Cottam, was executed for his Jesuit sympathies.

1576

23 April: Shakespeare's twelfth birthday was, coincidentally, the day when James Burbage with his business partner John Brayne (who had built The Red Lion in Whitechapel in 1567) took a twenty-year lease on land in Shoreditch to build a playhouse called, simply, 'The Theatre'.

This date also marked the seventeenth wedding anniversary of James Burbage, who married Ellen Brayne (c.1542 to c.1613) on 23 April 1559. Ellen was the sister of John Brayne (1541–86).

The word 'theatre' stems from the Greek word, '*theatron*' meaning 'a place for viewing' (theates = spectator, tron = place). Hitherto, the public had referred to places of entertainment as playhouses. Eventually, when indoor theatres were invented, they would all be called 'theatres'.

James Burbage's original occupation had been carpentry, the same as actor Harrison Ford's had been.

Much of the wood used to construct theatres came from what was described as 'owld ship tymber'.

John Brayne advanced the sum of £700 to his brother-in-law, James Burbage, to build 'The Theatre'. In return, Brayne owned some of the property, with both men sharing the profits equally.

The Theatre was a polygonal building. It consisted of three galleries with a capacity for 1,500 patrons, surrounding an open yard 'for the groundlings' with a thrust stage. It was plastered and coloured black and white with a tiled roof.

To find the site of the original theatre, walk north from London Bridge along Gracechurch Street (which becomes Bishopsgate Street), and you'll come to The Theatre on the left side of Shoreditch Road on the edge of Finsbury Fields.

Until James Burbage built the first stand-alone playhouse in Europe, London was considered to be just another town on the touring schedule. Venues in London included the inn yards of The Saracen's Head, The Red Lion, The Bull, The Boar's Head, The Cross Keys and The Bel Savage.

In 1576/7 Philip Henslowe began building another house of entertainment called the Curtain playhouse. He was careful to stay outside the city walls and the Curtain was less than two hundred yards to the east of The Theatre.

Outside the City walls, the Shoreditch area was known as 'the suburbs of sin' because of the proliferation of brothels and gaming houses. After 'The Curtain' was erected, the district became London's theatrical hub.

A printer called James Roberts had exclusive rights to produce pre-publicity posters for playhouses. Playbills were displayed on posts in the streets.

A court document contained the information that '...John Shappere alias Shakespere of Stratford-up-Avon...' was accused of usury resulting in John Shakespeare resigning from public office. This documentary evidence was not discovered until 1983 by the researcher, Wendy Goldsmith.

John Shakespeare's name remained on the Stratford council's rolls for a further ten years. If he hoped that in time he would be able to return to public life and recover his financial situation, such aspirations were never realised.

1577

Thomas Jenkins became Schoolmaster at King's New School, Stratford (until his resignation in 1579). He was a Latin and Greek scholar from St John's College, Oxford. His chief influence on William Shakespeare was giving him an introduction to the poetry of Ovid.

The Curtain playhouse opened its doors to the public just outside the City of London in what is now called Hewett Street. The name 'The Curtain' was coined because of the address of the building site that had a wall acting as a windshield, called a curtain. In fact, the lane was called Curtain Close, Shoreditch. Henry Lanman, Gentleman, was the proprietor. There were no 'Proscenium Arch curtains' in those days. Years later, Shakespeare immortalised The Curtain when, during the premiere of *Henry V*, he described the venue as 'this wooden O'. Until recent discoveries were made, *Henry V* was thought to have premiered in The Globe Theatre.

24 March: Church worshippers in Stratford-upon-Avon came under the strict supervision of Worcester. Heretic-chaser, Dr John Whitgift, was nominated as Bishop of Worcester. Sometimes 800 horsemen accompanied him on his journeys. He shared Queen Elizabeth's hatred of Puritans.

The first edition of *The Chronicles of England, Scotland and Ireland* was published. Cheshire-born Raphael Holinshed (born 1529) supervised the work with other writers contributing. This book, together with a revised second edition published in 1587, formed the primary source notes used by William Shakespeare for his history plays.

28 June: Peter Paul Rubens, the Flemish Baroque painter, was born in the German city of Siegen.

From the beginning of August, although building work was not completed, The Theatre staged fencing matches to provide desperately needed ready cash.

James Burbage (1534–97) was sometimes guilty of sharp practice. He was certainly considered a rough diamond with a short temper and was involved in brawls. Upbraided for his 'unconscionable behaviour', Burbage responded with, 'I care not a turd for conscience.'

The Reverend Thomas White said in a sermon, 'The cause of plays is sin, if you look to it well; and the cause of sin are plays; therefore the cause of plagues are plays.' (from E.K. Chambers, *William Shakespeare: A Study of Facts and Problems*, 2012 edn.)

15 November: Sir Francis Drake set off from Plymouth on his attempt to circumnavigate the world.

1578

At the age of fourteen, boys left school and began to work – sometimes taking up apprenticeships. When Shakespeare became fourteen in April, his father was experiencing financial difficulties and if it had not been possible to pay the extra five pounds to continue the boy's education, the likelihood is that William would have followed his father into the leather business, to start a seven-year apprenticeship as John Shakespeare himself had done.

However, some early biographers suggested that Shakespeare left school to become a clerk to a lawyer. There is not a shred of evidence that he did so.

John Aubrey wrote a collection of manuscripts containing gossip about famous men called – *Brief Lives* between 1680 and 1693. Within that work he stated, 'I have been told heretofore by some of the neighbours that when he was a boy he [Shakespeare] exercised his father's trade but when he kill'd a Calfe he would doe it in a high style, and make a Speech.' So much for Aubrey; he thought Shakespeare's father was a butcher.

According to contemporary gossip, many of Aubrey's conjectural observations were written under the black cloud of a throbbing hangover.

Here are three more enlightening passages from John Aubrey's shaky pen:

1) This William, being inclined naturally to Poetry and acting, came to London, I guesse about 18: and was an Actor at one of the Play-houses, and did acte exceedingly well: now B. Johnson was never a good Actor, but an excellent Instructor.

2) He began early to make essayes at Dramatique Poetry, which at that time was very lowe; and his Playes tooke well. He was a handsome, well-shap't man: very good company, and of a very readie and pleasant smoothe Witt.

3) His Comedies will remaine witt as long as the English tongue is understood, for that he handles mores hominum [the ways of mankind]. Now our present writers reflect so much on particular persons and coxcombeities that twenty yeares hence they will not be understood. Though, as Ben Johnson sayes of him, that he had little Latine and lesse Greek, he understood

Latine pretty well: for he had been in his younger yeares a schoolmaster in the countrey.

It is possible there may be some evidence for the schoolmaster rumour, as will be revealed shortly.

Another story comes from Poet Laureate, Nicholas Rowe (1674–1718). He heard it from the actor Thomas Betterton (1635–1710), who worked with William Davenant – self-proclaimed illegitimate son of Shakespeare – so there may be a grain of truth in it. It goes thus:

Shakespeare had by a Misfortune common enough to young fellows, fallen into ill Company; and amongst them, some that made a frequent practice of Deer-stealing, engag'd him with them more than once in robbing a Park that belong'd to Sir Thomas Lucy of Charlecote, near Stratford. For this he was prosecuted by the Gentleman, as he thought, somewhat too severely; and in order to revenge that ill Usage, he made a Ballad upon him. And tho' this, probably the first Essay of his Poetry, be lost, yet it is said to have been so very bitter, that it redoubled the Persecution against him to that degree, that he was oblig'd to leave his Business and Family in Warwickshire, for some time, and shelter himself in London.

(from Chambers, *William Shakespeare: A Study of Facts and Problems.*)

Modern scholars tend to dismiss the deer-poaching anecdote, claiming that at the time of Shakespeare's youth there were no deer in either of Sir Thomas Lucy's estates. Peter Ackroyd writes in *Shakespeare: The Biography*: '...There are difficulties with the story as it stands. There was no park in the grounds of Sir Thomas Lucy's house, Charlecote; it was then a 'free warren', and deer were not brought onto the estate until the eighteenth century. As a result of this discovery the site of Shakespeare's alleged misdeed was moved, two miles across the Avon, to another of Lucy's parks called Fullbrooke...'

The Lucy family descendants are now called Fairfax-Lucy, the 'Fairfax' addition referring to a relation of the Parliamentarian general who refused to sign Charles I's death warrant. The Lucys have lived there for at least six hundred years, and retain the original archives. They claim that fallow deer have *always* been there. These were wild fallow deer, not to be confused with a herd of red deer that was introduced for a short time in the 1840s.

The strict Forest Laws that reserved rights of hunting to the ruling class were resented by the lower orders. Peasants accused of poaching were liable to hanging, castration or blinding. Sometimes, as an alternative form of hunting for the landowners, a culprit could be sewn into a deerskin, told to run and then be hunted down by ferocious dogs. If Shakespeare was caught stealing deer, it is small wonder that he disappeared from Stratford. This could account for the so-called 'Lost Years'.

Between 20 August and 6 September, Sir Francis Drake passed through the Strait of Magellan during his circumnavigation of the globe. To celebrate, he renamed his ship *The Golden Hind*.

It was customary, at the end of the sixteenth century, for women to wear dresses in public that exposed their breasts. (Peter Ackroyd, *Shakespeare: The Biography*, page 112.)

There were over a hundred brothels in London. It is certain that Shakespeare was familiar with some of them, for he mentions the sign of the 'blind Cupid': a logo often hung over the door of a bordello.

John Shakespeare found himself in arrears with his taxes due to his refusal to pay a levy for six additional soldiers. It is not clear why six additional soldiers had been demanded.

12 November: To raise cash, John Shakespeare sold seventy acres of property in Wilmcote to Thomas Webbe, signifying his gradual slide from grace.

1579

Alexander Aspinall took over as Schoolmaster at Stratford and lasted until 1582. He was a dominating Lancashire man with exemplary Oxford University credentials. He stood for the council and at one point became Deputy Town Clerk. His pomposity led to his colleagues referring to him as the 'Great Philip Macedon' (Stratford Corporation MSS). In 1590, he obtained permission from the corporation to convert part of the old schoolhouse into a dwelling for himself. A kinswoman of Alexander Aspinall was Alexander Houghton's wife, Maud Aspinall. In 1594, Alexander married Anne Shaw, a widow and neighbour of the Shakespeares in Henley Street. The Aspinalls still resided there eighteen years later, when William Shakespeare retired.

John Shakespeare was forced to mortgage Mary Arden's estate – known as 'Asbies'. In future years he tried to regain possession on at least two occasions.

4 April: Anne Shakespeare, William's sister, was buried at the age of eight. The parish register records a payment of eight pence for 'the bell and paull for Mr Shaxpers daughter.'

17 June: During his circumnavigation of the world, Francis Drake went ashore on land he named 'Nova Albion' (New England) and claimed it in the name of Queen Elizabeth I. Today it is known as California – a name coined later by Spanish explorers from a reference to a mythical land described in a novel of that time called *Las Sergas de Esplandián*.

In 1579, Shakespeare was fifteen, and his younger brothers, Gilbert and Richard, were thirteen and five respectively.

20 December: John Fletcher, the playwright, was born in Rye, Sussex. His father, Richard Fletcher, was Dean of Peterborough and as such was present at the execution of the thirty-five-year old Mary, Queen of Scots in the Great Hall at Fotheringay Castle, Northamptonshire, when John was aged eight.

Fotheringay Castle was razed to the ground in 1627.

6 July: To confuse historians, in 1579 another man named William Shakespeare was drowned in the River Avon. In the St Nicholas' Churchwardens' Accounts, transcribed and printed by Mr Richard Savage, of Stratford-on-Avon, the register states: '*1579. July Sexto die huius mensis, Sepultus fuit Guliemus Shaxper, qui demersus fuit in Rivulo aquæ, qui vel vocatur Avona.*' (Here was buried William Shakespeare who was drowned in the water of a river called Avon.)

24 July: Having been an assistant for two years, Edmund Tilney (1536–1610) was promoted to become The Master of the Revels, a post he would continue to hold for nearly thirty years until his death in 1610.

One of Tilney's responsibilities was to vet plays before giving them a licence as being suitable for public performance. He charged seven shillings for each play he had to read. From time to time, it seems he allowed the payment of these fees to lapse. Burbage was particularly favoured in this regard. The Office of the Revels was situated in the old Palace of St John's in Clerkenwell, a suburb north of Newgate. There, in the 'great chamber' the actors and musicians 'auditioned' their plays for approval. The plays that Tilney finally chose were claimed to be 'the best that were to be had' and were 'often perused and necessarily corrected and amended by all the aforesaid officers.'

It was not the concern of the Master of the Revels to worry about licentious or blasphemous material. His purpose was to prevent corrupting the public with seditious ideas. Any play with political content decreed to agitate the court was censored and never released. Although censorship was a bone of contention for artists, the office of the Master of Revels brought respectability to actors and the theatre in general, because it gave the acting companies a measure of royal protection.

No play could be produced without a licence signed by Tilney on the last page of a playbook.

Plutarch's Lives of the Noble Greeks and Romans was written at the beginning of the second century AD. It is a social history of the ancient world. Sir Thomas North, a sea captain, translated it into English from the French of Jacques Amyot. The first edition appeared in 1579 and was dedicated to Elizabeth I. This book formed the source from which Shakespeare drew the materials for *Julius Caesar*, *Coriolanus* and *Antony and Cleopatra*. In the latter play, Shakespeare copied whole speeches from North's translation almost verbatim. Sir Thomas (1535–1604) has been described as 'the first Master of English prose'.

John Aubrey (1626–97) made the following entry in his diary: 'Shakespeare had been in his younger yeares a Schoolmaster in the Country'. In the margin Aubrey noted: 'from Mr Beeston'. William Beeston was the son of Christopher Beeston, a player who worked with Shakespeare in his acting company, so the legend may be credible.

17 December: It was reported that a Stratford girl called Katherine Hamlet was found drowned in the River Avon near Tiddington. At first it was thought to be a suicide, but the Church gave her the benefit of the doubt and she received a Christian burial in Stratford.

Scena Secunda
1580–90

 1580

In Tudor times among the most common gifts to be exchanged were gloves. Presents were given on New Year's Eve rather than Christmas. Another favourite gift was an orange punctured with expensive cloves. Apparently, when this was added to a flagon of wine, it imparted spice to the drink.

 February: The Civic authorities in London grew alarmed at the rise in popularity of mass entertainment. The following observation was made:

There are 'unlawful assemblies of the people to hear and see certain interludes called plays exercised by the said James Burbage and divers other persons unknown at a certain place called The Theatre in Holywell in the aforesaid country. By reason of which unlawful assembling of the people great affrays, assaults, tumults and quasi-

89

insurrections and divers other misdeeds and enormities have been then and there done by very many ill-disposed persons to the great disturbance of the peace.'

6 April: At six in the evening, England was hit with the largest earthquake ever recorded in the country: measuring nearly 6.0 on the Richter scale, according to modern estimates. Its epicentre was somewhere under the Straits of Dover. As it happened in Easter week, it was considered to be a bad omen. Many accounts of the event were published for the eyes of an avid English public. Richard Tarlton, a comic actor who would later join William Shakespeare's acting company, wrote a piece that was contained in Abraham Fleming's collection of 27 June entitled: *A Bright Burning Beacon, forewarning all wise Virgins to trim their lampes against the coming of the Bridegroome. Conteining A generall doctrine of sundrie signes and wonders, specially Earthquakes both particular and generall: A discourse of the end of this world: A commemoration of our late Earthquake, the 6 of April, about 6 of the clocke in the evening 1580. And a praier for the appeasing of Gods wrath and indignation. Newly translated and collected by Abraham Fleming.*

The April earthquake was blamed by the authorities on the playhouses. 'The cause is the players of plays, which are used at The Theatre and other such places – is a great hindrance of the service of God, who hath with His mighty hand so lately admonished us of our earnest repentance.'

3 May: Edmund Shakespeare (William's youngest brother) was baptised.

29 May: John Shakespeare was fined £40 for missing a court appearance in Stratford.

Newington Butts playhouse was built outside the city limits on the far side of Southwark, a quarter of a mile away from today's new Southwark Playhouse.

12 June: Edmund Campion landed at Dover. He was a Jesuit sent by the Pope to help with a religious conversion of the English people back to Catholicism. Edmund was lightly disguised but customs officials had been issued with 'likenesses' of him. Government spymasters had advance warning of an infiltration of Catholic Counter-revolutionaries. Campion was allowed into England and agents shadowed him, hoping he would lead them to the 'lion's den'. Informants kept in touch with the authorities as Campion made his way towards the safe house near Stratford at the ancestral home of the Arden family. Several other Jesuits were holding secret masses in a concerted effort to sway the religious beliefs of the people. The government agents gradually closed in.

The company called 'Lord Strange's Men' began as a troupe of acrobats. Over a period of about six years, Henry Stanley, fourth Earl of Derby, transformed it into an acting company. The players were led by John Symons, who was known as 'The Tumbler'. They played intermittently at court from 1580 to 1586. Symons left the company in 1588.

Playwrights were happy to take the £6 fee for writing a play, yet seemed reluctant to watch it in production. George Chapman actually refused to be bothered, saying, 'I see not my own plays.'

It was the time of naval adventures. England continued hostilities with the Spanish. After one particular excursion, Sir Francis Drake brought back booty worth £600,000.

According to Peter Ackroyd, Shakespeare makes use of sixty-six terms for the vagina, among them, 'ruff', 'scut', 'crack', lock', 'salmon's tail', 'clack dish' and, of course, other 'country matters'. Since the word 'nothing' is alleged to be an Elizabethan slang term for vagina, one can only speculate over the possible double-entendre in the title *Much Ado About Nothing*.

Until 1580 the published scripts of plays cost sixpence and had to be purchased from an accredited London bookstall. The profits went to the publisher, not to the author.

1581

Shakespeare was seventeen years old in April. There is a tradition placing Shakespeare in the county of Lancashire at this time.

It has been claimed that Shakespeare was employed as a young tutor at Alexander Hoghton's home in Lancashire. The evidence is circumstantial but there are definite clues. His schoolmaster, John Cottam, had left Stratford to become a 'servant' (as a tutor) for Hoghton and was in a position to recommend his former pupil, William, as an assistant. John's younger brother, the Catholic priest Father Thomas Cottam, had lived there incognito, pretending to be a gardener. Whoever they employed, the Hoghton family needed to find someone with impeccable references on whose discretion and loyalty they could rely.

When Hoghton seemed in danger of imminent arrest, he wrote a last will and testament, signed on 3 August 1581, in which seventeen-year-old Shakespeare, (spelt here Shakeshafte), is bequeathed to Sir Thomas Hesketh, thus:

> ... it is my mind and will that the said Thomas Hoghton of Brynescoules my brother shall have all my instruments belonging to music, and to all manner of play clothes if he be minded to keep and do keep the players.
>
> And if he will not keep and maintain players, then it is my will that Sir Thomas Hesketh, knight, shall have the same instruments and players' clothes. And I most heartily require the said Sir Thomas to be friendly unto Fulk Gyllome and William Shakeshafte now dwelling with me, and either take them unto his service or else to helpe them to some good master, as my trust is he will.

Gyllome refers to Fulke Gillam who was from an old family of Catholic pageant organisers responsible for producing the Chester mystery plays. (The will was proved on 12 September 1581.)

Shakespearian scholars have not made up their minds whether 'william Shakeshafte' mentioned in this will referred to William Shakespeare, the poet. On balance, they think it probably did. In which case, Shakespeare went with Fulke Gillam across the River Ribble to serve at Hesketh's Rufford Hall. Here, he may have been a junior teacher, participated in plays and played musical instruments. There is a lack of documentary evidence. On the other hand, there is nothing to suggest he was anywhere else.

If Sir Thomas Hesketh acceded to the request in Alexander Hoghton's will, Shakespeare may have become one of the troupe of players employed in private performances at Rufford Hall. Hesketh and Lord Strange were colleagues and Shakespeare soon became a member of a theatrical company, one of Lord Strange's Men. The circumstances leading to his transfer are unknown.

Twenty years later, in 1599, when Shakespeare became a co-owner of the Globe playhouse, one of the trustees was Thomas Savage, a goldsmith, whose wife was a Hesketh from Rufford Hall. John Heminges, a close acting colleague of Shakespeare, rented a house in Addle Street from the same Thomas Savage in the parish of St Mary's Aldermanbury, London.

The Hoghton family nurtured a long held tradition that Shakespeare had been one of their servants in the sixteenth century. Sir Thomas Hesketh's Rufford Hall is set in secluded gardens directly off the now busy A59 road near Ormskirk. Its spectacular Great Hall contains a carved 'moveable' wooden screen and a dramatic hammer-beam roof.

Tradition has it that Shakespeare stayed at the hall for six months in the 1580s but the theory wasn't taken seriously until the production of Honigmann's publication *Shakespeare: The Lost Years* in 1985, in which he states that there was good evidence that it was the real William Shakespeare who was at Rufford.

There are connections that can strengthen the case. A friend of the Lancashire families was Henry, the fourth Earl of Derby whose son, Ferdinando, had his own company of actors.

ACTUS SECUNDUS, SCENA SECUNDA

The acting company of Lord Strange's Men was established in Lancashire. Ferdinando Stanley, later the fifth Earl of Derby, was the patron. Shakespeare's early plays were staged by this company, making it likely that Lord Strange's Men gave Shakespeare his first provisional contract.

18 March: A royal directive barred the employment of unlicensed schoolmasters. If Shakespeare was then an assistant tutor, the simplest solution for him would have been to cease formal teaching and change his title to a servant or 'a player'. The Heskeths often entertained Lord and Lady Strange and since Strange had his own company of players, this would have provided Shakespeare with the means of becoming a professional actor. 'Player' was the common word for 'actor', a term which was less frequently used.

4 April: Queen Elizabeth went aboard the *Golden Hind* at Deptford and knighted Francis Drake (1540–96). He was the first Englishman to circumnavigate the planet. It had taken him thirty-four months to put a girdle round the earth. The earlier global circumnavigation made in the years 1519 to 1522 by the Magellan-Elcano expedition has been disputed on the ground of technicalities.

Sir Francis Drake was an English hero but in Spanish eyes, he was considered to be a pirate. They called him *El Draco*, Latin for 'The Dragon'. King Philip II offered a reward of 20,000 ducats for Drake's life; that is equivalent to about seven million dollars in the early twenty-first century.

5 September: In Stratford-upon-Avon it was Election Day, but John Shakespeare did not turn up. He had not attended a council meeting for months.

At some point on this day, John Shakespeare signed a declaration that he was a Catholic in the Jesuit Testamenta (a document drawn up by Edmund Campion under instruction from the leader of the Counter-Reformation movement, Cardinal Borromeo) and hid it in the loft at Henley Street.

Many years later, in 1757, this document was discovered. In it John Shakespeare attested his obedience to 'the Catholicke, Romaine and Apostolicke Church', claiming that his patron Saint was St Winifrere, whose shrine was in the Holy Well in Flintshire. The testament is written on a standardised form provided by the Jesuit priest, Edmund Campion, on the occasion when he visited Stratford in 1581. However, there remains a feeling of uncertainty as to the authenticity of this document.

September: Richard Hathaway died in Shottery (about a mile away from Stratford) at Hewland Farm – which he bequeathed to his son, Bartholomew. He left Anne Hathaway the sum of £6 13s 4d to be paid 'atte the day of her maryage'. The will was proved on 9 July 1582. Hewland Farm is better known today as Anne Hathaway's cottage. It contains twelve rooms.

The Master of the Revels, Edmund Tilney, of the Lord Chamberlain's department, was given the following brief: 'To vet all plays – 'tragedies, comedies or shows to order and reform, authorise and put down' should he disapprove (as referred to earlier). Tilney preferred the written word to masques, probably because plays were cheaper. He is credited with creating the Queen's company of actors two years later.

1 December: Edmund Campion, an English Jesuit priest who rejected Anglicanism, was hung, drawn and quartered as a traitor at Tyburn, following torture by 'Scavenger's Daughter' and the 'Duke of Exeter's Daughter' (see below).

The 'Scavenger's Daughter' was conceived as the perfect complement to the 'Duke of Exeter's Daughter' (the rack) because it worked in the opposite way to the rack by compressing the body rather than stretching it. This form of torture was invented by Sir Leonard Skeffington, Lieutenant of the Tower of London, during the reign of Henry VIII. A mispronunciation of his name led to the nickname of the compressing device, which consisted of one single iron bar that connected iron shackles closing around the victim's hands, feet and neck. These were then winched together, forcing the head to the knees of the victim in a sitting position, compressing the body in order to force the blood from nose and ears.

The Scavenger's Daughter is rarely mentioned in documents and the device itself was probably used in some secrecy. The best-documented use of it was on the Irishman Thomas Miagh, charged with being in contact with rebels in Ireland. It may be in connection with The Scavenger's Daughter that Miagh carved on the wall of the Beauchamp Tower in the Tower of London: 'By torture straynge my truth was tried, yet of my libertie denied. 1581. Thomas Miagh.'

🕮 **1582**

23 April: William Shakespeare's eighteenth birthday.

🕮 30 May: Father Thomas Cottam had been a Jesuit novitiate in Rome. He returned to England and was executed at Tyburn for disseminating Catholicism. Thomas was the brother of John Cottom (he chose to spell his name differently) who, since 1579 had been the schoolmaster at the King's Free School in Stratford.

🕮 24 July: In the London courts; John Shakespeare released William Burbage from his obligations regarding a dispute over the lease of his Henley Street house.

🕮 27 November: On this Tuesday, at the consistory court in Worcester, a special licence was issued for the marriage of William Shakespeare. Every diocese has its consistory court – a type of ecclesiastical court within the Church of England.

🕮 Fulk Sandells and John Richardson, friends of the Hathaway family, signed a surety of £40 as a financial guarantee for the wedding of 'William Shagspere and Anne Hathwey', so the likelihood is that Sandells and Richardson 'gave away the bride'.

🕮 The surety was made in the consistory court of Worcester to free the bishop from liability in case of 'lawful impediment by pre-contract or consanguinity, which might proceed hereupon with only one publication of banns.'

28 November: On Wednesday, the Episcopal register recorded the marriage bond had been granted:

*Dat. 28 die Novem. Anno regni dominae nostrae Eliz. Dei gratia Angliae Franc. Et Hiberniae Reginae fidei defensor &c.25.*2 The condition of this obligation is such that if hereafter there shall not appear any lawful let or impediment by reason of any precontract, consanguinity, affinity or by any other lawful means whatsoever, but that William Shagspere on the one party and Anne Hathwey of Stratford in the diocese of Worcester, maiden, may lawfully solemnize matrimony together, and in the same afterwards remain and continue like man and wife according unto the laws in that behalf provided...

27 November: Tuesday. There is another entry in the Episcopal register at Worcester with the issue of a marriage licence in which the names have been incorrectly recorded — probably because of another entry earlier in the day relating to 'Whateley'. For the record, this is how the earlier entry was written:

'*Anno Domini 1582 — November — 27 die eiusdem mensis. Item eodem die supradicto emanavit Licentia inter Willelmum Shaxpere et Annam Whateley de Temple Grafton.*' ('In the year of the Lord 1582 — November — 27 day of the same month. Also mention is made of a licence the same day between William Shaxper and Anne Whateley of Temple Grafton.')

In fact, this concerned another ecclesiastical matter with regards to somebody called Whateley who happened to make a deposition

THE BOOK OF SHAKESPEARIAN USELESS INFORMATION

that morning. It has been suggested that the confusion arose because the cleric wrote his note following a long liquid lunch.

William Shakespeare's age was eighteen years and seven months. By the canon of the Holy Scriptures of the Christian Church it was a requirement that 'infants' under twenty-one required the express consent of their parents and guardians. It follows that William needed to obtain his father's permission to get married. Anne Hathaway was pregnant and due for a dowry of £6 13s 4d upon her marriage, so it is probable that John Shakespeare gave his blessing to the marriage without prevarication.

To sum up, by the time he was eighteen, William Shakespeare was married to a pregnant woman seven years older than himself. What is more, his father was on the verge of ruin. William's prospects must have seemed bleak.

It is assumed that the wedding took place in a village called Temple Grafton, five miles west of Stratford, where the vicar was John Frith. It was a small church with no pews. In such circumstances it was usual for weddings to take place in the church porch. Frith acted under the guidance of the Bishop of Worcester, Dr John Whitgift, whose ecclesiastical regime was strict.

According to a report written in 1586, John Frith, the vicar, was 'an old priest and unsound in religion, he can neither preach nor read well, his chiefest trade is to cure hawks that are hurt or diseased for which purpose many do usually repair to him.'

John Frith, was identified by the government in 1586 as a Roman Catholic priest, even though he had outwardly affected Protestant ways. It is reasonable to speculate that the reason Shakespeare chose the church in Temple Grafton as the site of his wedding, as opposed to the then Protestant church in his hometown, was because he wanted to marry in a Catholic ceremony.

During the nineteenth century it became generally accepted that Shakespeare's marriage took place at Luddington, but there is no evidence for this.

There is yet another church where the ceremony might have been performed: St Martin's in Worcester. Again, there is no documentary evidence because at some point the marriage lists for 1582 have been excised from the parish register.

The reading of banns in the Worcester diocese was proscribed between Advent Sunday (2 December 1582) and the octave of Epiphany (13 January), so it is likely that the banns for William Shakespeare's marriage were read on St Andrew's Day, Friday, 30 November, when there was a full moon. William and Anne could then have married on the following day: Saturday 1 December 1582.

Anne Shakespeare left Hewland Farm to live at the Shakespeare family home in Henley Street.

There is no record that Mrs William Shakespeare ever went to London.

Thomas Whittington was Richard Hathaway's shepherd. In Whittington's will he claimed that Mrs Shakespeare owed him forty shillings — a statement that has foxed scholars ever since. In Richard Hathaway's will it is written: 'Item, I owe unto Thomas Whittington, my shepherd, fower poundes six shillings eight pence.'

As mentioned before, Anne Shakespeare is also referred to as Agnes. At that time, the name 'Agnes' was pronounced 'Annie' or 'Annice'.

The bride need not necessarily have worn a white dress — her own best dress would have sufficed, probably cotton or flax. White dresses were not yet fashionable for weddings. As for William's wedding outfit: it was *de rigueur* to sport a codpiece, and it was usual to wear breeches, hose and a doublet, with neck and cuff ruffs.

After the feasting, Anne and William returned to Stratford, where they took residence in John Shakespeare's crowded Henley Street house.

It was not possible for a married man to enter university or be apprenticed to a trade. Speculation places William as a clerk during the years 1583 and 1584. It seems logical that he tried to make money using his skills at reading and writing.

During October, the changeover from the Julian calendar to the Gregorian calendar took place in most Continental countries except England. Ten days were skipped and it was decreed that the day following Thursday 4 October, 1582, would become known as Friday

15 October, 1582. Being a directive of Pope Gregory, the English ignored it as a Catholic plot.

📖 One hundred-and-sixty-nine years passed before England implemented the change from the Julian to Gregorian calendar. The system was not synchronised until 1751. This has resulted in confusion over the exactitude of dates ever since.

📖 **1583**
23 April: This was William Shakespeare's nineteenth birthday, and little more than a month later, on 26 May, Susannah Shakespeare, the first of William and Anne's three children, was born.

📖 29 May (Trinity Sunday): Susannah Shakespeare was baptised by the Reverend Henry Haycroft, Protestant vicar of the Church of the Holy Trinity, Stratford-upon-Avon. Haycroft was transferred to the tiny village of Rowington in 1584.

📖 Elizabeth I's spymaster and *éminence grise*, Sir Francis Walsingham, brought together the twelve best actors from existing companies to form the Queen's Men. The amalgamation was actually for political reasons. From now on, the plays presented in the Queen's name were selected for their propaganda value, emphasising the monarch as head of the Church, with the intention of spreading the word of Protestantism throughout the country.

📖 Until this time James Burbage had been the leading actor of the Earl of Leicester's company.

A hautboy was an early version of the oboe. Plays had musical accompaniment played principally by drums, trumpets and hautboys.

In August Dr John Whitgift was appointed Archbishop of Canterbury, in which function he remained until 1604. A mean-spirited man in private life, he wrote a series of articles in which he tried to prove that everything is preordained by God. Elizabeth I suppressed the thesis, but it was an issue widely discussed, not least by Shakespeare in his plays.

25 October: A young man called John Somerville from Edstone near Stratford was arrested. Armed with a pistol, he boasted he was going to assassinate Elizabeth I. Somerville's father-in-law was Edward Arden, the head of Shakespeare's family on his mother's side. This triggered the Privy Council to send their troubleshooter, Thomas Wilkes, to Stratford to investigate the Ardens on their home turf.

2 November: Wilkes arrived and set up his local headquarters at the Charlecote home of Thomas Lucy. The next day Wilkes and Lucy assembled an armed posse and raided Park Hall, that had been the country-seat of the Ardens since William the Conqueror's era.

Today a sewage works marks the spot where Park Hall stood, to the northeast of Birmingham.

Edward Arden, his wife Mary, and their daughter Margaret were taken to the Tower of London along with Somerville and his supporters. Through the last two weeks of November, gaolers were kept busy. First the prisoners were incarcerated in 'the room of little ease' in the Tower, where it was too small for a person to lie down. They were then stretched on the rack. Finally they were compressed again in the Scavenger's Daughter device. It made no difference whether they confessed or not. Somerville was found strangled in his cell prior to the execution, but he was beheaded anyway. Edward Arden was hanged at Smithfield on 20 December. His death was typically appalling. Upon sentencing, he was told that 'you will be hanged by the neck, and being alive cut down, and your privy members to be cut off, and your bowels to be taken out of your belly and there burned, you being alive.' Dismembered heads were displayed on poles at the southern end of London Bridge, which in those days was situated to the east of our modern London Bridge. William Shakespeare would have had little choice but to see his cousin's head whenever he crossed the river to the theatre. He probably preferred to go by boat.

More than one hundred shops were built on Old London Bridge, some of them cantilevered precariously over the river for its whole length of 900 feet.

In Shakespeare's plays even prostitutes wore ruffs – small ones. Socially, the size of one's ruff was significant – the larger the ruff the more important the wearer and the more underpinning it required, sometimes requiring the use of wire and pasteboard. For some reason the size of ruffs continued to grow. A contemporary remarked 'every day worser and worser'.

Phillipp Stubbes wrote his *Anatomy of Abuses* in 1583: 'The devil, as he in the fullness of his malice first invented these great ruffs, so

105

hath he now found out also two great stars to bear up and maintain his kingdom of great ruffs: the one arch or pillar whereby his kingdom of great ruffs is underpropped, is a certain kind of liquid matter which they call Starch, wherein the devil hath willed them to wash and dive his ruffs well, which when they be dry will then stand stiff and inflexible about their necks... The other pillar is a certain device made of wires, crested for the purpose... and this he calleth a supportasse or underpropper.'

1584

Francis Throckmorton (1554–84) was a nephew of one of Queen Elizabeth's trusted diplomats and unwisely he had tried to liaise between Mary, Queen of Scots and the Spanish Ambassador. Throckmorton was captured and tortured, after which he confessed to organising an invasion of England to be led by Henry 1, Duke of Guise, and a plot to kill the queen. Throckmorton was executed for high treason.

23 April: William Shakespeare's twentieth birthday. Nobody has a clue where he was or what he was doing. But he may have been connected to Lord Strange's Men.

Lord Strange's Men were on a tour that included Coventry.

Queen Elizabeth granted Walter Raleigh a royal patent to explore and colonise 'the remote and barborous lands' of North America.

As soon as a play was accepted and approved by the Master of the Revels, the manuscript was returned to the company where it was stitched and bound with a hard cover.

Copyists wrote out each character's lines on a separate roll, indicating the cue by giving the last couple of lines of the preceding character's speech. According to Judith Cook in *The Golden Age of the English Theatre* (p. 112): 'each individual part was copied out on a roll of paper (hence the term roll-call) and handed to the actor, his appearance in the relevant scenes and his words marked only by the cues, the last words of the character before him and the first of the one who came after.'

During times of paper shortages – as in the world wars of the twentieth century – similarly abbreviated scripts were distributed amongst the actors. These pages were called 'sides'. These were still used by certain weekly repertory companies as late as the 1950s, as your chronicler can attest.

The original playhouses in late Elizabethan times were built with three separate acting areas: 1) the front stage with the rear concealed by a traverse curtain, 2) the whole stage – back and front – with the traverse curtain open, and 3) the 'upper' stage reached from the rear that could be used, for example, as a balcony or as the battlements of a castle. This explains the curious stage direction sometimes found in old play scripts: 'Enter Above'.

Over the stage area of the early playhouses was a blue canopy supported on columns called 'the heavens'.

Many of the stage costumes worn by actors were discarded robes handed down to them from wealthy patrons. Whole wardrobes were bequeathed to theatrical companies in some wills.

1585

2 February: William Shakespeare's twin children Hamnet and Judith were born. They were named after nearby neighbours Hamnet and Judith Sadler, who lived on the corner of the High Street and Sheep Street.

Lord Strange's Men were playing in Beverley.

The Queen's Men continued to tour; dates included Scotland, Dublin, Leicester, York, Norwich, and many of the stately homes of lords living in Lancashire, Yorkshire and East Anglia.

Lanman's business at the Curtain playhouse was doing so well that he and Burbage joined forces and agreed to pool profits from their ventures at the Curtain and The Theatre for the next seven years.

In March, Philip Henslowe bought a twenty-year lease on a large plot of land called the Little Rose Estate that lay on the Bankside area of the Thames opposite the city. The land was owned by the parish of St Mildred's in Bread Street in the city. Building began on the Rose playhouse eighteen months later. More than 200 plays were performed there between 1592 and 1603. The leading actor was Edward Alleyn, for whom Christopher Marlowe wrote many leading roles.

Sir Walter Raleigh (1554–1618) was knighted for suppressing Irish rebellions.

A descendant of Joan Shakespeare (William's sister) reported 'that Shakespeare owed his rise in life, and his introduction to the theatre, to his accidentally holding the horse of a gentleman at the door of the theatre on his first arriving in London; his appearance led to enquiry and subsequent patronage.' (James Halliwell-Phillipps, *Outlines of the Life of Shakespeare, 1883*.)

Most university-educated writers considered themselves superior to the typical expectations of theatre patrons. Such 'university wits' disparagingly dismissed the public as 'penny knaves' (as coined by Robert Greene). In order to display their erudition these writers penned stage directions in Latin. Actors set about replacing them with plain English. However, some examples survived, such as: *Dramatis Personae* and *Exeunt*.

Until the mid-1580s, Elizabethan theatre operated without scenery. These really were radio plays with minimal movement. Gradually the 'realist' school of that time demanded that details should be historically and topographically correct. The odd tree or bush emerged and such props became part of the growing expense in mounting productions. One of the appendices within Stanley Wells's book, *Shakespeare & Co.* is entitled 'An Inventory of Theatrical Properties'. This was penned on 10 March 1598 on behalf of the Lord Admiral's Men and is preserved at Dulwich College. Included within this document are such items as: '1 golden fleece, 2 rackets and 1 bay tree' and 'Mercury's wings; Tasso picture; 1 helmet with a dragon, 1 shield with 3 lions; 1 elm bowl,' and '1 cauldron for the Jew.' Et cetera.

1586

John Shakespeare was removed from the Board of Aldermen. At about the same time there were further accusations of usury against him (defined as charging borrowers interest above 10 per cent).

🕮 25 March: Margaret Clitherow, a Roman Catholic who hid priests in her home and secretly held mass, was pressed to death in York.

🕮 A Puritan survey of Warwickshire condemned 64 per cent of incumbents as 'dumbe'. There remained thirty approved preachers including Stratford's current vicar, Richard Barton. He is described within a Puritan survey of 1586 quoted in the 'Church Timeline' of the Holy Trinity Church Parish Office (Old Town, Stratford-upon-Avon, CV37 6BG) as: 'a preacher, learned, zealous and godly and fit for the ministry. A happy age if our age were provided with many such.'

🕮 11 August: After being implicated in the Babington Plot, Mary, Queen of Scots was arrested while out riding and taken to the village of Tixall. Spain immediately responded by declaring war on England and assembling an armada to invade her shores.

🕮 20 September: Tuesday. Plotters involved in the Babington conspiracy were found guilty of high treason and condemned to die in a mass execution. Anthony Babington had been enlisted by a priest named John Ballard in a plot to murder Queen Elizabeth, by putting gunpowder under her bed, after which they intended to release Mary Queen of Scots from Chartley Hall, where she was being held captive.

Seven Catholic men were bound to hurdles in the Tower of London – one of them, John Ballard, on a single sled, the others two-a-piece – and then dragged westward on their final journey through the city's autumnal streets to a scaffold in the open fields situated somewhere to the north west of what is now Lincoln's Inn Fields, then known as Cup Field. Babington and Ballard were drawn and quartered. The others were hanged. The authorities fenced off the site to stop horsemen blocking the view, and also raised the gallows 'mighty high' so that everyone could see justice being done. Thousands of people gathered to watch them die.

25 October: Mary, Queen of Scots was sentenced to death.

John Brayne died. He not only built The Red Lion venue but had also financed the construction of The Theatre. James Burbage immediately halted repayments of the debt he owed Brayne, whose widow, Margaret Brayne, together with her former business partner, Robert Myles, showed up in person at The Theatre to demand half of everything in the building. Richard Burbage, James's son, physically assaulted them. Robert and Margaret left empty handed and filed several lawsuits. However, their disputes were superseded by the new litigation of the Alleyns – the original owners of the land, after the Burbages dismantled The Theatre overnight and rebuilt it as the Globe on the South Bank. At the time of Margaret Brayne's death the lawsuits had not been settled. In her will she left the money she expected to accrue from court judgements to Robert Myles.

1587

10 January: A partnership was drawn up between Philip Henslowe and John Chumley in which they were to 'beniffyte somes of moneye proffitte and advantage of a playhouse now in framing and shortly to be erected...' The Rose playhouse was being built.

Mary, Queen of Scots had abdicated the Scottish throne in 1567 following the murder of her husband, Lord Darnley (in which it was suggested she was implicated) and her subsequent marriage to her husband's killer, the Earl of Bothwell.

Mary's grandmother was Henry VIII's sister, making her Elizabeth's auntie. Catholics were keen that Mary Stuart should be Elizabeth's successor to the throne. As mentioned above, the 'Babington plot' was hatched with the intention of doing away with Elizabeth and replacing her with Mary. When Elizabeth's spies brought the plot to her attention, Mary's fate was sealed.

8 February, soon after dawn: Thirty-five-year old Mary, Queen of Scots, blindfolded with a white veil embroidered with gold, was beheaded at Fotheringhay Castle, Northamptonshire. The executioner, a man named Bull, botched the first two strokes of the axe. After her head had been severed with the third stroke, he stood up holding Mary's head by the hair, as was the custom. Apparently it takes about fifteen seconds for a detached head to lose consciousness. The reason for holding up the head was not so much to let the crowd witness its detachment as to allow the still-conscious head to see its own body. In this case, Bull discovered he was clutching only an auburn wig, and the grey-haired skull of Mary, Queen of Scots clattered to the ground. It is claimed that following this incident, Richard Fletcher, father of John Fletcher, the writer, knelt on the scaffold steps and shouted, 'And so perish all the Queen's enemies.'

After the execution, a Skye terrier called Armageddon, Queen Mary's pet dog, was found hiding under her skirts and had to be parted forcibly from his dead mistress.

ACTUS SECUNDUS, SCENA SECUNDA

The Queen's Men presented *The Famous Victories of Henry Vth* with William Shakespeare in the cast. This was an early version of the play.

In his book, *Tarlton's Jests*, the clown, Richard Tarlton, claimed to have appeared in this production.

Richard Tarlton was Queen Elizabeth's favourite jester and renowned for his witty repartee against hecklers. He died in 1588 and part of his epitaph reads:
'...he of clowns to learn still sought
But now they learn of him they taught.'

13 June: The Queen's Men opened a tour at Thame in Oxfordshire. Following one of the performances, two of the actors had a sword fight in which John Towne killed the leading man, William Knell. Towne's plea of self-defence was accepted at a subsequent inquest. It has been suggested that this may have been the occasion when Shakespeare stepped in to fill Knell's roles and established himself as a journeyman actor.

The next two dates of this Queen's Men tour were Abingdon and then Stratford. As a junior member, Shakespeare would have been given minor roles and menial tasks, such as writing out the 'rolls' of the script from which actors learned their parts. Perhaps, as he did so, he made suggestions and improvements to relieve the sensitivities of the censor. His 'improvements' may have progressed into being trusted with major re-writes.

William Knell's widow, Rebecca, went on to marry John Heminges, who became one of Shakespeare's closest companions.

Rocco Bonetti ran a fencing school in Blackfriars used by actors and their apprentices, as well as by military men.

September: The Admiral's Men performed the First Part of *Tamburlaine the Great* by Christopher Marlowe. It was a tremendous success and marked a revolutionary approach to dramatic writing. Tamburlaine was played by Edward Alleyn (1566–1626), the actor who later founded Dulwich College.

October: The Rose playhouse in Southwark was up and running, attended by such a huge clientele that complaints were lodged by local residents about plays being performed on Sundays.

Philip Henslowe was thirty-two when he opened the Rose playhouse. His carpenter, John Griggs, constructed it as a fourteen-side polygon, copied from the earlier Theatre design. The stage was 47 feet (14m) wide. The outer sides of the fourteen bays were set one rod apart. A Tudor 'rod' was 16 feet and 6 inches.

The Rose became the London base of the Admiral's Men for several years.

The building site chosen for the Rose was on a messuage (house with outbuildings and land) called the 'Little Rose', leased from the parish of St Mildred in 1585. The word 'rose' in Tudor times was contemporary slang for 'prostitute'. It contained substantial gardens and two buildings; John Cholmley, a grocer, used one as a storehouse, while Henslowe leased the other as a brothel. It was situated by the Paris Gardens in the parish of St Saviour's on Bankside in Southwark.

When it was first built, the Rose playhouse had an audience capacity of 1900. Five years later, after remodelling, it could hold 2,400 patrons.

In 1989, an archeological dig took place on the site of the Rose, revealing 'orange pips, Tudor shoes, a human skull, a bear skull, the sternum of a turtle, sixteenth-century inn tokens, clay pipes, a spur, a sword scabbard and hilt, money boxes, quantities of animal bones, pins, shoes and old clothing.' (Eccles: *The Rose Theatre*, page 94.)

Raphael Holinshed wrote a comprehensive history of England, Ireland and Scotland. In 1587 it was revised and brought up to date. Shakespeare mirrored his stage adaptations on much of this material, sometimes matching it word for word. Holinshed was a friend of the Arden family thus it is likely that Shakespeare knew him.

John Shakespeare made renewed efforts to regain his wife's former family home, Asbies. At the same time, his younger brother, Henry, became a defaulter, failing to repay a loan from the Catholic landowner, Nicholas Lane, whose attorney, Thomas Trussell sued John Shakespeare in Henry's place. This led both sides into heavy costs over the recovery of £22.

From what little we know of William Shakespeare's uncle Henry, it seems he was a man of independent mind. Henry was excommunicated at one point for failing to pay church tithes. It transpired that he refused to wear a cap on Sundays. On another occasion he was fined for breaching the 'Statute of Caps'. The statute was made in 1571 on behalf of the trade of cappers to bolster the wool industry.

More than one hundred English settlers arrived in North America to establish a colony on Roanoke Island, off what is now North Carolina. They disappeared. In 2015 it was claimed that some of the settlers interbred with native Americans and that traces of their presence have been found further afield.

1588

In March, Rebecca Knell, aged sixteen and widow of the actor, William Knell, who had been killed in a fight the previous year, remarried. Her new husband was John Heminges, who became a close colleague of William Shakespeare. Heminges was one of the compilers of the First Folio in 1623.

As rumours began to spread of an impending Spanish Armada, a large proportion of the English population headed for the south coast, hoping to witness a sea battle. The Queen's Men followed the crowd and toured through Dover, Hythe, Romney, Lydd, Rye and Lyme Regis, and by the end of June they were in Plymouth where the queen's galleons were patrolling the coast, as Francis Drake waited patiently on Plymouth Hoe with little else to occupy his time other than playing bowls.

Shakespeare made three separate references to the game of bowls – more than for any other sport. He also touched upon tennis, football, fencing, tilting and wrestling.

8 July: The Pope proclaimed Philip of Spain as King of England following the excommunication of Queen Elizabeth in a Papal Bull (*Regnand in Excelsis*) in 1570. (A 'bull' is the leaden seal of a Papal document.)

29 July: The English Fleet defeated the invasion of the Spanish Armada. The Spanish had assembled their fleet two years previously in 1586 but sailing was delayed due to a shortage of balls for their 3,000 cannons. Eventually 123,000 cannon balls were delivered and Philip's astrologer gave the go-ahead for the invasion. However, this gave Sir Francis Drake and Queen Elizabeth two years to prepare for the attack.

The war with Spain did not finish with the defeat of the Armada. It continued for another ten years and only petered out when James I entertained the Spanish ambassador with a lavish entertainment of Shakespeare's plays.

30 August: The following recusants were hanged at Tyburn: Margaret Ward (the pearl of Tyburn), John Roche, Edward Shelley, Richard Martin, and Richard Flower. This was the penalty for helping a Catholic priest, Father William Watson, to escape from prison.

John Symons, also known as 'the Tumbler', left the Earl of Derby's company and joined a competing acrobatic troupe known as

Queen Elizabeth's Men. William Kempe, Thomas Pope and George Bryan joined Derby's company.

An early version of *The Taming of a Shrew* set in Greece was documented, although it is not believed to be Shakespeare's work.

Shakespeare wrote the first draft of *The Troublesome Reigne of John King of England*. This was first printed in 1611 by Valentine Simms, believed to be an associate of the author. Later, Shakespeare wrote a greatly revised version.

1 September: John Shakespeare paid another visit to Barton-on-the-Heath, in the vain hope of inducing John Lambert to surrender Asbies, the old Arden home.

4 September: The death of Robert Dudley, the Earl of Leicester (born 1532). For years he was surrounded by those who suspected that he had caused the death of his wife (Amy Robsart) in 1560 by arranging for her to be thrown down a staircase. These rumours prevented him from sealing his liaison with Queen Elizabeth. Following his death, the company of Leicester's Men disbanded.

During the last week of September, William's father, John Shakespeare, filed a bill of complaint at the Queen's Bench at Westminster for the repossession of a house in Wilmcote that was being unlawfully occupied by Edmund Lambert – a cousin. The case was suspended, not to be raised again until eight years later. The court records show that John and Mary Shakespeare were to present themselves '*simulcum Willielmo Shackespere filio suo*' (together with their son, William Shakespeare).

October: A series of tracts by Martin Marprelate were widely circulated, causing uproar. Martin Marprelate was the pseudonym for a Puritan writer who attacked the Established Church. The establishment hit back by commissioning John Lyly, Thomas Nashe and others to write a number of plays defending the attitude of the Protestant Church with its liberal approach to entertainment. The plays are now lost. Marprelate kept up a virulent attack on the bishops saying, 'Why, you enemies to the State, you traitors to God and his Word, you Mar-Prince, Mar-Law, Mar-Magistrate, Mar-Church, and Mar-Commonwealth, do you not know that the world should rather go a-begging than that the glory of God, by maiming His church, should be defaced?'

The man behind the nom-de-plume, John Penry, was eventually found, charged with inciting rebellion and hanged in May 1593.

17 November: Bells peeled across England not only to celebrate Elizabeth I's accession day but also to rejoice at the defeat of the Spanish Armada.

Many Spanish sailors were shipwrecked along the shores of England and Wales. Some remained and set up home. Many Welshmen have names that betray their Spanish roots as, for example, Delacassa.

1589

The Two Gentlemen of Verona was written during this period and Edmond Malone (1741–1812) a Shakespearian scholar, theorised that this play was among the first of Shakespeare's dramatic efforts. In 1778 Malone wrote 'An Attempt to Ascertain the Order in Which the Plays Attributed to Shakespeare Were Written'.

The 'benefit' system for authors meant that – subject to negotiation – a share of the box-office profits of the third performance of each new play went to the author. The majority of plays never achieved a third performance.

26 February: Thomas Quiney was born. He was destined to marry William's youngest daughter, Judith, in controversial circumstances (see Year 1616).

In July, John Spielman, a German entrepreneur, was granted the monopoly of making paper at his Dartford-based mill. The patent specified he alone could 'buy and deal in linen rags, old fishing nets and leather shreds ... fitt for making all sorts of white paper. Nobody else was permitted to build a paper-mill without Spielman's consent. All persons were forbidden to make any paper in any mills...alreadye made erected or used for broune paper mills save with the license and assent of Spielman.' Needless to say, paper remained an expensive commodity.

Spielman became known as 'Goldsmyth of our Jewelles' to Elizabeth I and James I. He manipulated the favour and patronage of successive monarchs to ensure that he had a virtual monopoly of the paper industry.

As mentioned above, paper was expensive and was used sparingly. Peter Ackroyd, in his book, *Shakespeare: The Biography*, suggests that Shakespeare wrote on both sides of folio-sized sheets of paper for this reason. Shakespeare managed about fifty lines per page.

Thomas Lodge's prose tale of *Rosalynde, Euphues Golden Legacie* was printed in 1590, and probably inspired Shakespeare to write *As You Like It*. Lodge was something of a snob and sneered at the 'penny-knaves' who went to plays. He would have been surprised that his own work was turned into one of the most successful plays of all time.

September/October: Following an order from the Lord Mayor of London to stop any more theatrical performances within the city of London, Shakespeare was by this time a member of Lord Strange's Men, who performed in London at The Cross Keys Inn. This coaching inn stood inside the city walls on the corner of Gracechurch and Bishopsgate Street on the road to Shoreditch.

18 September: Christopher (Kit) Marlowe had a sword fight with innkeeper William Bradley. Thomas Watson, Kit's companion, intervened and fatally stabbed Bradley. Marlowe and Watson were sent to Newgate prison but were released after a fortnight, as it was argued that they acted in self-defence.

Hog Lane, the area where Marlowe was involved in the fatal quarrel with Bradley, was then a rural community, surrounded by fields, windmills and butts for archery practice.

Thomas Nashe, considered a great Elizabethan pamphleteer, had seen a performance of *Hamlet* by this time. He wrote caustically of Shakespeare: '…an English Seneca who by candle-light yields many good sentences…' He pointed out that 'To Be or Not To Be' is a crib from Cicero who was supposed to have said, '*id aut esse aut non esse.*'

9 October: Shakespeare's name was mentioned in a complainant's bill for a case brought before the Queen's Bench at Westminster. (Jonathan Bate, *Soul of the Age*, 2009.)

In November, the Lord Mayor of London ordered Strange's Men to stage no more performances within the city. They responded immediately by going to the Cross Keys Inn to mount a performance.

In the last decade of the sixteenth century there were no more than 300 people, including actors, working in various capacities for the theatrical companies. In London it was not unusual to present a different play every night, six days a week.

The major companies included the Queen's Men, the Lord Admiral's Men, Lord Strange's Men, the Earl of Warwick's Men, the Earl of Essex's Men and the Earl of Sussex's Men – most of them with a stock company of twelve to fifteen actors plus production staff and the admission gatherers with their earthenware boxes, and so on. Also, there were the boys' companies such as the Children of St Paul's and the Children of the Chapel Royal. Shakespeare's progression through the ranks of his profession probably touched on these companies.

Rehearsals for a Royal Command performance took place at the Master of the Revel's offices in Clerkenwell. Here is an extract from one of the few extant accounts of the cost:

'...24 torches and 170 candles set around the hall on a series of plates. 400 sticks of firewood and 2 loads of coal...' The bill included rushes to keep the floor clean and warm, also a porter with three assistants (each receiving twelve pence per day) 'for their attendance and service in the rehearsals.' (Julian Bowsher, *Shakespeare's London Theatreland*, 2012)

Occasionally extra coal had to be purchased at great expense to speed up the drying process of newly painted cloths and pieces of scenery.

It is clear from the inquisition post-mortem of the Earl of Warwick (the Lord of the Manor) in 1590, that Mr John Shakespeare still owned the two houses in Henley Street.

Actus Tertius

Scena Prima

1590–9

🕮 **1590**

It has been estimated that three-quarters of all the plays written between 1590 and 1615 have been lost.

🕮 Writers were paid £6 on average for a playscript, which became the property of the company. During the course of twenty years, by 1610, the price of a play doubled.

🕮 John Shakespeare sold all his property with the exception of the Henley Street house.

🕮 Lord Strange's Men reached a reciprocal agreement with the Admiral's Men to share actors and to pool the income of performances from both The Theatre and the Curtain. At its zenith, Lord Strange's company consisted of twenty-seven actors including William

Shakespeare, Augustine Phillips, Will Sly, Thomas Pope, George Bryan, Richard Cowley, Edward Alleyn and Richard Burbage.

Richard Tarlton, the comic actor, lived with his lady, Em Ball, in Holywell Street, a few doors away from Richard Burbage.

Christopher Marlowe and Robert Greene lived in a cul-de-sac in the liberty of Norton Folgate, north of the parish of St Leonard, Shoreditch and east of the parish of Spitalfields. Many actors lived in the area, particularly in Hog Lane (now Worship Street), an area notorious for its thieves and prostitutes.

Henry VI, *Part 2* was written at about this time. It has the largest cast of any Shakespearian play. The Henry VI trilogy was not put together in chronological order. It did not enter the Stationers' Register until 12 March 1594. *Henry VI*, *Parts 2* and *3* were originally titled *The Contention of the Houses of York and Lancaster* and *Richard Duke of York*.

Some of the actors with whom Shakespeare worked could not read and had to learn their lines by rote from someone dictating the script to them.

A supply ship led by John White anchored at Roanoke Island to aid the new colonists, only to discover they had vanished, leaving a chiselled name on a gatepost reading: 'Croatoan'. 425 years later, an archaeologist called Mark Horton from the University of Bristol announced the discovery of Elizabethan artifacts on an island some seventy miles south of Roanoke, where a native Indian tribe, the Croatoans, once lived. Some of the Croatoan descendants display grey-blue eyes and fair hair, suggesting the probability that the lost colonists integrated with the natives.

1591

It has been estimated that, on average, each company produced fifteen new plays every year and that a new play took three weeks to rehearse.

The original handwritten play script was called 'The Book'. Similarly, today the script of a film is often referred to as 'The Property'.

Peter Ackroyd in *Shakespeare: The Biography* wrote that '... Shakespeare is supposed at various times of his career, to have collaborated with Jonson and Fletcher, Peele and Munday, Nashe and Middleton. There is no reason at all why he should not have done so.'

Open-air plays were produced without breaks in their continuity – rather like a two-hour movie seen in the cinema today.

The Puritan movement, culminating in the rise of Oliver Cromwell, was taking root at this time. Maypoles were banned in Coventry but the ban did not come into effect in Stratford until 1619.

From the beginning of the year until May, the Admiral's Men played at The Theatre. One of the plays presented was *Dead Man's Fortune* starring Edward Alleyn with Richard Burbage – the only time these two actors are known to have acted together.

Starting in 1745 and continuing well into the twentieth century, it was standard practice to play the National Anthem at the end of every performance while the cast and the audience stood to attention. In Shakespeare's time, an anthem had not been formally devised. In fact, 'God Save the King' was written to celebrate the defeat of the Gunpowder Plot in 1605. In Elizabethan times, the ritual following the end of a play, once the announcement for forthcoming attractions had been made, was for the actors to kneel on the stage while prayers were intoned for the monarch. To bend the knee (e.g. to kneel) was corrupted to 'break a leg' over time, and this became used as an expression to wish an actor a successful outcome for his performance. However, every actor has his own pet theory on the origin of this saying.

Once prayers had been said at the end of a performance, dancing followed. The principal comedian of a company, such as Will Kempe, performed jigs that became progressively suggestive and bawdy.

In the open-air playhouses, performances usually began at two in the afternoon but if an audience was thin, the start of a play might be delayed until four o'clock in the hope of attracting stragglers. When the second Lord Hunsdon took control, he pledged with the authorities that plays would conform to the two o'clock opening, so that audiences would not have to go home in the dark.

To proclaim that a theatre was open and preparing for a show, a flag was hoisted from the roof and a fanfare of trumpets would follow. Thereafter, drummers took up the call, parading round the venue, giving rise to the expression 'drumming up business'. Years later, in response to the protests of local residents, George Carey, the second Lord Hunsdon, forbade noisy demonstrations.

Henry VI, Part 3 was written at about this time. It was the success of the *Henry VI* trilogy that established Shakespeare's reputation as a playwright. The bookseller Thomas Millington issued a printed version in 1595. This is the play that the pamphleteer, Robert Greene mocked on 20 September 1592, so it was obviously in production before that date.

10 December: Outside his own house at Gray's Inn in London, Swithun Wells, with his fellow Catholic priests, Edmund Gennings, and Polydore Plasden, were hung, drawn and quartered. On the scaffold, Swithun Wells said to Topcliffe, 'I pray God make you a Paul of a Saul, of a bloody persecutor one of the Catholic Church's children.' In 1970, Pope Paul VI canonised them.

Autumn: *Richard III* was first performed by a conglomerate of the Admiral's Men and Lord Strange's Men with Richard Burbage playing King Richard. The play was highly successful. It may have been called *Buckingham* originally because in his diaries, Philip Henslowe refers to a play of this name being performed in December 1593 and January 1594. Later performances were given by the Lord Chamberlain's Men (also known as the Chamberlain's Men) at the Globe playhouse. It was not registered by the Stationers' Company until 20 October 1597.

A quarrel between Edward Alleyn and James Burbage resulted in Alleyn decamping from The Theatre. Alleyn moved south and crossed the Thames to the Rose playhouse in Southwark, taking with him several of the actors. Shakespeare remained at The Theatre with Burbage, Condell, Tooley, Beeton and John Sincler (nicknamed 'Sinco').

1592

Academics designate the seven years between 1585 and 1592 as 'Shakespeare's lost years' (Bowsher, *Shakespeare in London*, 2012).

William Shakespeare's knowledge of legal terminology was extensive. Consequently, it has been suggested he may have spent time as a clerk in a lawyer's office.

When Shakespeare first came to London there were twenty-six licensed brewers producing ales with names such as Stride Wide, Huffe Cup, Mad Dog, Angels' Food and Lift Leg.

The Battle of Alcazar (also called *Muly Molloco*), a play by George Peele, was presented fourteen times between 21 February 1592 and 20 January 1593 under the auspices of Lord Strange's Men. Later, at the turn of the century, it was presented by the Admiral's Men. In Edward Alleyn's production the property master supplied 'three vials of blood and the liver, heart and lungs of a sheep' for a disembowelling scene (Marchette Chute, *Shakespeare of London*, 1951).

February to June: Lord Strange's Men were at Henslowe's Rose playhouse where they acted in a repertory of twenty-three plays, one of which was called *A Knack to Know a Knave* that some claim to have been partly written by William Shakespeare.

26 February: The first performance of *The Jew of Malta* was produced at the Rose. Christopher Marlowe, the writer, missed the premiere, as he had been arrested on a coining charge. 'Coining' referred to several offences relating to gold and silver coins, from clipping coins to provide coin metal for forgeries, to colouring coins to make them appear of higher value. Coining was a hanging offence.

Philip Henslowe set about restructuring the Rose playhouse, with extensive remodelling of the stage area.

3 March: Henslowe recorded 'a performance of Harey VI' (*Henry VI*) by Lord Strange's Men at the Rose playhouse. It earned £3 16s 8d on its first showing: a triumph. This is the first documentary evidence confirming Shakespeare's presence in London. He was twenty-seven. Holinshed's Chronicles were his source material.

May: According to the Henslowe diaries, *Henry VI, Part 1* played fifteen times in May and June. 16,344 patrons saw the show from the galleries alone, meaning that the total number of admissions to this play was in the region of 30,000.

Shakespeare never let chronological facts get in the way of a good story. In *Henry VI*, Lord Talbot, Constable of France, dies before Joan La Pucelle (Joan of Arc). In reality he died twenty-two years after she did.

June: Following the rioting of apprentices in Southwark – which the Privy Council blamed on the evil influence taught to them by the theatres – all 'profane spectacles' were forbidden until 29 September.

23 June: Plague closed London theatres. Pembroke's Men went on tour. The dates included Edinburgh, Newcastle-upon-Tyne, Carlisle, Plymouth, Exeter, Winchester, Bath, Ludlow, York, Bristol, Southampton, Ipswich, Norwich, Coventry and Stratford.

Robert Southwell, the poet, came from Norfolk. He left England to study as a Catholic priest in Rome. At the age of twenty-six, he returned to England to face the greatest wave of anti-Catholic sentiment yet. He set up a secret publishing house to advise and comfort fellow Catholics. The queen and her council were furious. They wanted to find Southwell and make an example out of him. Enter Richard Topcliffe. Born in 1531, Topcliffe's uncle was Katherine Parr's first husband, so he was well connected. He had been a Member of Parliament at various times for both Beverley and Old Sarum. He had a penchant for torture and relished interrogating recusant Catholics, gypsies and vagabonds. Topcliffe seduced a Catholic girl, impregnated her, and persuaded her to reveal Southwell's hiding place. The prisoner was taken to Topcliffe's house in Westminster where a torture room had been rigged up. This allowed the Privy Council to declare that Southwell was only under house arrest. Southwell's wrists were manacled and his arms were held up and the manacles stapled to the wall with his feet off the ground. He was hung like this on ten concurrent occasions for several hours at a time. Eventually, Southwell was hung, drawn and quartered.

Topcliffe boasted that he had touched the Queen's breasts and 'that he felt her belly and said unto Her Majesty that she had the softest belly of any womankind.'

23 July: Meanwhile, in Stratford, John Shakespeare appraised the goods of two neighbours – of Ralph Shawe, wool-driver, and Henry Field, tanner.

Actors 'doubled' and played several parts in each production. If there were minor roles to be filled, they were cast from outside the company. The payment for this was one shilling per performance. (Chute, *Shakespeare and His Stage*).

Richard Burbage (1567–1619) was the first actor to play Richard III, Lear, Hamlet, and Othello. It is probable that he created the roles of Romeo, Macbeth, Coriolanus, Prospero, Henry V and Antony. He also played major roles in plays by Jonson, and Beaumont and Fletcher, and excelled in tragedy.

Edward the Third was written about this time. Many scholars believe it to be the work of Thomas Kyd with additional material by Shakespeare, thus explaining why it did not appear in the first folio of 1623. It is unknown when the play was originally produced but it appeared in print, anonymously, in 1596.

In Stratford John Shakespeare was fined for not attending church.

Throughout August, theatres remained closed following the ban imposed after the riots in June. The theatre owners made a special plea to reopen on behalf of 'the poore watermen' who usually ferried theatregoers to the south bank. The council relented and the theatres were in rehearsal when another wave of plague swept the country.

🕮 13 August: The Privy Council put out a warning that the latest outbreak of the plague would force all places of entertainment to close.

🕮 William Shakespeare changed employers. He ceased being an actor with Lord Strange's Men and joined the company of the Earl of Pembroke's Men.

🕮 21 August: In Stratford-upon-Avon, Thomas Trussell, an attorney, drew up the inventory for the estates of Ralph Shawe and Henry Field, and denominated his associate as 'Mr. John Shaksper, Senior', for no clear reason, but possibly to distinguish him from another John Shakespeare – a local cobbler. The attestation is witnessed only by an inked cross.

🕮 During the year, Sir Thomas Lucy and others continued to assemble lists of Warwickshire recusants that had been 'heretofore presented'. Among these they included several members of the sorely oppressed family of the Ardens of Park Hall, and in Stratford-on-Avon 'Mr. John Shackspere' and eight others. Probably some friendly clerk, wishing to spare them fines, added: 'it is sayd that these last nine coom not to Churche for feare of process for debte.' However, it is possible it might refer to the other John Shakespeare – the shoemaker who, having been Master of the Shoemakers' Company, might have been called 'Mr.' In the earlier undated draught from which this was taken the Commissioners state: 'wee suspect theese nyne persons next ensuinge absent themselves for feare of processes, Mr. John Wheeler, John his son, Mr. John Shackespeere,' etc.

3 September: Robert Greene, a University graduate and writer, died. During his last illness he wrote *A Groatsworth of Wit* in which he made coruscating comments about Shakespeare: '... with his tiger's heart wrapped in a player's hide supposes he is as well able to bombast out a blank verse as the best of you; and being an absolute Johannes factotum is his own conceit the only Shake-scene in the country.' Roughly translated, 'Johanne factotum' means 'jack of all trades'. The sentence regarding a 'tiger's heart wrapped in a player's hide' parodies Shakespeare's line in *Henry VI*: 'a tiger's heart wrapped in a woman's hide.'

Robert Greene had a wife, Dorothy, who survived him. He also had as his mistress a notorious prostitute called Emma Ball, sister of the cutpurse known as 'Cutting' Ball. This was the same Em Ball who had lived with the comic actor Richard Tarleton (1530–88). Emma and Robert Greene had a son whom they tastelessly christened Fortunatus, who was buried in St Leonard's, Shoreditch, on 12 August 1593.

3 September: Coinciding with Robert Greene's death at the age of thirty-two, two books of his reminiscences were published: *Greene's groats-worth of wit* and *Greene's vision, 'written at the instant of his death'*. Soon after the death of Robert Greene, his publisher, Henry Chettle, published a rebuttal of Greene's maligning comments by 'praising Shakespeare's honesty and his facetious grace in writing.'

Ben Jonson left Flanders, where he had been serving in the army, and returned to England.

When Shakespeare arrived in London he lodged in Shoreditch where there was a wide choice of inns. He could have stayed at the

White Hart by St Botolph's Church or The Dolphin Inn that could 'lodge and with ease feed two or three hundred people and their horses at short warning.' Alternatively, there were The Bells, The Cross Keys, The Wrestlers, The Angel, The Vine, The Four Swans, The Green Dragon and The Black Bull, to name but a few.

The 'going rate' for London inns was one penny per night for bed and breakfast without stabling.

7 September: The London council put the plague orders into effect. All theatres within seven miles of London were to remain closed until 3 June 1594.

Ammunition was expensive so when a gun had to be fired, 'training blanks' were generally used. However, this was not possible for cannons, for which actual balls had to be employed. Unfortunately, this was still an inexact science and the results were unpredictable. The original Globe playhouse was burnt down because of a misfired cannon ball.

Over time, sound effects were introduced and continued well into the late twentieth-century, using some of the early primitive methods. These included the sound of wind by means of turning a wheel under a sheet of canvas, rain – simulated by peas rolled in a drum, and a sheet of thin metal being shaken to evoke thunder.

Philip Henslowe's stepdaughter married Edward Alleyn, one of the most popular actors of the day.

In his concise biography on Shakespeare, Bill Bryson considers that the memoranda Philip Henslowe scribbled on the reverse sides of his account books from 1592–1603 were not so much diaries as 'a catch-all of preoccupations including a recipe for curing deafness, notes on casting spells, even advice on how best to pasture a horse.'

At the end of each week, money collected in 'the Box Office' was divided among the actors following deduction of expenses.

Shakespeare's principle income came from his work as an actor. For handing in a complete playscript he received no more than £6 or £7. Collaborative efforts with other writers brought his share down to around £2. Shakespeare wrote about forty plays over twenty years, so his total income as a writer would have been no more than £300. That is, around £14 per year. It was his involvement as an actor-shareholder that made him a rich man.

Despite claiming to write for the common man, some university-trained writers could not resist demonstrating their erudition by penning stage directions in Latin. Actors tended to replace these with plain English, though certain examples survive to this day such as *Dramatis personae* and *Exeunt*.

Costumes were the biggest budgetary consideration and armour was an expensive part of the wardrobe. Sometimes an armourer's apprentice had to be hired to help the actors get in and out of the equipment.

Sword-fighting on the streets was common, and actors on the stage had to sword-fight realistically. Comic actor, Richard Tarleton, despite being vertically challenged, was made 'Master of the Fence' in the 1580s – the highest award the fencing schools could grant.

Edward Alleyn was also Master of the Queen's Bears and conducted some of the bear-fighting tournaments himself.

It was not yet usual for actors to go out on provincial tours during the winter and it is conjectured that William Shakespeare spent the end of 1592 and the beginning of 1593 writing his narrative poem *Venus and Adonis*.

October: In Stratford-upon-Avon thirty-seven people were accused of opening their shops on the Sabbath or holy days, seven charged with fornication or adultery, one for receiving evil company in their house and another for making slanderous libels.

The play, *Sir Thomas More* may have been written at about this time. The 'plotter' of plays, Anthony Munday, wrote the scenario based on Holinshed's Chronicles but the authorities cast this play to one side until such time as a writer could be found to tone down the threat of civil disobedience inherent in the subject matter (of a court official opposing the will of a monarch) that was feared might disparage the official Protestant religion of England. Master of the Revels, Edmund Tilney, wrote on the manuscript: 'Leave out the insurrection wholly with the cause thereof, and begin with Sir Thomas More at the Mayor's sessions with a report afterwards of his good service done, being Sheriff of London, upon a mutiny against the Lombards only by a short report and not otherwise, at your own peril.' Shakespeare complied and managed to water down any possibility of incitement to riot. Other writers were brought in: Henry Chettle, Thomas Dekker, and Thomas Heywood. Even so, the material was still considered too sensitive for a public performance. A handwritten script survives in the British Library. 147 lines have been identified as being in Shakespeare's own hand, the only writing of his known to survive apart from six signatures. The first production was at Nottingham Playhouse in 1964 with Ian (now Sir Ian) McKellen as Sir Thomas More.

Queen Elizabeth visited her godson, Sir John Harington, at his house in Kelston near Bath. There he had invented the first flushing lavatory, which he named Ajax. The queen was so impressed she ordered one to be built for herself. Meanwhile, her subjects, blissfully unaware of such developments, continued to sit on their jordans (chamber pots), then emptied them into the streets below whilst calling out, '*gardez-l'eau*', which today is truncated into the word 'loo', as mentioned earlier. Geese had a hard time of it: goose-down was popularly used before toilet paper was invented.

When Shakespeare joined the Chamberlain's Men, it was compulsory for him to attend St Helen's Church in Bishopsgate on Sundays. St Helen's was second only to Westminster Abbey in terms of tombs and monuments. Churches in England developed a system of handing out metal tokens to the congregation. Each worshipper had to return it to the communion table on the following Sunday. Failure to turn up without a good excuse was met with a hefty fine. An adult male taxpayer who failed to go to church regularly was immediately suspected of being a recusant.

Travellers between Stratford and London invariably stayed overnight in Oxford. The following is an account of a delegation from Stratford who went to London on corporation business:

> Charges laid out when we went to the court – 1592.
>
> Paid for our horsemeat the first night at Oxford: 2 shillings and 8 pence
>
> And for our own charges the same night: two shillings and two pence.
>
> The second night at Iselipp for our suppers: two shillings and fourpence.
>
> For horsemeat the same night at Iselipp: two shillings and eightpence.
>
> The third day for our bayt and our horses at Hooke Norton: twelve pence.
>
> And for walking our horses at Testseworth and elsewhere: three pence.
>
> Sum for this journey: eleven shillings and one penny.'
>
> (James Halliwell, *A Life of William Shakespeare*, 1848.)

John Aubrey (1626–97) in his strained working relationship with Anthony Woods (1632–95) speaking of William Davenant, related the following: 'His mother was a very beautiful woman, of a good wit and conversation, in which she was imitated by none of her children but by this William. The father, who was a very grave and discreet citizen (yet an admirer and lover of plays and playmakers, especially Shakespeare, who frequented his house in his journies between Warwickshire and London), was of a melancholick disposition, and was seldom or never seen to laugh.'

As well as carrying a sword, Shakespeare would have worn a tall hat – the taller your hat, the higher your social status.

Thomas Vincent was called a 'book-keeper' at The Globe. Today he might be described as Prompter or the 'Stage Manager on the Book'. There has been speculation that Shakespeare started out as Vincent's assistant.

1593

Plague wiped out 15 per cent of the population of England.

January: London's Privy Council issued the following Order: 'Forasmuch as by the certificate of the last week it appeareth the infection [the plague] doth increase we think it fit for all manner of concourse and public meetings of the people at plays, bear-baitings, bowlings and other like assemblies for sports be forbidden...'

The effect of this order was to keep the London theatres closed. Save for a few weeks in the winter, they remained closed for eighteen months.

2 February: With all London playhouses shut, Pembroke's Men went on tour to Ludlow, Bath and Bewdley. At Bath the company received 14 shillings. In Bewdley and Ludlow the company received 20 shillings from each venue. In Shrewsbury it received 40 shillings.

To rein in the possibility of seditious printing, only twenty-two printers were licensed to publish material in the City of London. One of these was a friend of Shakespeare called Richard Fields, who also hailed from Stratford. When his father Henry Fields died in 1591, John Shakespeare was the council member who appraised his goods.

18 April: *Venus and Adonis*, the first epic poem by Shakespeare, was published and sold at sixpence per copy. The printer was Richard Fields of Blackfriars. London was flooded with posters declaring that copies of *Venus and Adonis* could be purchased at the 'sign of The White Greyhound' in St Paul's Churchyard at the shop owned by John Harrison, senior, one of the major London publishers. William had taken the storyline from Ovid's *Metamorphoses*. *Venus and Adonis* was an instant hit, going through ten editions during Shakespeare's lifetime.

In its 1,194 lines, *Venus and Adonis* contains many allusions to sexual intercourse:
'Backward she push'd him as she would be thrust...'
'Panting he lies, and breatheth in her face...'
'Be bold to play – our sport is not in sight...'
When Venus mourns the death of Adonis, Shakespeare wrote the deathless line: '"Ay me!" she cries, and twenty times "Woe, woe!" / And twenty echoes twenty times cry so.'

Venus and Adonis conforms to 'the Greek unities' taking place in one location over twenty-four hours. It was dedicated to the Earl of Southampton, who was nineteen in the spring of 1593. The Earl, described as decidedly effete, inherited great wealth from his father and struck up a close relationship with an older man, the Earl of Sussex.

The Stationers' Company had offices in a hall on the south-west of Paul's Churchyard. When unauthorised or banned books were discovered, the Stationers' Company formally burnt them in the hall kitchen.

12 May: Thomas Kyd, a colleague of Christopher Marlowe, was arrested for the alleged distribution of 'inciteful' posters against Protestant refugees from the Continent.

18 May: A warrant was issued for the arrest of Christopher Marlowe, for his alleged contribution to inciting violence against Protestants.

20 May: Christopher Marlowe presented himself to the Privy Council to give himself up but it was not sitting that day so he went home again.

29 May: At four o'clock in the afternoon, John Penry, a Puritan, having been found guilty of sedition and inciting rebellion, was hanged at St Thomas-à-Watering, now known as Walworth Common on the Old Kent Road. The Thomas-à-Becket pub is adjacent to the place where the old gallows stood.

John Penry has become a symbol of Welsh Protestantism. The fact that Christopher Marlowe is recorded to have died less than twenty-four hours later than Penry did, just over two miles away in Deptford, has led to speculation that Marlowe faked his own death and pretended that Penry's dead body was his own.

30 May: Christopher Marlowe was killed in Deptford. Dame Eleanor Bull, a widow, owned a large house where she hired out

rooms for private meetings. It was rumoured to be 'a safe house' for Government agents. Christopher Marlowe had previously received a commendation from the Privy Council for his 'good service' to the queen. He was reputed to be a spy working for Sir Francis Walsingham's intelligence service. On this day, he had a meeting at Dame Eleanor's house with Ingram Frizer, Nicholas Skeres and Robert Poley (this was a private house, not a tavern). Dame Eleanor's sister, Blanche, was the god-daughter of Blanche Parry, who had been nanny to Queen Elizabeth in her infancy.

Marlowe and Ingram Frizer argued over whose turn it was to pay the bill. Marlowe grabbed Frizer's dagger and cut him on the head twice. Frizer seized back his dagger and with a single stab into Marlowe's right eye, killed him instantly (see below for more details).

Until recently academics gave serious consideration to the theory that Christopher Marlowe faked his own death and went abroad to live in exile under the assumed name of Monsieur Le Doux. Geoffrey Caveney, in collaboration with Peter Farey, scotched the rumour and pointed out that Monsieur Le Doux was, in fact, the nom-de-plume of European scholar Catharinus Dulcis (1540–1626).

Within a few months, a rumour was circulating that the fight between Marlowe and Frizer resulted from a homosexual lovers' tiff arising from jealousy. In *Palladis Tamia* published in 1598, Francis Mere wrote: 'Marlowe was stabbed to death by a bawdy serving man, a rival of his in his lewd love' as some sort of divine justice for his 'epicurism and atheism'.

ACTUS TERTIUS, SCENA PRIMA

🕮 1 June: The Coroner of the Queen's Household, William Danby, presided over an inquest on Christopher Marlowe's death. It was established that all of the four men meeting at Dame Bull's house had been special agents working under Francis Walsingham – the Elizabethan equivalent of our MI5. Skeres and Poley had been undercover agents in the Babington Plot. Poley was actively on a mission carrying secret papers to the queen that very day (he did eventually deliver them on 8 June). Witnesses claimed that Marlowe and Frizer had argued over the bill for refreshments. Frizer was sitting at a table and Marlowe was lying on a couch behind him. 'Malicious words' were exchanged. Marlowe rose, took Frizer's dagger and tried to stab him. There was a struggle, Frizer wrested the knife away as he turned to face Marlowe and stabbed him fatally in the eye. Frizer's plea of self-defence was accepted and he was let free. At various times both men had been engaged by the Royal Court as secret agents. Immediately following the inquest, Marlowe was buried in an unmarked grave at the Church of St Nicholas in Deptford. Or so it was alleged. The conspiracists say the buried body was actually that of John Penry.

🕮 Fortunately, Marlowe's greatest writing rival, Shakespeare, was out of London on tour at the time, so no slur could be levelled against him.

🕮 Marlowe, Kyd and other alleged homosexuals were not overt in their predilection for such sexual activities, because sodomy was a capital offence.

🕮 Marlowe was twenty-nine when he died. Lyly wrote nothing after the age of thirty-seven. Greene died at the age of thirty-two,

147

Peele at thirty-nine, and Kyd at thirty-eight. Shakespeare did not reach his writing peak until he was thirty-two and continued working until he was fifty-two.

By mid-July, 15,000 Londoners had succumbed to the plague.

July: Lord Pembroke's Men performed in Rye on the south coast of England, where they made thirteen shillings and fourpence.

1593–97: According to court records, William Shakespeare owed outstanding tax in Shoreditch. It was noted that he had moved away from Shoreditch and was now lodging in Bishopsgate (see Appendix D)

On tour, up north, the Pembroke Men's company collapsed financially to such an extent that the actors had to pawn their costumes to pay expenses. William Shakespeare was a member of the bankrupt company. Some players joined the Earl of Sussex's Men. It is probable that Shakespeare was amongst them, in which case he would have had to 'go on the road' again. Dates that they performed on included Newcastle and Winchester.

25 September: Following Ferdinando Stanley, Lord Strange's accession to his father's title, Strange's Men (pronounced 'Strang') became known as the 'Earl of Derby's Men'.

28 September: In a letter to Edward Alleyn, Philip Henslowe wrote: 'As for my lord of Pembroke's, which you desire to know where they may be, they are all at home, and have been this five or six

weeks; for they cannot save their charges with travel, as I hear, and were fain to pawn the apparel.' In other words, the show had folded and Shakespeare was 'resting'.

Most of the scene divisions that are published in today's editions of Shakespeare's plays are thanks to the gratuitous intervention of an eighteenth-century editor, Nicholas Rowe. These divisions tend to obstruct the unbroken flow of the narrative. Shakespeare often used a rhyming couplet to indicate the end of a scene. The actors then carried on in the new location or time zone without pause. 'Scene divisions' and 'Intervals' came about because of the introduction of scenery and lighting in indoor theatres. (See August 1608).

The wife of Edward Alleyn was Philip Henslowe's stepdaughter. She was 'carted' (arrested) as a prostitute but it is thought that the real reason for charging her was because during a plague outbreak she didn't close down the brothel that she controlled.

1594

The knock-on effect of a disastrous harvest the previous autumn was causing near starvation in parts of England. Poorer peasants were reduced to eating acorns.

24 January: First mention of *Titus Andronicus* in Philip Henslowe's 'Diaries'. He recorded a performance by Sussex's Men as *Titus & ondronicus* [sic] probably at The Rose playhouse, taking three pounds and eight shillings at the box office. There were other performances on 29 January and 6 February. On the latter date, the play was entered by the printer, John Danter, in the Stationers' Register under the title *A*

Noble Roman Historye of Tytus Andronicus. Copies of the play were sold at the 'Sign of the Gun' outside the north door of St Paul's.

John Masefield (Poet Laureate, 1930–67) wrote this about *Titus Andronicus*: 'Shakespeare certainly never touched this job for love… It is possible that the play was brought to him by his theatre-manager, with such words as these: 'This piece is very bad, but it will succeed, and I mean to produce it, if I can start rehearsals at once. Will you revise it for me? Please do what you can with it, and write in lines and passages where you think it is wanting. And whatever happens please let me have it by Monday.'

29 January: The second performance of *Titus Andronicus* earned two pounds at the box office. Two more performances of *Titus Andronicus* took place on 5 June and 12 June.

Some scholars believe that *Titus Andronicus* was a collaboration between Shakespeare and George Peele. They claim that *Troilus and Cressida* is a first rough draft and that the play is unfit for production. Experts also theorise that *King Henry VIII* was written by John Fletcher assisted by Massinger (J. W. Marriott, *The Theatre*, 1945).

The misfortunes of *Titus Andronicus* were sung in the streets to the tune of 'Fortune My Foe'. This ditty had hitherto accompanied ballads describing murders. It became known as 'the hanging tune'.

Elizabeth I translated some of the works of the Roman poet, Seneca. Shakespeare's *Titus Andronicus* is a dramatic reconstruction of

Seneca's *Thyestes*. He wove in Ovid's story of *Philomena* to portray the rape of Lavinia.

The Mayor and the London council continually tried to suppress plays on the grounds that the crowds they attracted were a public nuisance. However, the queen wanted to see plays and her word was law. In order that there would be a supply of suitable dramas for her to see during the Christmas season, it was necessary that they be tried out in public first.

This gave playhouses such a good excuse to perform plays on a daily basis that the council complained that every playhouse in London was filled with companies declaring themselves to be the Queen's Men.

Fashionable weddings often ended with a play. The Stationers' Company made a charge of ten shillings for the use of their Hall at the Priory of St John's for special events.

6 February: *Titus Andronicus* was entered into the Stationers' Register by the printer John Danter as 'A booke intitled a Noble Roman Historye of Tytus Andronicus' It also states that the play had already been tried out by the Earl of Derby and the Earl of Pembroke.

6 February: In the afternoon a stage performance of *Titus Andronicus* at the Rose playhouse took two pounds in admission charges.

Shakespeare never wrote a contemporary play.

The Earl of Sussex's Men returned to London.

Plague forced the theatrical companies to stay on the road for a year-and-a-half. By the spring of 1594, two acting companies dominated the London stage. First, there were the Admiral's Men with Edward Alleyn as its star. Alleyn, backed by his wealthy father-in-law, Philip Henslowe, ran the Rose playhouse. Their patron was the High Admiral of England, Charles, Lord Howard of Effingham, who had commanded the fleet against the Spanish Armada.

The chief rivals of the Admiral's Men were the Chamberlain's Men, of which Shakespeare was a leading member. This had been formed following the death of Lord Strange, fifth Earl of Derby, in 1594. It was compulsory for a theatre company to have a noble patron and his death left a vacancy, filled by a first cousin of Elizabeth I, Henry, Lord Hunsdon, who held the important Court position of Lord Chamberlain. Consequently the troupe of actors changed its name to the Chamberlain's Men.

This new company, the Lord Chamberlain's Men, consisted of ten actors plus six boys – acting apprentices – who would play the female parts. The boys' parents paid £8 for them 'to be taken into service'. Each master actor in charge of an apprentice promised to pay his lad fourpence per day and teach him 'in playinge of interludes and plaies'.

Lord Hunsdon, aged seventy, vouchsafed that all plays would henceforth start promptly at 2.00 p.m. and that the performances would finish in time for the audiences to return home before dark. He also declared that there would be none of the loud trumpet fanfares and the banging of drums that usually announced the commencement of a performance, as a sop to the people who lived in the area.

As mentioned above, Hunsdon was the queen's first cousin and had a curious background. Henry Carey, first Baron Hunsdon, was the illegitimate son of Henry VIII. His mother was Mary Boleyn (Elizabeth's aunt). His meteoric rise in the aristocracy merely confirms this. Elizabeth bestowed favours on him and made him her chief Privy Councillor. It was a great relief to the actors that their patron was so politically powerful. Carey's marriage to Ann Morgan resulted in sixteen children. At the age of sixty-six he began an affair with Emilia Lanier (Lanier was her later, married name) (1569–1645), daughter of a Venetian-born Jewish court musician, that resulted in further illegitimate offspring, another son: the grandson of Henry VIII. Emilia was twenty-three when she became pregnant with Lord Hunsdon's child in 1592. Hunsdon was forty-five years older than her. He paid her a large sum of 'hush money' and then married her off to her own first-cousin – once-removed, Alfonso Lanier, a queen's musician. They were married in St Botolph's Church, Aldgate on 18 October 1592. Lanier then gave birth to Carey's son, another Henry, in 1593.

Lord Hunsdon had complete control over the royal household and the Office of the Revels had to comply with his instructions. He was 'extremely choleric by nature' and famous for 'his custom of swearing'. In many respects he reflected the qualities of Henry VIII, who was allegedly his real father.

Shakespeare remained with the Chamberlain's Men for the rest of his life. The historian, A.L. Rowse, described him as 'actor, shareholder, patented member, principal playwright and one of the housekeepers of the Globe.' Later, when James I (James VI of Scotland) ascended the throne, the company changed its name to the King's Men.

The Chamberlain's Men grew to comprise about fifteen actors including Augustine Phillips, who lived in Southwark with his wife Ann and their five children.

Three of the leading members of the Chamberlain's Men resided in Shoreditch near The Theatre. Richard Burbage and Richard Cowley lived with their respective families near each other in Holywell Street (aka Halliwell Street).

Edmond Malone, the eighteenth-century scholar, noted that Philip Henslowe recorded how Shakespeare lived close to the Bear Gardens near the Elephant Inn on the corner of Horseshoe Alley. This memorandum has since been lost. There were at least 300 inns in the vicinity of Southwark.

John Heminges and his wife Rebecca, with their fourteen children, and Henry Condell and his wife Elizabeth, with their nine children, lived on the west side of town in the Parish of St Mary Aldermanbury, within the walls of Cheapside.

Shakespeare first lived on Bishopsgate Street in lower Shoreditch before moving to Southwark as a neighbour of Augustine Phillips.

Afterwards he took rooms to be near Heminges and Condell. Shakespeare was always on the move around London, where for twenty years he rented rooms. This might be interpreted to mean that he felt he was a man of Stratford who was merely 'visiting' London.

Heminges acted as a business manager for his colleagues and helped execute their wills. Heminges and Condell were to be the principal movers behind issuing the first folio of Shakespeare's works in 1623.

The Lord Chamberlain's Men made a temporary home in Newington Butts, south of London Bridge, in a makeshift theatre that had been an archery range. Then they moved to the city of London to act at the Cross Keys Inn as a temporary measure, before a short residency at The Theatre in Shoreditch.

Shakespeare became a neighbour of Thomas Morley (1558–1602), who wrote musical settings for some of Shakespeare's plays. Morley is closely associated with the song 'There was a lover and his lass' from *As You Like It*. He became organist at St Paul's Cathedral in 1590.

Solo songs in Elizabethan plays were usually accompanied by the lute, an instrument handled by the player similarly to the technique employed by a modern guitarist.

In the tax assessment roll of St Helen's parish, Shakespeare's goods (including books) were valued at 13s 4d. (See Appendix D.)

12 March: A play was entered in the Stationers' Register by the bookseller Thomas Millington and printed in quarto by Thomas Creede later that year as 'The First part of the Contention betwixt the two famous Houses of Yorke and Lancaster, with the death of the good Duke Humphrey: And the banishment and death of the Duke of Suffolke, and the Tragicall end of the proud Cardinall of VVinchester, vvith the notable Rebellion of Jacke Cade: And the Duke of Yorkes first claime vnto the Crowne.' This describes the theme of what is today called *Henry VI, Part 2*.

15 March: There is a record of payment made by the Royal Treasurer of the Chamber: 'To William Kempe, William Shakespeare and Richard Burbage, servants to the Lord Chamberleyne, upon the Councille's warrant dated at Whitehall XVth Martij 1594, for two severall comedies or enterludes shewed by them before her majestie in Christmas tyme laste part viz St Stephen's daye and Innocents daye. £13 6s 8d, and by way of her Majesty's reward, £6 13s 4d.' In all, £20.

It is probable that the *Henry VI* plays were written a couple of years earlier. Robert Greene's pamphlet *Greene's Groatsworth of Wit* (entered in the Stationers' Register on 20 September 1592) mocks Shakespeare as 'an upstart crow, beautified with our feathers, that with his "tiger's heart wrapped in a player's hide", supposes that he is as well able to bombast out a blank verse as the best of you.' This is a parody of *Henry VI*, where York refers to Margaret as a 'tiger's heart wrapped in a woman's hide!' and it proves that *Henry VI* was well known by September 1592, which means it must have been staged before 23 June, when the government closed the theatres to prevent the spread of plague.

April: During the first half of the month Shakespeare acted at the Rose playhouse. A short time later, when he joined The Chamberlain's Men, he changed lodgings yet again. He moved from Shoreditch to Bishopsgate. This was marginally a more respectable area.

Robert Cecil set up an official enquiry under the auspices of the 'High Commission in Causes Ecclesiasticus' against the so-called 'School of the Night', the name given to a nebulous cult of scholars alleged to indulge in blasphemous and atheistic matters. This irreligious group revolved around Walter Raleigh and his half-brother, Carew. Others involved included the mathematician/astronomer, Thomas Harriot (1560–1621) Thomas Allen (1560–1635) the playwright George Peele (1556–96) spymaster and literary patron Thomas Walsingham (1561–1630) and Ferdinando Stanley, Lord Strange, Earl of Derby. The enquiry dragged on for months but no conclusive evidence resulted from it. When Lord Strange died in April the matter was dropped.

16 April: In Lancashire, Ferdinando Stanley, fifth Earl of Derby, died unexpectedly, as mentioned above. Although a patron of the arts, he was known as 'the Wizard Earl' because he was suspected of dabbling in the occult and necromancy. His mysterious death was put down to the diabolical influence of a man called Hesketh, who had stuck pins in a waxen doll and hidden it under his lordship's pillow. His widow, Lady Alice, remarried in 1600. Her new husband was the dour Sir Thomas Egerton, a Court official.

2 May: *The Taming of the Shrew* was entered into the Stationers' Register under the title, 'The Shrew'.although the play is thought to have been produced in early 1592.

300 years later, George Bernard Shaw held Shakespeare in grudging respect. He wrote: 'Shakespeare is a wonderful teller of stories so long as someone else has told them first.'

9 May: John Harrison of the White Greyhound, St Paul's – printer – entered into the Stationers' Register *The Rape of Lucrece*, another epic poem. This confirmed Shakespeare's standing in London as a poet to be reckoned with.

5 June: *Titus Andronicus* was performed by the Admiral's Men together with the Lord Chamberlain's Men at the Newington Butts playhouse.

7 June: Queen Elizabeth's Jewish physician, Roderigo Lopez was executed. Lopez, who had fled from Portugal to escape the Inquisition, championed Don Antonio, the bastard pretender to the Portuguese throne. The Spanish saw in this an opening to use Lopez as a pawn to poison Elizabeth. Lopez was 'racked' and confessed. Richard Topcliffe – master of the rack – boasted that he could 'stretch a man one foot longer than ever God intended', rendering Lopez's confession as possibly worthless. The forces of law and order carried on regardless. Estaban Ferreira and Senor Tinoco shared Lopez's fate on the execution block.

Edmund Valentine Campos, who specialised in academic writing at that time, argued that certain facets of Lopez's character were used by William Shakespeare in *The Merchant of Venice*.

Following Lopez's hanging, drawing and quartering, Christopher Marlowe's *The Jew of Malta* was performed twice at Newington Butts, during the weeks beginning 8 June and 15 June. Throughout the weeks beginning 27 June, 6 July, and 13 July, further performances were staged at the Rose playhouse.

It is likely that Shakespeare's theatrical career started with the Queen's Men. He moved on to Lord Strange's Men, then to Pembroke's Men before finally becoming a member of the Lord Chamberlain's Men, with whom he remained for the rest of his career. (The company of the Lord Chamberlain's Men changed its name to the King's Men on James I's accession.)

William Shakespeare was a founder member of the Lord Chamberlain's Men and became a shareholder. The consortium included the following investors: Shakespeare, Heminges, Kempe, Phillips, Pope, Richard Burbage, Cuthbert Burbage and three people who were not actors. Each shareholder owned one tenth of the new building and its profits. Shakespeare not only became one of the principal actors of the new company but he also brought his plays to them. He was to remain with the core company of the Chamberlain's Men for the next sixteen years, even when it changed its title on the accession of James I.

Lord Hunsdon's son-in-law, Charles Howard, was Lord High Admiral. He became the patron of Edward Alleyn's theatrical group under the name the Admiral's Men.

June: The newly formed Chamberlain's company opened with six afternoon performances at the Newington Butts theatre. These comprised two performances of *Titus Andronicus*, two performances of *Hamlet*, two performances of *Esther & Ahasweras* (a Biblical play) and one performance of *The Taming of the Shrew*. These played on alternate afternoons with the Admiral's company performing on the other days.

Thereafter, the Chamberlain's Men, led by Richard Burbage, dominated the theatrical scene north of the river at The Theatre, while the Admiral's Men had the South Bank franchise. The Admiral's Men took control of Marlowe's plays.

John Roberts married the widow of a printer who, by decree of the Stationers' Company, 'possesse the right of the only imprinting of all manner of bills for players.' John Robert's marriage gave him the monopoly for printing advertising material that turned out widely distributed playbills, and posters that were hung in the street.

13 June: Philip Henslowe recorded in his diary that *The Taming of the Shrew* was given its first performance at Newington Butts play-house. Another version of this play called A Shrew is thought to have been in existence for at least two years.

15 August: Thomas Kyd died aged thirty-five. The atheist writer of The Spanish Tragedy – a hit in its day – remains something of an

enigma. He had shared lodgings with Christopher Marlowe and some claim he wrote the first drafts of both *Hamlet* and *King Lear*, later adapted by Shakespeare. It is believed that his play *Edward III* was written in association with Shakespeare.

29 September: By Michaelmas, the company of the Chamberlain's Men was performing at the Cross-Keys Inn on the corner of Bishopsgate Street and Gracechurch Street in London.

8 October: The Chamberlain's Men continued playing at the Cross Keys.

14 November: Ben Jonson married Ann Lewis at the Church of St Magnus the Martyr near London Bridge. Not much is known about Ann Lewis. Their first-born child was a girl named Mary who died after six months. Ten years later their eldest son Benjamin, died of the plague. Jonson fathered a second son, also named Benjamin, of whom Shakespeare is thought to have been the godfather. The second Benjamin died in 1635. Towards the end of his life, Ben Jonson claimed he had not 'bedded' his wife for over a decade.

Although not published until the First Folio of 1623, it is believed that *The Comedy of Errors* was written at this time. *The Comedy of Errors* is the only Shakespeare play not to contain a musical number or an interlude.

26 December: St Stephen's Day. At ten o'clock in the evening, the Chamberlain's Men, with William Shakespeare in the company, performed at Greenwich in front of Queen Elizabeth. Scenery and rigs

for the props and candles were transported by boat from the Revels Office down the River Thames to Greenwich. The queen paid a £20 fee to the company as well as covering the costs of costumes and properties for two plays. Ordinarily, payment was made by a warrant from the Privy Council for plays given on Thursday 26 and Friday 27 December.

Gray's Inn was the largest of four law schools. To become a qualified legal gentleman took seven years of residential training. This length of time had its drawbacks. One of the rules of Gray's Inn was 'that no laundresses or women victuallers should thenceforth come into the gentlemen's chambers of this Society, unless they were full forty years of age, and not send their maidservants of what age soever.'

28 December: (Saturday) – Innocents Day – *The Comedy of Errors* was first performed at Gray's Inn by the Chamberlain's Men.

Shakespeare imitated an atypical Plautus comedy with *The Comedy of Errors*.

Italian playwrights wrote according to a strict convention. The stage had to represent a city square. The backdrop consisted of a row of houses. In comedies, these houses included a) a church, b) a home, and c) a brothel.

Love's Labours Lost was written about this time.

In *Love's Labours Lost*, Shakespeare's creations, 'Longaville', 'Dumaine' and 'Berowne' are corruptions of the names of French soldiers who were in the news pamphlets of 1593. The Duc de

Longueville, The Duc de Mayenne and Marechal Biron were the talk of London town.

Shakespeare's *The Rape of Lucrece* was published.

James Burbage was a wheeler-dealer come plague or come shine. He sold fruit, nuts and drink without a licence, so he was breaking city laws. He was indicted and banned from catering. When The Theatre was shut he sold food illegally at Holywell Street despite Middlesex Justices summoning him on many occasions (in 1591/92/93/94).

1595

England suffered its second bad harvest in a row and in the spring there were food riots. Fish and butter were beyond the reach of the working man's pockets. Angry apprentices invaded the markets at Southwark and Billingsgate to intimidate traders into selling food at reasonable prices.

10 January: Richard Fletcher was translated to the Bishopric of London. As Dean of Peterborough, he had presided over the funeral of Mary, Queen of Scots. His son, John Fletcher (sixteen at this time) would become one of Shakespeare's writing collaborators, and follow Shakespeare as house playwright for the King's Men.

21 February: Robert Southwell, the poet, was hanged, drawn and quartered at Tyburn for high treason. He was a distant cousin of Shakespeare through the Arden connection. Before he was caught and put to death, Southwell wrote open letters to Shakespeare,

beseeching him to work on religious subjects rather than on love stories. Southwell clearly felt that '*Venus and Adonis* is a waste of a wonderful talent.'

15 March: Having performed on two occasions at court during the Christmas period, Burbage, Shakespeare and Will Kempe as 'servants to the Lord Chamberlain' for 'plays performed before Her Majesty' went to the court treasurer to collect their fee. This is the first documentary evidence to attach Shakespeare to a specific theatrical company.

25 March: A book on fencing, including Paduan fighting techniques, was published. Entitled *Vincentio Saviolo, his practise, in two bookes, the first intreating of the use of the Rapier and Dagger, the second of Honor and honorable quarrels*, it is thought to have influenced Shakespeare's sword-fighting scenes in *Romeo and Juliet*. The main source for the play was Arthur Brooke's poem, *The Tragical History of Romeus and Juliet* in which Juliet was aged sixteen. It is a puzzle to scholars as to why Shakespeare made her even younger. There is the possibility that the boy actor, Robert Goffe, who played Juliet, had an exceptionally youthful appearance.

With the beginning of summer came public discontent and the riots continued following years of bad harvests. People took matters into their own hands and refused to pay for butter at five pence per pound. They snatched it from the retailers, refusing to pay more than threepence per pound. A curfew was decreed. Public assemblies were banned. Playhouses were closed.

ACTUS TERTIUS, SCENA PRIMA

1 June: Philip Henslowe lent £9 to his nephew, Francis 'to lay down for his half share with the company which he doth play withal.' This was in anticipation of opening the second playhouse now being built on the South Bank. The Swan was to open on Bankside 500 metres upstream, intending to vie for business with Henslowe's Rose playhouse. It was situated on the east side of modern Hopton Street, the largest of London's playhouses and the only one for which a pictorial record of the interior survives. Unfortunately, the plague stopped play for the time being.

26 June: With playhouses shut, Shakespeare had no visible means of livelihood.

29 June: An angry mob tore down the pillories in Cheapside and a gallows was erected outside the Lord Mayor's residence. Over a thousand men, mostly apprentices marched on Tower Hill to pillage the shops of gun-makers. Subsequently, a number of arrests were made and five leaders of the riot were hanged. Community Service was not an option in those days.

The builder of the Swan, Francis Langley, made a fortune as a wool inspector, in which capacity he was not above a little extortion. He also owned a brothel, fenced stolen goods and, on the side, dabbled as a slum landlord.

Theatre life was rough. One of the Lord Admiral's Men, an actor called John Singer, in his capacity as an admission gatherer, killed a playgoer who argued over the penny he had to put into the box to gain entry.

According to Henslowe's Diary, the Admiral's Men had a 'read-through' of scripts at The Sun Inn in New Fish Street, where so much wine was drunk that they were barred from ever entering this City tavern again.

The Lord Chamberlain's Men had no choice but to leave London and tour such places as Ipswich and Cambridge, receiving 40 shillings per venue.

Love's Labours Won was probably produced in this year. In 1598, when the bookseller Cuthbert Burby published it in quarto, he stated on the Stationers' Register that the play had been newly corrected and augmented by William Shakespeare.

29 August: *Richard the Second* was entered into the Register of the Stationers' Company. The scene in which Richard II is deposed was omitted for fear of offending Queen Elizabeth, as the Tudors believed that kings and queens were ordained by God. It was not until 1609 that the deposition scene was reinserted.

1 December: *Edward the Third* was entered into the Stationers' Register. This play spans the historical gap between Christopher Marlowe's *Edward II* and the early Shakespeare play *Richard II*. Although no attribution exists, scholars say that Kydd probably rewrote a rough draft by Christopher Marlowe and that Shakespeare added his own contribution later.

9 December: The first recorded performance of *Richard the Second* took place at Sir Edward Hoby's Canon Row house for a vetting process in front of Sir Robert Cecil.

A Midsummer Night's Dream was written at about this time.

1596

1 January: The Chamberlain's Men were in Rutland to perform *Titus Andronicus* at Burley-on-the-Hill in the manor belonging to Sir John Harington, Baron of Exton. The tour continued until Saturday, 6 January.

23 January: Richard Byfield, who held strong Puritan views, took over as vicar of Stratford-upon-Avon.

The Anglo-Spanish War continued to be fought in a spasmodic manner at sea. War was never formally declared, but it continued intermittently from 1585 to 1604.

Sir Walter Raleigh spoke with a broad Devonshire accent. Speech analysts, upon examination of Shakespeare's idiosyncratic spelling, have concluded that he spoke with the equivalent of a West-Midlands accent, although the letter 'r' was invariably rolled and included within words. Some suggest he spoke with an accent somewhere between Birmingham and Boston, Massachusetts.

January: Sir Francis Drake, aged fifty-six, died of dysentery off the coast of Portobello, Panama. Dressed in full armour, he was buried at sea in a lead coffin that has not yet been found.

The twenty-one-year lease on The Theatre playhouse in Shoreditch was coming up for renewal. The Burbages baulked at a huge hike in the proposed rent. What is more the owner, Giles Allen, offered only another five years, after which he wanted to redevelop the site.

4 February: James Burbage purchased the Blackfriars Theatre property for £600. Burbage reconstructed the upper part of the former Blackfriars Dominican Priory in the City of London that included the old Parliament Chamber, and converted it into a theatre for use as an indoor venue for the cold winter months. The space was 70 feet long and 46 feet wide.

The acting company was absolutely forbidden from playing at Blackfriars by the Privy Council under orders of their own patron, Lord Hunsdon. Plays were restricted to those acted by children's companies for the time being. Burbage leased the theatre to Henry Evans for £40 per annum, for use mainly by the boys' choir of the Chapel Royal.

Local residents hated the idea of a new theatre in Blackfriars and they launched a petition with thirty-one objections, fearing '...the gathering together of all manner of lewd and vagrant persons.'

When he joined the Chamberlain's Men, Shakespeare moved his lodgings to St Helen's parish on the east side of town until he migrated south of the river. It seems he never stayed in any one place for long.

One of the many fine old houses in the Bishopsgate Street area of St Helen's was Crosby Place, once the residence of Richard III. It was now the home of the Lord Mayor.

Tax collection was in the hands of the parish. Shakespeare was on the lists of St Helen's for the subsidy that had been voted by Parliament in 1593. When the second assessment was made in 1596 there were seventy-three taxable residents and the value of Shakespeare's goods was rated at £5. Over in St Leonard's parish, Richard and Cuthbert Burbage were rated as having even fewer possessions than Shakespeare. Even in those days people lied about what they actually owned.

William Shakespeare's Uncle Henry, John's brother, died.

According to the list of plays that Francis Meres documented in 1598, *The Life and Death of King John* was produced at about this time.

2 July: The fifty-gun Spanish ship *St Andrew* was captured by the English at Cádiz. In the play *The Merchant of Venice*, Salerio says, 'See my wealthy Andrew docked in sand, veiling her high-top lower than her ribs to kiss her burial.' Because of this allusion scholars tell us the play must have been written shortly after the news of this victory reached London at the end of July. James I gave the ship back in 1604.

22 July: Plague closed the playhouses.

23 July: Henry Carey, first Baron Hunsdon, the Lord Chamberlain, aged seventy, died at Somerset House. Finding themselves without a patron, the players were at the mercy of the Mayor of London and his council. Thomas Nashe wrote to a friend: 'Now the players are piteously persecuted by the Lord mayor and the aldermen, and however in their old Lord's time they thought their state settled, it is now so uncertain that they cannot build upon it.'

The next Lord Chamberlain was William Brooke, tenth Baron Cobham (1527–97) who was not a big fan of theatrical companies. In league with the Lord Mayor of the City of London, he closed down the inn-theatres, such as The Bel Savage and The Cross Keys.

📖 Meanwhile, the Chamberlain's Men came under the patronage of George Carey, second Baron Hunsdon, and for the next seven months the company was known as Lord Hunsdon's Men.

📖 1 August: Lord Hunsdon's Men, with Shakespeare in the company, put on a play at the Faversham Market Hall in Kent.

📖 11 August: Hamnet Shakespeare (the boy twin) was buried in Stratford. If Shakespeare received the awful news in time to attend his only son's funeral, a carrier must have been dispatched from Stratford to Kent to leave a message at one of the towns on the touring circuit with instructions to pass it on when the theatre company arrived. For Shakespeare to have been able to return to Stratford from the south-east of England, he must have had to ride several horses into the ground to complete the 200-mile journey in time.

📖 The Master of the Revels was the scrutineer of plays submitted for Royal Command performances. The plays selected were 'the best to be had' and were 'often perused and necessarily corrected and amended by all the aforesaid offices'. In all but name he was a censor protecting against sedition and ensuring that Protestantism remained the dominant religion.

📖 Edmund Tilney held the powerful political post of Master of the Revels throughout Shakespeare's career. Tilney's office consisted of thirteen rooms in the old palace of St John's in Clerkenwell – a suburb of Newgate. It contained a great chamber for the special rehearsal of those plays deemed suitable for performances before the queen.

20 October: William Shakespeare re-applied to the College of Heralds for a coat of arms on behalf of his father, claiming worthiness because Thomas Shakespeare of Balsall with his wife Alicia were illustrious ancestors. When Henry VII defeated Richard III at Bosworth Field in 1485, parcels of land taken from Richard's Warwickshire portfolio were distributed amongst the men who had helped Henry Tudor to victory. In his application, William Shakespeare alluded to his forefather's contribution to that victory. Thomas Shakespeare had joined the chapel at Knowle in 1486.

A coat of arms was granted to 'the said John Shakespeare, Gentlemen, and ... his children, issue & posterity'. At last he could be called 'a gentleman'. The cost to the Shakespeares was thirty guineas. Robert Cooke of the Heralds' Office designed these arms to his coat: 'Gold on a bend sables, a spear of the first steeled argent, and for his crest or cognizance a falcon, his wings displayed argent, standing on a wreath of his colours, supporting a spear gold, steeled as aforesaid and, set upon a helmet with mantles and tassles.' The motto was '*Non sanz droict*': meaning 'Not without right' – an ancient battle-cry.

Ben Jonson took a dim view of Shakespeare's aspiration to join high society and lampooned his mentor in his next play, *Every Man Out of His Humour*. Jonson penned a clown called Sogliardo buying a coat of arms all covered in yellow with the motto 'Not without mustard'.

The coat of arms could be displayed on the front door of the Shakespeares' home and on all their personal items. It appears on Shakespeare's tomb in Stratford.

Granting a coat of arms conferred 'gentlehood' on the bearer. Gentle (from the French *gentil*) means high-born. Hence the Shakespeares established themselves as gentlefolk and Master Shakespeare became a proper gentleman. This called for a bigger ruff and a taller hat.

Three years later another claim was made: to quarter the Shakespeare coat of arms with those of Arden. This involved dividing the shield in two so that it contained both coats of arms, thereby linking the Shakespeare family with the older, Arden family. This time the claim did not succeed.

The Herald's office was run by Sir William Dethick and William Camden (a scholar who tutored Ben Jonson). Camden wrote a legal tome in Latin called '*Britannia*'. He made a list of contemporary English poets starting with Sidney and Spenser and ending with 'William Shakespeare and other most pregnant wits of these our times, whom succeeding ages may justly admire.'

24 October: Henry Condell, a leading player, married Elizabeth Smart at St Laurence Pountney's Church. Elizabeth was a city heiress with twelve valuable houses in the Strand, west of Somerset House. Not bad for the son of a fishmonger.

9 November: George Peele, the louche dramatist, expired at the age of forty. According to Francis Meres, he 'died of the pox.'

The bawdy-house keeper of Clerkenwell's 'stews' answered to the name of Lucy Negro.

In an age where syphilis was the second biggest killer after the plague, the notion of homosexuality became regarded as 'a soft option'. It was widely regarded that sexual intercourse with loose women was largely responsible for venereal disease, therefore love amongst men was safer.

There were at least 300 inns and brothels in the vicinity of the Swan playhouse. Skittles, bowling, fencing contests and blood sports were growing in popularity daily, much to the concern of the authorities. The gaming available turned the area into the Las Vegas of its age. Playgoers from the north shore used the landings at The Paris Garden Stairs or The Falcon Stairs, both short walking distances from the playhouse.

William Wayte and his stepfather, Mr Justice William Gardiner, tried to close down the Swan playhouse. Francis Langley, the owner of the Swan, reacted violently and threatened the objectors. He had previous form, having been charged by a tribunal for extortion.

29 November: Shakespeare was summoned to keep the peace along with Francis Langley, Dorothy Soer and Anne Lee. The playwright was particularly unhappy that the Swan playhouse was threatened with closure. Shakespeare's alliance with the opportunistic

Francis Langley places a different light on the playwright, who is usually described as 'gentle'. Langley was listed along with Shakespeare on a writ of attachment addressed to the sheriff of Surrey to keep the peace. 'Be it known that William Wayte seeks sureties of the peace against William Shakespeare, Francis Langley, Dorothy Soer the wife of John Soer and Anne Lee, for fear of death and mutilation of limbs...' This suggestion of thuggery by the Swan of Avon was glossed over in earlier biographical ventures.

Francis Langley fenced diamonds stolen from a treasure ship and sold them to the queen for £1,500. As well as the Swan playhouse, he built the Boar's Head playhouse, north-east of the tower outside the city walls. He also ran a brothel, gaining the reputation to be a tricky man with whom to deal. It is mooted by some that Shakespeare was in the pay of Langley as his protector and bodyguard.

Shakespeare's other known associates were no less insalubrious. Dorothy Soer owned a tenement building in Paris Garden Lane, an area renowned for its houses of ill-repute. Shakespeare may have rented rooms from her. Edmond Malone (1741–1812), an Irish scholar, claimed he had documentary evidence that Shakespeare 'lived in Southwark, near the Bear Garden in 1596.'

1597

2 February: James Burbage died. He left the Theatre playhouse to Cuthbert Burbage and the Blackfriars property to his other son, Richard.

John Shakespeare (William's father) was mentioned in the local Stratford records when he sold some property to George Badger, a draper.

Many years later, a document dated 1597 was discovered in the loft of Henley Street. It was a testament of faith promulgated by a Jesuit priest, Edmund Campion, in which John Shakespeare attested his obedience to 'the Catholicke, Romaine and Apostolicke Church'. He claimed that his patron saint was St Winifrere, whose shrine was in the Holy Well in Flintshire. Following many years of academic argument, today this document seems to be accepted as genuine.

The first edition of *Romeo and Juliet* (First Quarto), printed by John Danter, appeared in early 1597. Its text contains numerous differences from later editions and is referred to as the 'bad quarto'.

5 March: The death of William Brooke, tenth Baron Cobham, left a vacancy for a new Lord Chamberlain. Cobham's death was something of a relief in theatrical circles because he was in the process of closing down the companies.

17 March: George Carey, second Baron Hunsdon, followed in his father's footsteps and became Lord Chamberlain. Being the grandson of Henry VIII, albeit on the wrong side of the blanket, he carried a lot of clout in court circles. He took over patronage of his late father's company. Lord Hunsdon's Men reverted to its former title as the Lord Chamberlain's Men. This provided the players with protection from the mayor and the Privy Council, who considered theatrical companies to have disruptive influences.

The prologue of *Romeo and Juliet* contains the following reference:

'... now the two hours' traffic of our stage;

The which of you with patient ears attend,

What here shall miss, our toil shall strive to mend.'

The 'two hours' traffic' infers that the production will take two hours to perform.

Romeo and Juliet is estimated to be the most-filmed play of all time.

Although there is no documentary evidence regarding a performance of *Henry IV, Part 1* until March 1600, it seems likely that it first saw the light of day at The Theatre in early 1597, performed by the Lord Chamberlain's Men.

The character of Sir John Falstaff was originally named 'Oldcastle' and was modelled on John Oldcastle, a famous Protestant martyr with influential living descendants, who instantly objected to their ancestor being depicted as a buffoon. The late William Brooke, Lord Cobham, was a descendant of Oldcastle. The Brooke family objected and Shakespeare obligingly renamed the character 'John Falstaff' because a historical figure called Sir John Fastolf, inveighed against for his cowardice at the Battle of Patay, had no living descendants. Unfortunately, the word Falstaff is one syllable shorter than Oldcastle, making the poetic passages scan less well.

The character is called Falstaff in all surviving texts of the play. In the quarto text of *Henry IV, Part 2* (1600) one of Falstaff's speech prefixes in Act I, Sc 2 is mistakenly left uncorrected, 'Old.' instead of 'Falst.' In Act 3, Sc 2, Falstaff is said to have been a 'page to Thomas Mowbray, Duke of Norfolk', a true reference to the historical Oldcastle. In *Henry IV, Part 1*, Act I, Sc 2, Prince Hal calls Falstaff 'my old lad of the castle'. To remove doubt and to eliminate the risk of reprisal, Shakespeare adds in the epilogue: 'for Oldcastle died martyr, and this is not the man.'

The character of Falstaff was also originally called Oldcastle in *The Merry Wives of Windsor*. There are signs in the text of last-minute alterations. Falstaff was played by Will Kempe.

In April, the ground lease of The Theatre expired and still Cuthbert Burbage could not come to terms with the owner for a renewal.

Giles Allen, the owner of site on which the Theatre stood, prevaricated in granting an extension of the lease by increasing the ground rent from £14 to £24 and wanted to take back possession of the land within five years. Burbage found this unacceptable. The theatre remained unoccupied throughout the summer.

23 April: Elizabeth I attended the Garter Feast at Windsor Castle (see 18 January 1602). George Carey, the new Lord Chamberlain, was invested as a Knight of the Garter and it is believed the first performance of *The Merry Wives of Windsor* was held to commemorate the occasion. It happened to coincide with Shakespeare's thirty-third birthday.

Tradition has it that Shakespeare wrote *The Merry Wives of Windsor* at the request of Queen Elizabeth, who wanted to see another play with Falstaff in it. It was alleged that Shakespeare tossed it off in just over a fortnight.

4 May: William Shakespeare bought New Place in Chapel Lane, opposite the Guild Chapel in Stratford for £60 'in silver'. The seller, William Underhill, was a Catholic who found himself in financial difficulties. A former lord mayor of London, Sir Hugh Clopton had built the house and the stone bridge of Stratford. There was a special pew in the church called the Clopton Pew.

6 July: Before the sale was finalised, Underhill became ill, realised he was dying, and made a verbal will. He died the following day but it took another five years before Shakespeare could call the place his own.

William Underhill's son, Fulke Underhill, was arrested for poisoning his father, and hanged in Warwick for the felony in March 1599. Meanwhile, the sale was hovering in legal limbo and had to be turned over to William's younger son, Hercules Underhill, by right of his father. The New Place property was not securely in William Shakespeare's name until Hercules came of age and a renegotiation had taken place in 1602.

New Place was the second biggest house in Stratford, on the corner of Chapel Street and Chapel Lane. It had ten fireplaces. The grounds incorporated an orchard and two barns. There were probably more rooms than fireplaces, as the latter were taxable.

After living with her parents-in-law for fifteen years, Anne Shakespeare (née Hathaway) moved into her own home at New Place.

Shakespeare followed up this purchase by buying another cottage opposite New Place – possibly for a servant.

Emilia Lanier's husband was enrolled as one of Sir Walter Raleigh's 'volunteers' and sent abroad from 10 July until the end of October. This had probably been arranged by the late Lord Hunsdon in order to unencumber his mistress, Emilia, from the marriage he'd fixed up for her.

The Lord Chamberlain's Men performed at the Curtain playhouse and presented both parts of *Henry IV*.

Shakespeare acquired 107 acres of tenanted farmland north of Stratford for £320.

26 July: At the Swan playhouse, Thomas Nashe presented Ben Jonson's early play called *The Isle of Dogs*. This caused outrage in court circles. The piece was described as 'a lewd plaie stuffed with seditious and slanderous matter.' The Privy Council was so incensed that on 28 July it decreed: 'no plaies shalbe used within London... during this tyme of summer.' Richard Topcliffe, master of the rack and chief interrogator, was called in. Ben Jonson was jailed in Marshalsea Prison. Gabriel Spenser and Robert Shaw, both actors, were also imprisoned. No copy of the play has been found.

28 July: The Privy Council's watchdogs renewed their perennial plea for the 'present staie and fynall suppressinge of stage

plays.' They requested of the Justices of Middlesex and Surrey that all 'playhouses be plucked down.' Theatre owners were to be required 'so to deface the same as they maie not be ymploied agayne to suche use.' The upshot of this was that the Swan playhouse was closed by order of the government and apparently never regularly used again.

The city authorities regarded 'plays and entertainments' as a nuisance because of the convergence of low-lifers such as pickpockets and prostitutes. Strict laws were implemented to lessen the disruption of traffic and discourage absenteeism. Curfews were imposed to ensure people were home before nightfall.

A punishment meted out to strolling players imposed under the 1572 Act wherein 'all fencers, bearwards, common players of interludes, and minstrels (not belonging to any baron of this realm, or to any other honourable person of greater degree),' wandering abroad without the licence of two justices at the least, were subject 'to be grievously whipped and burned through the gristle of the right ear with a hot iron of the compass of an inch about' was now reduced to impressment in the service of the fleet. A sigh of relief could probably be heard throughout the underworld.

Henry IVth, *Part 2* was written during this period.

29 August: *The Tragedie of King Richard the second* was entered into the Stationers' Register. It was published by Andrew Wise and printed by Valentine Simms.

ACTUS TERTIUS, SCENA PRIMA

🐚 August/September: The Lord Chamberlain's Men kept their distance from London They went on tour visiting Rye, Dover, Marlborough, Faversham, Bath and Bristol. According to tradition, in pre-Roman times, Bath had been founded by King Bladud who, like Icarus, thought he could fly, only to become fatally disillusioned. His son, King Lear (sometimes spelt Lier) succeeded him.

🐚 8 October: Ben Jonson was released from Marshalsea prison, where he had been imprisoned for co-writing the seditious play, *The Isle of Dogs* (see above).

🐚 The inquisitor sent to question Ben Jonson was Richard Topcliffe, who had himself spent time in Marshalsea prison because of the cruelty he inflicted in the course of his interrogation techniques. He was feared by all after the details became known of how, earlier in the decade, he had tortured Robert Southwell. Ben Jonson was lucky to get away with little more than a stern warning.

🐚 When Ben Jonson went on his 'foot voyage' to Scotland in July 1618, his still anonymous travelling companion kept a journal of the journey in which he writes that spending an evening with Ben Jonson was like being confined in a small room with someone banging a big drum. (From The Aldersey Collection at Cheshire Archives.)

🐚 11 October: Henslowe's new playhouse, the Rose, opened.

🐚 Edward Alleyn retired from acting, sold his stock in the Lord Admiral's company and began buying real estate in Dulwich. In 1605 he joined Henslowe as joint Master of the Bears. His wife, Joan, died in 1623. Six months later he was married again to a girl half his age, Constance Dunne, the daughter of John Dunne, Dean of St Paul's. The Dean disapproved of the marriage, withheld a dowry and would not let her take possession of her late mother's jewellery and mementoes.

20 October: *The Tragedy of King Richard the Third* was entered into the Stationers' Register. Later it was published by Andrew Wise and printed by Valentine Simms.

November: *An Excellent conceited Tragedie of Romeo and Juliet* was printed in an unauthorised edition printed by John Danter.

Collectors of property tax in St Helen's, Bishopsgate, noted that Shakespeare had an outstanding debt of five shillings. However, the records state that he was one of those who was 'dead, departed and gone out of the said ward.' Shakespeare had moved digs again.

In his absence, Shakespeare was taxed thirteen shillings and fourpence on his goods, a rate of about 13 per cent. The two tax collectors in St Helen's parish were Thomas Symons (a skinner) and Ferdinando Clutterbook (a draper). They were hot on the trail of Shakespeare when he moved out of the district. By 1599, he was in the tax jurisdiction of the Sheriff of Surrey.

At Westminster Hall in London, Shakespeare started a lawsuit for the recovery of property in Wilmcote, where his mother had lived. The case was presented against the Lambert family, who refused to vacate the rented premises. The sum in dispute was £40, a large amount of money at that time. The case was not resolved until

1600 when, it is presumed, the Shakespeare family received the outstanding £40.

At Christmas the first recorded performance of *Love's Labours Lost* was presented at court for Queen Elizabeth.

An unauthorised quarto version of *Romeo and Juliet* of poor textual quality was printed by John Danter. In this version it is stated that 'it hath been often and with great applause played publiquely.' It was printed again in 1599 with many improvements by Thomas Creede and published by Cuthbert Burby.

Cuthbert Burby was made a 'freeman' of the Stationers' Company on 13 January 1592. He was a respectable publisher working at the Royal Exchange and in St Paul's Churchyard at the sign of the Swan. He published the first quarto of *Love's Labour's Lost* in 1598 and a quarto of *Edward III* in 1596, which is included amongst Shakespeare Apocrypha.

The original cast of *Romeo and Juliet* included Richard Burbage as Romeo, Master Robert Goffe as Juliet and Will Kempe as Peter. In the 1599 published edition, Kempe is actually named instead of the character.

The age of consent to marry was fourteen for a boy and twelve for a girl.

30 December: Disputes with the landlord of the Theatre playhouse in Shoreditch resulted in the company moving to the nearby Curtain playhouse.

Doctor Simon Foreman was an astrologer and mystic who kept copious diaries of his consultations. As well as examining Emilia Lanier, he was visited by Jennet Davenant and her sister, Ursula Shepherd. All six offspring of Jennet had died in childbirth. Ursula, fearing the same fate, sought Foreman's advice but he was of no comfort, foreseeing Ursula's false pregnancy and death. He advised Jennet to leave plague-ridden London. Subsequently, John and Jennet Davenant moved to Oxford, where they became landlords of the Cross Inn. This Tavern had 'twelve hearths and twenty windows'. Above were opulent bedrooms for travellers including the 'Painted Room' in which, according to legend, Shakespeare stayed on his stopovers between Stratford and London. It was in the 'Painted Room' that Jennet is supposed to have sustained Master Shakespeare with victuals and other needs of his while her husband was abroad buying wine.

1598

Abraham Sturley, (1550–1614), the bailiff of Stratford, wrote to Richard Quiney, alderman, saying: 'our countryman mr Shaksper is willinge to disburse some monei upon some od yardeland or other att Shottri or neare about us; he thinketh it a veri fitt patterne to move him to deale in the matter of our tithes... Bi the instruccions you can geve him thereof, we thinke it a faire mark for him to shoote att, and not unpossible to hitt. It obtained would advance him in deede, and would do us muche good.' (E.A.J. Honigmann, *Shakespeare's Impact on His Contemporaries*, 1982.) Whether or not Shakespeare followed through on this purchase is uncertain, though he was to buy other property in Stratford over the succeeding years.

ACTUS TERTIUS, SCENA PRIMA

A series of poems by William Shakespeare went into public circulation, described as 'sugred Sonnets among his private friends'.

4 February: The Queen's Council ordered a survey throughout England to check on the amount of wheat and barley being held in private hands. Following two years of bad harvests, grain was in short supply. Malt derives from barley and other grain. Wheat and barley were known as corn and malt in Elizabethan times. 'Malt hoarders' were subject to the wrath of brewers and the authorities. It was discovered that in Stratford-upon-Avon every major householder was hoarding grain. 'Shakespeare of Chapel Street Ward' had ten quarters (eighty bushels) of malt stored in his thatched barn – well over the legal limit.

25 February: Andrew Wise entered *The historye of Henry the iiijth (Henry IV, Part 1)* into the Stationers' Register. Two further editions were brought out later in the year, both printed by Peter Short, the second of which is now designated the first quarto. The tavern scenes seem to have been inspired by another play being produced at the time called *The Famous Victories of Henry Fifth*, the authorship of which is unknown.

10 March: *Love's Labour's Lost* was first published in quarto by the bookseller Cuthbert Burby and printed by William White. The title page states that the play was 'Newly corrected and augmented by W. Shakespere' suggesting it is a revision of an earlier version.

28 March: Philip Henslowe put Edward Alleyn and Thomas Heywood under two-year contracts to act for the Admiral's Men.

🕯 10 July: John Barrose was a Burgundian fencer who challenged all comers, before his success at killing opponents led to him being hanged. His exploits were immortalised in Ben Jonson's play *Every Man in His Humour*, first performed at the Curtain playhouse two months later.

🕯 22 July: *The Merchant of Venice* was entered into the Stationers' Register by the printer James Roberts. Its original title in the First Folio was '*The Comicall History of the Merchant of Venice, or otherwise called the Jewe of Venyce*'.

🕯 Under the Venetian Republic, Jews were compelled to live in the Cannaregio Sestiere area of Venice instituted in 1516, and called a 'ghèto', from which the English word, 'ghetto' is derived.

🕯 Churchman and avid theatregoer, Francis Meres (1566–1647), kept a record of some of the productions he had seen in his 700 pages of jottings called *Palladis Tamia – Wit's Treasury*. He mentions *The Merchant of Venice* as one of Shakespeare's comedies. There is a reference in the play to the 'wealthy Andrew docked in sand', showing that Shakespeare could not have written the play earlier than 30 July 1596, when news reached England regarding the capture of the Spanish ship, *El San Andres*.

🕯 Fancis Meres wrote of seeing *The Comedy of Errors*, one of Shakespeare's 'six excellent comedies' and added, 'the sweet witty soul of Ovid lives in mellifluous and honey-tongued Shakespeare.'

Additionally, Meres mentioned a play entitled *Love Labours Wonne*. This may be an alternative name for another play such as *Taming of the Shrew* or it could mean there was a sequel to *Love's Labours Lost* that has not survived.

English historian, John Stow (1525–1605) published his *Survey of London*, describing life in Elizabethan times. Roads were being improved to accommodate the new coaches that were starting to be built. Stow complained of 'a terrible number of coaches – a world run on wheels...'

The leading boy actors in the Lord Chamberlain's Men company included Nick Tooley (Burbage's apprentice) and Alexander (Sander) Cooke (John Hemming's apprentice). From 1598 another boy actor called Ned joined the company. This probably referred to Edmund Shakespeare, who could well have been the apprentice of his elder brother, William.

Much Ado About Nothing was written. Contemporaneously, this play was sometimes billed as *Benedick and Beatrice*.

When an audience disapproved of a performance they would start 'mewing'. The wailing of a thousand voices making the sound, 'Mew, Mew, Mew' tended to discourage performers. Today the 'mew' has transmogrified into 'boo' but is still described as a 'catcall'.

4 August: When William Cecil, first Baron Burghley, died, aged seventy-seven, Queen Elizabeth became remote and felt isolated. He had been her chief adviser and closest political friend.

September: The first performance of *Every Man In His Humour* by Ben Jonson took place at the Curtain playhouse. The Lord Chamberlain's Men original cast, listed as 'Principal Comedians', included (in billing order): William Shakespeare, Richard Burbage, Augustine Phillips, John Heminges, Henry Condell, Thomas Pope, William Sly, Christopher Beeston, William Kempe and John Duke. Shakespeare played the character of Kno'well.

Nicholas Rowe (1674–1718) recorded in 1709 that following his jail sentence for writing the *Isle of Dogs*, Ben Jonson was not exactly flavour of the month with the production companies. *Every Man In His Humour* was initially rejected by the Lord Chamberlain's Men but tradition has it that Shakespeare read it, liked it and persuaded his company to try it out. Shakespeare himself played the part of Kno'well in it, as mentioned above, and the play revived Jonson's fortunes. Henceforth, Shakespeare took a paternal interest in Ben Jonson, his junior by eight years.

22 September: Shortly after *Every Man in His Humour* opened, Ben Jonson fell out with an actor of the Admiral's Men, Gabriel Spenser (also known as Spencer). A duel with swords was arranged near The Theatre in Hogsden Fields of Shoreditch (now Hoxton). Gabriel Spenser was killed by Ben Jonson, who was charged with manslaughter. He pleaded 'benefit of clergy'. In effect, this required him to display his devotion to God by reciting sections of the Bible from memory. Fortunately, he convinced his peers and he was released, but not before he was branded on his left thumb with the letter 'T' for Tyburn, to remind him that should he transgress a second time, he would be hanged.

25 October: Stratford alderman Richard Quiney came as a representative to London with a petition to the queen requesting a reduction in tax. He lodged at the Bell Inn in Carter Lane. After four months of fruitless lobbying in the capital, he was running short of funds. He wrote a letter to William Shakespeare, which said: 'Loveinge Countreyman, I am bolde of yowe as of a ffrende, craveing yowre help with xxx li (£30) ... Yowe shall ffrende me muche in helpeinge me out of all the debettes I owe in London, I thancke god, & much quiet my mind...' et cetera.

It is the only letter to Shakespeare known to exist. It was never actually sent and was found amongst Quiney's papers after his death. Quiney died following a tavern brawl with Greville's men in 1602, and this letter was archived with the rest of his papers by Stratford Corporation. As it happens, Quiney's petitioning had a favourable outcome. Queen Elizabeth agreed to relieve Stratford's tax problem, and the Exchequer reimbursed Quiney for his London expenses.

Eighteen years later, Richard Quiney's son, Thomas, went on to marry William Shakespeare's youngest daughter Judith, much to her father's chagrin.

More than a third of the householders living in the Clink consisted of watermen. Altogether, there were two thousand highly competitive, licensed boatmen.

The boat trip from one side of the Thames to the other – between Blackfriars and Paris Garden Stairs – had a statutory fare of one penny. Many of the watermen were old sailors and on being given a mere one extra penny as a gratuity their language was sometimes salty. They had a reputation for surliness. The boats were described by one visitor as being 'charmingly upholstered with embroidered cushions laid across the seats, very comfortable to sit on or lean against. Generally speaking the benches seat only two people next to one another.' (Chute, *Shakespeare of London*, 1951, *page 207*)

The watermen (sometimes referred to as wherrymen), claimed that up to 4,000 people crossed the river every day to visit the Globe, the Rose or the Swan.

The parish church of Southwark was called St Saviour's, where many actors were buried, including Shakespeare's youngest brother, Edmund, and James I's favourite player, Lawrence Fletcher.

The prostitutes in the area were known as 'Winchester Geese', as the brothels in the district of Southwark fell under the control of the Bishop of Winchester, who made a pretty penny out of taxing the ladies of the night. The Church encouraged prostitution because it reduced the incidence of sodomy and masturbation – considered mortal crimes by religious-minded men. In the vernacular of that time to 'be bitten by a Winchester Goose' meant 'to contract a venereal disease'. 'Goose bumps' was slang for the first symptoms of venereal disease. Many prostitutes were buried in Cross Bones, an unconsecrated graveyard.

September 1598 (through to mid-1599): The Lord Chamberlain's Men played at the Curtain playhouse near Finsbury. *Henry V* premiered during this period, indicating that the words 'this wooden O' spoken in the Prologue refer to the Curtain rather than the Globe, as has sometimes been thought.

ACTUS TERTIUS, SCENA PRIMA

1 December: William Shakespeare sold a load of stone to Stratford Corporation to help repair the bridge over the River Avon. It is said that the stone had come from the foundations of New Place, which was undergoing repairs. The Bill of Sale taken from the chamberlain's accounts reads as follows: 'Wyllyn Wyatt Chamberlin Pd to Mr. Shakespere for one load of stone xd.' (ten pence).

William Shakespeare, Heminges, Kempe, Phillips, Pope, Cuthbert Burbage and Richard Burbage, together with three others, each invested an equal sum of money to rebuild the Theatre following the expiry of the lease. Each investor owned one-tenth of the new building.

28 December: Throughout Christmas heavy snow settled thickly. Negotiations to renew the Theatre lease had dragged on for a year. The Lord Chamberlain's Men ran out of patience with the protracted delay. The Burbage brothers and a carpenter named Peter Street brought a gang of a dozen men to Finsbury Fields and overnight, despite the vehement opposition of the landowner, they dismantled The Theatre. Piece by piece they carried it across the frozen River Thames to the marshy land on the South Bank that they had recently leased for thirty-one years. The building was quickly reconstructed and renamed the Globe. The procedure took four days.

One of the trustees of the new arrangement for the Globe playhouse was a goldsmith by the name of Thomas Savage. He hailed from Rufford in Lancashire, where Shakespeare as a young man is alleged to have been a teacher's assistant after he escaped Sir Thomas Lucy's punishments for stealing deer. Shakespeare became one of the 'housekeepers' of the new theatre. In fact, he paid a fifth share into the kitty to become part-owner.

From 1598 to 1608 Shakespeare lived in the Liberty of the Clink, an area in Southwark on the south bank of the Thames. The liberty was exempt from the authority of Surrey's high sheriff and was under the jurisdiction of the Bishop of Winchester, who was usually treasurer to the monarch.

Shakespeare stayed in the parish of St Saviour's close to the Bear Garden for ten years.

The ward of Southwark was divided into three areas and The Liberty of the Clink was one of them. It was reputed to have more brothels than any other similarly sized area in London. A special 'overspill' graveyard for fallen women was known as the Single Women's Churchyard.

The Liberty of the Clink in Southwark was built up mostly of terraced tenement buildings called 'rents'. The alley behind the Globe playhouse was known as Brend's Rents (after Sir Nicholas Brend). Shakespeare's contribution of rent to the landlord Brend was only one-tenth of the total but he was treated as the senior member of the syndicate. Brend's lawyers described the Globe as a playhouse 'in the possession of William Shakespeare and others'.

The Clink was famous for its prison, a sort of oubliette in the cellars of an old manor, originally Winchester House. In 1161, it was decreed that whoever was the incumbent bishop held the power to license prostitutes and brothels.

There were five prisons in Southwark: the Clink, the Counter, the King's Bench, the White Lion and the Marshalsea. The last is best remembered as the prison where Charles Dickens's father was incarcerated in 1824 for a debt to a baker.

A taproom or bar run by John Heminges was attached to the outside of the Globe playhouse. It served bottled ale, oranges, apples, nuts, gingerbread and pipes of tobacco, selling at threepence per pipe.

On the South Bank the playhouses were usually closed on Thursdays and Sundays because the adjacent bear pits were opened on these days. Bear baiting was a popular spectator sport.

Social rank was precious to the Elizabethans. The York Herald, Sir Ralph Brooke, addressed the Garter of Arms, Sir William Dethick, questioning his wisdom in granting coats of arms to people possibly unworthy of them. He tabled a list of twenty-three 'mean persons', of which Shakespeare's name ranked fifth, (a reference to John Shakespeare in Stratford). Dethick responded: 'the man was a magistrate of Stratford-upon-Avon: a Justice of the Peace. He married the daughter and heir of Arden, of a good substance and ability.'

1599

John Shakespeare was reinstated on the Town Council in Stratford.

February: Cuthbert Burbage and his brother Richard signed a thirty-one year lease for the land on which the Globe playhouse was situated. The owner Sir Nicholas Brend had previously used the site to house a popular brothel. The other shareholders included: William Shakespeare, John Heminges, Augustine Phillips, Thomas Pope and Will Kemp. The building of the Globe made Burbage pre-eminent amongst his peers. He and his brother Cuthbert secured 50 per cent of the venture, with Shakespeare and the four other 'housekeepers' taking 10 per cent each.

May: The cost of reconstruction was in the region of £400. A legal survey of the land on which the Globe playhouse was built described it as being 'in occupatione Willielmi Shakespeare et aliorum' – 'in the possession of William Shakespeare and others.' (Chute, *Shakespeare and his Stage*).

1 June: For reasons that remain obscure, the Archbishop of Canterbury banned all satire written in verse. The Bishop of London helped enforce theatre censorship. The ecclesiastical authorities disapproved of the tendency for plays to portray the mores of the time in a satirical manner.

4 June: At Stationers' Hall a bonfire was made of all banned books, including the entire works of Thomas Nashe. When he heard of this, Nashe was said to be a broken man. He died two years later at the age of thirty-three.

7 June: One of Philip Henslowe's playwrights, John Day (1574–1638) killed another writer, Henry Porter, in Southwark. Day pleaded self-defence. Ben Jonson described him as 'a rogue'.

Oxford and Cambridge universities issued statutes forbidding students from attending professional plays. During the final years of Queen Elizabeth's reign, the London companies were paid to perform at the universities.

12 June: After careful consultation with astrologers, this day was deemed to be the most auspicious moment to open the new Globe playhouse. It was a day when the summer solstice coincided with the new moon. The axis of the Globe was in direct alignment with the midsummer sunrise.

The Globe was built along similar lines to The Theatre but it contained a capacity for 3,000 people, many more than the playhouse it replaced. On the opening afternoon admission prices were doubled. Shakespeare's *Julius Caesar* was the choice to inaugurate the building.

The name of the playhouse, the Globe, may have been suggested by the recent circumnavigation of the globe by Sir Francis Drake.

At some considerable distance, in Scotland, James VI arranged for a company of English players to erect a similar playhouse and perform in Edinburgh.

Sir George Buck made notes in his copy of a play called *George a Greene*. The first title-page inscription reads: 'Written by ... a minister, who acted the pin[n]ers part himself. Test. Shakespeare.' The second page reads: 'Ed. Juby saith that this play was made by Ro. Gree[ne].' Scholars point out that Buck obviously knew Shakespeare personally and consulted with him.

Sir George Buck was a noted antiquarian and became Master of the Revels under King James I. Shakespeare evidently made friends in high places.

Thomas Platter was a Swiss tourist visiting London in 1599. He noted that:

> Since the city is very large, open, and populous, watch is kept every night in all the streets, so that misdemeanor shall be punished. Good order is also kept in the city in the matter of prostitution, for which special commissions are set up, and when they meet with a case, they punish the man with imprisonment and fine. The woman is taken to Bridewell, the King's palace, situated near the river, where the executioner scourges her naked before the populace. And although close watch is kept on them, great swarms of these women haunt the town in the taverns and playhouses.
>
> Daily at two in the afternoon, London has two, sometimes three plays running in different places, competing with each other, and those which play best obtain most spectators. The playhouses are so constructed that they play on a raised platform, so that everyone has a good view. There are different galleries and places, however, where the seating is better and more comfortable and therefore more expensive. For whoever cares to stand below only pays one English penny, but if he wishes to sit he enters by another door and pays another penny, while if he desires to sit in the most comfortable seats, which are cushioned, where he not only sees everything well, but can also be seen, then he pays yet another English penny at another door ... During the performances food and drink are carried

around the audience, so that for what one cares to pay one may also have refreshment.

Refreshments were supplied by outside catering establishments, called tap houses, sometimes franchised by the theatre owners. John Heminges owned a tap house adjoining The Globe playhouse. (Bowsher, *Shakespeare's London Theatreland*, 2012)

Thomas Platter also commented that: 'The actors are most expensively and elaborately costumed; for it is the English usage for eminent lords or knights at their decease to bequeath and leave almost the best of their clothes to their serving men, which it is unseemly for the latter to wear, so that they offer them then for sale for a small sum to the actors.'

Queen Elizabeth posted the Earl of Essex to Ireland.

Romeo and Juliet was published for the second time in two years with many amendments. This version was entitled *The Most Excellent and Lamentable Tragedie of Romeo and Juliet*, printed by Thomas Creede and published by Cuthbert Burby. It is 800 lines longer than the earlier quarto.

The plot of *Romeo and Juliet* is taken primarily from Virgil, and Shakespeare's version leans heavily on a book by William Painter called *Palace of Pleasure* (1567).

Shakespeare continued to owe tax in London, according to the 'Pipe Roll', which lists old debts of tax owed. Thirteen shillings and fourpence was the outstanding amount. According to a note in the margin, this matter was sent to the Bishop of Winchester for his attention because although it was the Sheriff of Surrey's responsibility, the Bishop alone had authority over the area of the Clink in Southwark. Shakespeare was residing in the Bishop's manor. '...William Shakespeare, who lives in the parish of St Helen's, owes 13 shillings and 4 pence for the first subsidy (tax) of 1599.' (See Appendix D.)

Henry V was written during this period.

As You Like It was also written about this time. It is a reworking by Shakespeare of an earlier play called *Rosalynde* by Thomas Lodge.

William Shakespeare's *Passionate Pilgrim* was published by William Jaggard. This was an anthology of twenty poems attributed to Shakespeare, only five of which are considered authentic. Three of them were taken from *Love's Labour's Lost*. Suggestion has been made that some of the other poems may be extracts from the lost play, *Love's Labour's Won*.

September: Thomas Platter recorded in his journal that on 'September 21st after lunch, about two o'clock, I and my party crossed the water, and there in the house with the thatched roof witnessed an excellent performance of the tragedy of the first Emperor Julius Caesar with a cast of some fifteen people; when the play was over, they danced very marvellously and gracefully together as is their wont, two dressed as men and two as women.'

Shakespeare was made a housekeeper at the Globe playhouse. As part owners of the theatre, housekeepers divided up between them half the proceeds from the gallery.

The comic actor Will Kempe left the company shortly after the Globe opened for business. Robert Armin was Kempe's replacement. It is conjectured that Kempe fell out with Shakespeare regarding acting styles. Kempe was the old style of clown actor, whereby he 'did a turn' within the play for light relief. Shakespeare appeared to require the comedy scenes to be integral within the structure of the plays.

In addition to William Shakespeare's name appearing on the title pages of poems and plays, during his lifetime his name was given as that of a well-known writer at least twenty-three times.

When a play was being acted in the playhouses, stopping the action for any length of time was virtually unknown.

From 1599, with the gradual switchover from daylight performances to night-time indoor theatres, artificial lighting became a necessity. Huge candelabra were hoisted above the stage area and oil stoves strategically placed for warmth. Candles generally have a life of not much more than an hour and plays had to be stopped in order to replace them. Also, oil wicks needed to be trimmed. It was because of these unforeseen interruptions that 'Intervals' came into existence. Until the advent of indoor theatres, scripts were played without pause, like modern films. Afterwards, playwrights and editors rewrote scripts to insert cliffhanger climaxes.

🕮 Lighting became more reliable with the introduction of gas. When the Savoy Theatre in London became the first to be entirely lit by electricity on 28 December 1881, the need for interventions in the dramatic structure was lessened. Consequently, the number of intervals were reduced. In the twenty-first century most plays are written with only two acts.

🕮 The daily pay for a skilled artisan was fixed by law at sixpence halfpenny. A builder's labourer received between six and eight pence per day. In practice, a master builder could earn as much as five shillings a week.

🕮 The words playwright and dramatist were not in general use. The author of a play was known as 'the maker'.

🕮 In his book, *The Moon's A Balloon* David Niven wrote: 'The word "playwright" is spelt that way for a very good reason. Shipwrights build ships, wheelwrights fashion wheels, and playwrights construct plays. If they construct them badly, they quickly fly apart at the seams.'

Scena Secunda

Rehearsal Protocol

When a royal command performance was imminent, a tried and tested play was re-rehearsed in 'the great chamber' at the priory of St John's converted by the Office of the Revels. New plays were avoided as too much of a risk. Rehearsals took place at night. A costing for one of these court 'specials' is extant. Here is a typical winter's audit:

2 dozen torches
15 dozen candles
4000 faggots (firewood)
2 loads of coal
Several sacks of rushes (as floor covering)
1 Porter plus 3 assistants 'for their attendance and service in the rehearsals' at twelve pence each per day.

The Revels Office paid for scenic artists to be brought to Whitehall for their designs to meet the approval of the Lord Chamberlain.

Acting companies always kept at least two tailors on the payroll to carry out running repairs and alter garments for new production requirements.

Copyists wrote out the dialogue for the various characters on sheets of paper that were each six inches wide. These were joined together from top to bottom in a continuous roll, often showing only the key cue lines of the preceding speech. These became known as roll-calls.

The rooms in which copyists wrote were called scriptoriums.

The musical instruments most commonly used in Shakespeare's day included the lute, the cornet, the hautboy (a kind of oboe), drums, fiddles and trumpets.

Discipline amongst the actors was kept by means of a system of fines:
1) Turning up late for rehearsal: 12 pence.
2) Not turning up at all: 2 shillings.
3) Not being ready in costume for an entrance: 3 shillings.
4) Being drunk: 10 shillings.
5) Failing to materialise for a performance unless 'by a just excuse of sickness': 20 shillings.

ACTUS TERTIUS, SCENA SECUNDA

A hired actor's daily rate was one shilling.

Actors were not allowed to wear their stage costumes in the street. The penalty for wearing theatrical apparel outside of the theatre was £40: an enormous sum.

Scena Tertia

Prices of Admission

Standing room (in the pit in front of the stage): one penny.

Sitting on a bench (the stalls): two pence.

Sitting in the stalls with cushion: three pence.

Entrance was gained by paying a fee of a silver penny, to be placed into the cheap earthenware 'box' of a gatherer at the entrance. This box was similar to a child's piggybank, with a slot wide enough to take the coin. Another gatherer waited with a second box to take another penny if the customer wanted to ascend to a gallery, where a third gatherer waited with another money-box. For a third penny the theatergoer could acquire a seat with a cushion. Once the show was in full swing, the gatherers assembled in the manager's office where they smashed open their boxes to count the pennies. This was known originally as 'The Boxinge Office', and eventually it became 'The Box Office', a term we retain to this day.

Performances usually began at three o'clock in the afternoon to take advantage of the daylight. The main floor for the audience was called the pit, and in order to let in as much light as possible, this area had no roof.

Actus Quartus

Scena Prima
1600–6

1600

At the conclusion of a play it was customary for an actor to step forward and invite applause (as Puck does in *A Midsummer Night's Dream*). During Elizabeth's reign, this custom developed into a kind of encore in which the actors assembled on stage to perform a masque or a dance. There was no front-drop curtain in those days. The choreographers favoured vigorous steps like those of the galliard and the capriole (a huge leap). The lavolta was a dance movement involving an intimate, close hold between a pair of dancers in which the female partner was lifted above the man's head supported by a hand under her crutch whilst the couple turned 270 degrees. When plays were produced at court, members of the audience were invited to join in the dancing afterwards. Apparently, the lavolta was a favourite dance of the Virgin Queen (Elizabeth I).

Elizabeth I never personally attended public playhouses. Instead, theatrical entertainment came to her. She commissioned Royal Command performances at court, usually over the Christmas season. Plays for Royal Command performances invariably opened on St Stephen's Day – 25 December – at one of the monarch's palaces, such as York Place (now known as Whitehall), St James's (on the north side of Pall Mall), Hampton Court, Greenwich, Richmond and Somerset House (briefly known as Denmark House during the reign of James I).

At Christmas, Elizabeth paid the acting company a fee of ten pounds for each performance. When James I came to the throne his court demanded a greater quota of plays and paid much more for them.

Students at Cambridge presented a play called *The Return from Parnassus, Part 1*. There is a line within it that reads: 'Oh, sweet Mr Shakespeare! I'll have his picture at the court.'

There had been earlier versions of *Hamlet* in England. Shakespeare reworked his draft of the play using as his prime source *Gesta Danorum* by the thirteenth-century Danish chronicler, Saxo Grammaticus (1150–1220). This version recounts the legend of Amleth. The French humanist writer, Pierre Boaistau told the story again in 1559. An Italian writer, Matteo Bandello embellished it still further. At length it was adapted in the *histoires tragiques* by the sixteenth-century scholar Francois de Belleforest (1582).

Shakespeare filched other stories from Matteo Bandello (translated into English in 1575 by William Painter) including *Cymbeline* (story 19), *Much Ado About Nothing* (story 20), *Romeo and Juliet* (story

6), and *Twelfth Night* (story 28). *Edward III* (story 29) is thought to be a collaborative effort between Kydd and Shakespeare.

Legend has it that the Ghost of Hamlet's father, doubling with the Player King, were played by William Shakespeare. The first actor to play Hamlet was Richard Burbage. Following Burbage's death in 1619, when the same company revived the play, Hamlet was played by Joseph Taylor, who became a sharer in the King's Men in 1624.

2 February: The first known performance of *Twelfth Night* was played at Middle Temple.

6 March: The first known performance of *Henry IV, Part 1* was specially staged at Court for the Flemish ambassador, Ludovik Verreyken.

The builder, Peter Streete, completed the construction of the Globe playhouse on the South Bank in time for a summer opening.

Above the main entrance of the Globe playhouse was a sign bearing the motto '*Totus mundus agit histrionem.*' This does not quite translate into, 'All the world's a stage'. A reasonable translation is, 'The entire world plays the actor'.

February/ March: 'William Shackspere' sued John Clayton of Willington, Bedfordshire, in the court of King's Bench for a loan of £7, repayable on demand. This had been acknowledged by Clayton in Cheapside as far back as 22 May 1592. Thomas Awdley of the parish of St Magnus, London, appeared in court as 'Shackspere's attorney'.

In Thomas Awdley's final will, he appointed as one of his overseers 'my very good friend, Mr Thomas Greene' of the Middle Temple. Shakespeare rented out rooms at New Place, Stratford to Greene and his wife, the colourful Lettice. Greene referred to Shakespeare as his 'cousin' when, as solicitor in 1601, Greene assisted Richard Quiney in supporting the Corporation of Stratford against the Lord of the Manor, Sir Edward Greville (d. *c.* 1621). It has been the subject of conjecture as to whether they were really cousins or whether it was an expression of endearment. Quiney died in May 1602 after being 'wounded by a drunken band of Greville's men'.

22 June: The Privy Council limited theatrical companies to perform only twice a week – apart from royal command performances. This restriction did not last long.

The so-called 'Poet's War' of 1599–1600 started with a play by John Marston called *Histriomastix* that poked fun at Ben Jonson for painting his theatrical characters with particular 'humours'. Jonson, not known to take a slight lightly, came back with a play called *Cynthia's Revels* in which he pilloried Marston for having written for the choirboys of St Paul's. Marston riposted with a play called *What You Will*, lampooning Jonson as a failure. When Jonson challenged Marston to a duel and was ignored, Jonson went out in search of his adversary and found him in a tavern. Marston drew a gun. Jonson wrested it away from the other man and pistol-whipped him. Following this, Thomas Dekker wrote a satirical play to which Shakespeare probably contributed called *Satiromastix*. This was presented by the Lord Chamberlain's Men, consequently redeeming Jonson's honour and causing the feud to subside into friendly rivalry.

Jonson's play *Poetaster*, was produced, in which Shakespeare's application for a coat of arms was gently mocked.

The wooden timbers of the Globe playhouse were painted to resemble marble or jasper, and rich tapestries were draped everywhere to give the impression of pseudo-Roman luxury.

4 August: A staying order was entered in the Stationers' Register for *As yo like yt*, along with *Much Ado About Nothing* and *Henry V*. A play by Jonson – *Every Man in His Humour* was also entered. 'To be stayed' meant it was not to be published until the Stationers' Company was satisfied that the publisher in whose name the work was entered had undisputed ownership of the copyright.

In the First Folio of 1623, halfway through the printed version of *Much Ado About Nothing* the names of the characters were inadvertently substituted for the real names of the actors who played the parts. Hence we know that Dogberry was played by Will Kempe and that Richard Cowley played the part of Verges. A singer called Jack Wilson sang 'Sigh no more, ladies'.

14 August: *Chronicle History of Henry the fifth* was entered into the Register of the Stationers' Company by the bookseller Thomas Pavier. At the end of the year the first quarto was published by Thomas Millington and John Busby.

23 August: *Henry IV, Part 2* was entered into the Stationers' Register by Andrew Wise and William Aspley, thus: 'Entred for their copies vnder the handes of the wardens. Twoo bookes. the one called:

Muche a Doo about nothinge. Thother the second parte of the history of kinge henry the IVth with the humors of Sr John ffalstaff: : Wrytten by mr Shakespere. xij d.'. Two quarto versions appeared in 1600. The first (a) appears to have been printed from Shakespeare's foul papers. It omits the first scene of act 3, and 8 other passages. The second Quarto version (b) printed in the same year is identical to quarto 'a' except that it adds the missing first scene of Act 3.

Giordano Bruno was an Italian priest-philosopher who proposed that the stars were distant suns surrounded by their own exoplanets, and he raised the possibility that these planets could even foster life of their own. This was deemed heretical. In April 1583, he came to England with letters of recommendation from Henry III, the last French monarch of the Valois dynasty, and published his theories in London. He had philosophical discussions with the poet Philip Sidney. Bruno was also suspected of spying on Catholic conspirators, under the pseudonym 'Henry Fagot', for Sir Francis Walsingham. In 1600, back in Italy, Bruno was burnt at the stake for his supposed worship of the occult. Magic was a subject of intense controversy. Shakespeare incorporated some of Bruno's ideas into *The Tempest*.

8 October: The bookseller Thomas Fisher entered *A Midsummer Night's Dream* into the Register of the Stationers' Company.

Shakespeare changed the popular perception of fairies in *A Midsummer Night's Dream*. Puck was atypical as a mischievous sprite, but it was an innovation to portray other gentler fairies like Cobweb, Moth, Peasblossom and Mustardseed, who fluttered like butterflies.

ACTUS QUARTUS, SCENA PRIMA

28 October: James Roberts printed *The Merchant of Venice* for Thomas Heyes. First published in quarto it was described as 'The most excellent historie of the merchant of Venice. With the extreme cruelty of Shylocke the Jewe towards the said merchant, in cutting a just pound of his flesh; and the obtaining of Portia by the choyse of three Caskets.' Shakespeare's prime source for the story was *Il Pecorone* by Giovanni Fiorentino (1558). When the First Folio was published in 1623, the play was described as 'The Comicall Historie as it has beene divers times acted by the Lord Chamberlaine his Servants.'

In 1144, after a young boy disappeared in Norwich, the Jews were held responsible for his murder, and further accusations followed. They were perceived as being devilishly clever and uncompromisingly bloodthirsty. The typically lackadaisical English-man was frightened of them. By the year 1217 every Jew was compelled to wear a yellow badge. The words 'yellow' and 'Jew' became synonymous with the words coward and usurer.

The Jews were subjected to vicious persecutions, including charges of the ritual sacrifice of Christian children, culminating with their expulsion by Edward I in 1290. It would not be until 1655 that Jews were officially allowed to return to London following the petition of Jewish scholar Manasseh ben Israel to Oliver Cromwell.

Henry VIII had brought in certain Jews, usually musicians, but there were few models on whom Shakespeare could base Shylock except from earlier stage caricatures of Jews, and from the prejudiced information filtering from Jewish enclaves based in Spain and Venice.

Originally, Shylock was characterised as a figure of fun, being virtually indistinguishable from Pantalone of the Commedia dell'Arte. The actor playing him traditionally wore a false nose with a red fright wig and a red beard and a knife in his belt. It is likely that the first actor to play Shylock was Will Kempe, the comic.

One hundred-and-fifty years later, on 14 February 1741, Charles Macklin's characterisation of Shylock at Drury Lane astounded the audience by acting the part realistically, underscoring his malice and revengefulness.

When Jews in London converted to Christianity they frequently anglicised their names and they were referred to as Marranos.

1 November: *A Midsummer Night's Dream* was first published in quarto.

Robert Armin, who also answered to the nickname 'Snuff', was the son of a tailor. He started off as an apprentice goldsmith but became a protégé of the actor/clown Richard Tarleton. He created the Fool in *King Lear*, Feste in *Twelfth Night*, Lavache in *All's Well That Ends Well* and Touchstone in *As You Like It*. He wrote two books: *Foole upon Foole* and *Quips Upon Questions*, both published in 1600 under the pseudonym 'Clonnico de Curtanio Snuffe'.

Throughout the sixteenth century, alternative entertainment for the masses consisted of cockfighting and bear-baiting. Bears were scarce and expensive. As an alternative, a monkey would sit astride a pony and mastiffs (dogs) would be set upon it. The entertainment, such as it was, consisted in watching the monkey trying desperately to escape the fangs of the dogs. The dogs always won and in the end what was left were a dead horse and the remains of a monkey.

Sir Thomas Bodley (1535–1613) began his book collection in Oxford, using the site of the former library above the Divinity School, which was in near ruin. He claimed it would bring scandal to the library if any playbooks were admitted, and that it was highly undesirable that 'such kind of books should be vouchsafed a room in so noble a library.'

The First Folio of 1623 arrived there only because the Stationer's Company had agreed to supply the library with one copy of every book printed by its members.

1601

The Globe and the Hope playhouses were almost identical in size and shape.

In January, Valentine Orsino, Duke of Bracciano, visited Queen Elizabeth. Within twelve months, Shakespeare's company was rehearsing *Twelfth Night* with characters called Duke Orsino and Valentine, his servant.

Robert Devereaux, the Earl of Essex, was in his mid-thirties and a favourite of the queen until he began to believe so greatly in his own popularity with the public, he thought he could gain power himself. This displeased the queen and she removed his chief source of income – the sweet wine monopoly. Each court favourite had a royal perk, being a share of the tax or profit from perfumes, wine or spices et cetera.

The self-deluded Earl of Essex instructed his agent, Sir Gelly Meyrick, to pay £2 to the Lord Chamberlain's Men for a command performance at the Globe playhouse of *Richard II*. This play contained a politically incorrect scene, censored by The Office of the Revels, in which the monarch is deposed.

7 February: The play, *Richard II*, was produced in its entirety without cuts and the consequences were devastating.

8 February: In the aftermath of the uncensored *Richard II*, Essex set off with 300 troops to demand the queen's abdication. The young earl and his dwindling group of supporters rode as far as Ludgate before the revolution ran out of steam. Essex and his collaborators were arrested.

Queen Elizabeth may well have been fond of the handsome Earl of Essex but she was also critical of his incompetence, his disobedience and the stark failure in which they resulted.

By performing the uncut version of *Richard II*, the Chamberlain's Men were implicated in the seditious plot. A senior acting member of the company, Augustine Phillips, was delegated as spokesman and he convinced the prosecutors that the actors had been duped by their erstwhile patron. The defence was accepted and the Chamberlain's Men were let off the hook.

One of Essex's advisers, Henry Wotton, was not directly involved in Essex's downfall. Even so, within sixteen hours of his patron's apprehension Wotton fled to France. When James I came to the throne, he knighted Wotton and sent him abroad as a roving ambassador. However, on a mission in Augsburg in 1604, Wotton angered James by saying, 'An ambassador is an honest gentleman sent to lie abroad for the good of his country.'

24 February: Shrove Tuesday. The Lord Chamberlain's Men were commanded to give another play before the queen at Whitehall on the eve of Essex's execution.

25 February: Robert Devereux, Earl of Essex, was executed for treason. He was the last man to be beheaded on Tower Green in the Tower of London. It was a messy business, taking the executioner, Thomas Derrick, three strokes of the axe to remove Essex's head.

Four weeks later on Tower Hill, other Essex conspirators met the same fate: Sir Christopher Blount, Sir Charles Danvers, Sir Gelli Meyrick and Henry Cuffe.

Essex's collaborator, the Earl of Southampton, to whom Shakespeare had dedicated his first two epic poems, was spared the axe. Instead, he spent the next two years in the Tower of London.

27 February: Ann Line was executed at Tyburn. This led to Shakespeare writing *The Phoenix and Turtle*, which was published six months later. Six years earlier, Ann's husband Roger, refusing to accept the new Protestant faith, left England and died abroad. Ann and Roger, devout and faithful, swore a vow of chastity in their marriage. Shakespeare's poem embraced the idea of spiritual love between a couple who are physically apart. Lately, Ann had invited a priest into her

rooms to bless her candles. She was arrested for recusancy and hanged. Her body was thrown into a charnel pit near Tyburn but it was exhumed later in a secret ceremony and was reburied to the accompaniment of music by the Catholic musician, William Byrd.

Robert Chester's anthology called *Love's Martyr or Rosalind's Complaint* was published. It included William Shakespeare's sixty-seven-line poem *The Phoenix and the Turtle*. The book was dedicated to Sir John and Lady Salisbury. The other major poem was by Robert Chester. It is a widely held belief that Shakespeare's poem is an extended Liturgy for the Dead, indicating the writer's sympathies with Catholicism.

Some of Stratford's town councillors were indicted for inciting a riot. The group included the High Bailiff himself together with friends of Shakespeare, such as Richard Quiney and Henry Walker. They were all sent to Marshalsea prison in Southwark. Being men of substance they were shortly released on bail.

The accusation against them concerned 'enclosure'. An attempt was made by the Lord of the Manor – Sir Edward Greville – to turn public pasture into private grazing. Some senior council members and concerned citizens armed themselves with shovels and mattocks to uproot the newly built hedges that Greville had ordered to fence in the cattle.

In their legal battle against Sir Edward, John Shakespeare was brought to London. In his testimony he recalled the original charter given to Stratford by Edward VI eight days before he died. His statement bolstered the council's case against Greville and the argument went to arbitration.

In the spring, John and Jennet Davenant moved from London to Oxford and took ownership of The Tavern on the east side of the Cornmarket. Later the name was changed to The Crown. This was a four-storey building open for the purposes of drinking – specifically wine. It was not an inn for the accommodation of travellers, although William Davenant alleged that Shakespeare lodged there.

7 September: John Shakespeare, William's father, died aged seventy, leaving the title of 'gentleman' to his son, William. Although no will survives, all that remained of John's property – the Henley Street houses – were inherited by William, subject to a life interest for his mother, the widowed Mary. After attending his father's burial in Stratford, he returned to London leaving Mary in Henley Street together with his sister Joan, who had married a local hatter, William Hart. During Shakespeare's absences, the Harts stayed on at Henley Street to look after Mary until her death in 1608.

Fifty years after John Shakespeare's death, the Reverend Doctor Thomas Plume (1630–1704) recalled that Vice Admiral Sir John Mennes (1599–1671) claimed that he had once met John Shakespeare in his shop and described him as a 'merry cheeked old man' who said of his son that 'Will was a good honest fellow, but he durst have cracked a jest with him at any time.' Doubtless written in good faith, the anecdote must be misattributed, since Sir John Mennes was only two years old at the time of John Shakespeare's death.

According to Henslowe's Journals, stage costumes comprised the largest item of expenditure in any production.

Henslowe's account book mentions William White 'being paid for making crowns and things' at the Rose playhouse. The phrase 'property maker' had not yet been coined.

'High-corked shoes' or what today we might call 'platform shoes', were worn as everyday attire not only to give extra height but also to raise the feet above the excrement that littered the streets and byways.

27 October: As she neared the age of seventy, Elizabeth I convened her last parliament at which she gave a speech. Following Essex's execution she was in need of gaining public empathy. Historians often describe this as her 'golden speech'. It began thus: 'To be a king and wear a crown is a thing more glorious to them that see it than to them that bear it.'

Ann Hathaway's father wrote in his 1581 will: 'I owe unto Thomas Whittington my shepherd four pounds six shillings eight pence.' In 1601 when it came time for Whittington himself to write a will, it appeared he had only received half the money owed to him. He dispensed with the matter thus: 'Item I give and bequeath unto the poor people of Stratford forty shillings that is in the hand of Ann Shaxpere wife unto Mr Wyllyam Shaxpere and is due debt unto me being paid to mine executor by the said Wyllyam Shaxpere or his assigns according to the true meaning of this my will.'

1602

6 January: *Twelfth Night* had its first recorded performance at the Globe playhouse.

18 January: *The Merry Wives of Windsor* was entered into the Stationers' Register. In the margin there is a scribbled note that *Hamlet* had already been performed by the Lord Chamberlain's servants in London, Cambridge and Oxford. (Also see 4 November 1604).

By this time, Shakespeare was probably lodging at the house of Christopher Mountjoy – maker of headdresses – at the corner of Silver Street and Monkwell Street in Cripplegate Ward.

2 February: A lawyer, John Manningham, noted in his diary that he saw a revival of *Twelfth Night* at Candlemas performed by the Lord Chamberlain's Men at the Middle Temple. 'At our feast wee had a play called 'Twelve Night, or What you will,' much like the Commedy of Errores, or Menechmi in Plautus, but most like and neere to that in Italian called Inganni.' Manningham's suggested here that the source of the play was *Gl' Inganni* (The Deceived) by Curzio Gonzaga, first printed in 1537. Some scholars think Manningham meant *Gl' Ingannati*, a collaborative effort amongst Italian academics that was produced in 1531.

Contemporaneously, *Twelfth Night* was sometimes billed under the title *Malvolio*.

13 March: John Manningham (1575–1622) recorded the following anecdote:

> Upon a time when Burbage played Richard the Third there was
> a citizen grew so far in liking with him, that before she went
> from the play she appointed him to come that night unto her by
> the name of Richard the Third. Shakespeare, overhearing their

conclusion, went before, was entertained and at his game ere Burbage came. Then message being brought that Richard the Third was at the door, Shakespeare caused return to be made that William the Conqueror was before Richard the Third.

For the benefit of exceptionally dim readers, Manningham added, 'Shakespeare's name is William.'

The Inns of Court were regarded as England's 'third university', where lawyers were trained. Situated to the west of the city of London the chief buildings were Inner Temple, Middle Temple, Gray's Inn and Lincoln's Inn. Temporary stages for plays were set up at one end of the great dining halls.

Six months after John Shakespeare's death, Ralph Brooke, the York Herald, accused Sir William Dethick, the Garter King of Arms, of elevating twenty-three 'base persons' to the gentry, implying that his fellow Herald was guilty of taking bribes. One of these was Shakespeare's father, who had applied for arms thirty-four years earlier but had to wait for the success of his son before they were granted in 1596. Brooke included a sketch of the Shakespeare arms, captioned 'Shakespear ye Player by Garter'. John Shakespeare's grant was defended by Dethick and Clarenceux King of Arms, William Camden, the foremost antiquary of the time. As the most senior Herald, Camden upheld the Shakespeare claim citing John Shakespeare's experience as Bailiff of Stratford-upon-Avon and the military service said to have been undertaken by Shakespeare's great-grandfather, Thomas, in the days of Henry VII. As for the player, William Shakespeare, Camden wrote in his *Remaines Concerning*

Britaine – published in 1605, that Shakespeare was one of the 'most pregnant witts of these ages our times, whom succeeding ages may justly admire.'

1 May: William Shakespeare bought an estate from John and William Combe. His brother, Gilbert Shakespeare, handled the transaction on William's behalf. This consisted of 107 acres in the open fields of old Stratford, together with farmhouse, garden and orchard, twenty acres of pasture and common rights. This property was recorded as being within the environs of Bishopstone and Welcombe. Outlay: £320.

John and William Combe were close friends of Shakespeare. Several apocryphal stories circulated about William writing punning epitaphs for them in readiness for their demise.

The Stratford farmland was laid out on the old medieval system in a series of long, narrow strips that were worked side by side by tenant farmers. Shakespeare's purchase consisted of over 300 of these farming strips.

The names of the furlongs bought up by Shakespeare were rediscovered in 1994. They are described as:

> 12 acres at Clopton Nether furlong, 10 acres at Clopton Over,
> 1 acre at Whetegate, 6 acres at Lime furlong, 6 acres at Little
> Rednall, 8 acres at Great Rednall, 2 acres at the Nether Gill Pitt,
> 2 acres at the Over Gill Pitt, 4 acres at Homes Crosse, 2 acres
> at Hold Furlong, 4 acres at Stoney furlong, 4 acres at the Buttes

between Welcome Church way and Bryneclose way, 8 acres lying upon the top of Rowley, 10 acres lying under Rowley, 4 acres shooting and lying into Fordes Greene, 10 acres of leas ground at the Hame.

(Extracted from Folger Shakespeare Library, *Shakespeare Quarterly* – issue 45, 1994.)

Shakespeare's heirs sold back to the Corporation a half-share of this acreage in the year 1625.

31 May: For over a year, the Stratford bailiff, Richard Quiney, had been trying to prevent Sir Edward Greville, the lord of the manor, from enclosing farming strips as they comprised 'common land'. Quiney died in a final confrontation with Greville's henchmen. He was the only Stratford bailiff to be killed in office. He had nine children, one of whom, Thomas, became a vintner and married Shakespeare's daughter, Judith. Shakespeare's land acquisition would have been jeopardised by Edward Greville's land-grabbing attempt.

In Stratford, New Place had been in Shakespeare's possession for four years. However, the man from whom he purchased the property – William Underhill – had died shortly after the sale, poisoned by his eldest son, who was hanged for the crime. The Underhill estates were forfeit to the Crown until the younger son – Hercules Underhill – came to man's estate (reached the required age to inherit). On 6 June, Hercules came of age and Shakespeare immediately set out to confirm his own title to New Place. Shakespeare received the conveyance confirmation from Hercules during the Michaelmas term.

In Stratford-upon-Avon, Puritanism was gaining momentum. The Stratford Council declared there would be no more plays given in the Guildhall. Any councilor who licensed the actors to perform would be fined ten shillings. The man who was instrumental in implementing this order was bailiff on Stratford council – Daniel Baker. The King's Men were licensed to perform anywhere and could overturn this local decision had they wanted to. It appears they didn't bother to try.

26 July: *Hamlet* was entered into the Stationers' Register, described as 'latelie Acted by the Lo: Chamberleyne his servantes'. It is thought that the play was written in the summer of 1599.

Groundlings are fish that live at the bottom of a river and have big eyes that gape upwards. Hence, Shakespeare's references to 'groundlings', alluding to the standing audience in 'the pit'.

In early versions of the printed version of *Hamlet* the word 'groundlings' was altered to 'ignorant'.

None of the early texts of *Hamlet* were divided into Acts. The Five Acts with which modern readers are familiar derive from a 1676 quarto. These apparently arbitrary divisions stemmed from the need to change candles. The enforced pauses sometimes break up the dramatic action in an unsatisfactory manner.

Tradition has it that Shakespeare played the ghost of Hamlet's father – a part that is generally doubled with that of the Player King.

The Privy Council allowed idle and disorderly spectators at plays to be press-ganged for the army and navy.

6 August: Countess Alice of Derby entertained the queen at Harefield House. Lady Derby's first husband was Lord Strange, fifth Earl of Derby. She was also sister-in-law of the second Lord Hunsdon. The expense accounts read: 'Rewards to the Vaulters, players and dancers (of this £10 to Bur-bidges Players) in summe: £64 18 10.' Burbidge's (Burbage's) players included the thirty-eight-year-old William Shakespeare.

The queen arrived at Harefield on horseback accompanied by a huge entourage. She rode along the lanes, stopping at Dew's Farm. For the three-day junket, the feast included: 100 pigeons, 50 chickens, 20 pigs, 13 stags, 11 oxen, 65 muttons, 74 bucks, 150 lobsters and 15 swans.

Countess Alice's troupe wore as their insignia a flying silver swan. This was in the form of an armband or a brooch pinned to a hat.

The badge of the Lord Admiral's Men consisted of a noble white lion with a blue shoulder crescent.

28 September: William Shakespeare travelled to Stratford and purchased a half-acre with a cottage in Chapel Lane behind New Place. This was a property in the gift of the Manor of Rowington, which happened to be in the possession of the widow of the Earl of Warwick. Shakespeare had to appear in person before Lady Anne, Countess of Warwick, to secure copyhold tenure. He agreed to pay the manor a rent of two shillings per year as long as he remained in possession of the property.

26 December: The Lord Chamberlain's Men made their annual visit to the court at Whitehall with another play for the queen.

1603

During this year 25,000 London inhabitants died of the plague: one in five of the population.

When mortality rates from plague reached thirty per week, playhouses were closed automatically.

2 February: The Chamberlain's Men's performed at Richmond Palace, where a fourteen-foot square stage was erected 'for the plaiers to playe on'. It was to be the last performance that the company gave before the queen.

7 February: *Troilus and Cressida* was entered into the Stationers' Register, and issued by the bookseller and printer James Roberts. In the registration it said the play 'was acted by the Lord Chamberlain's Men.' However, there is no record of it ever being performed. It was published again in 1609 with contradictory information. The suggestion is sometimes made that this play is the first 'cowboys and indians' story.

Parliament passed an Act 'to restrain the abuses of players', forbidding irreverence or blasphemy in theatres.

Elizabeth I remained in Richmond and never returned to London.

When Queen Elizabeth realised she was dying, she lay on her bed and faced the wall, refusing to speak. This fading away took several days.

14 March: The theatres were closed out of respect when the players were made aware of the queen's impending demise.

24 March: Queen Elizabeth I died aged sixty-nine. She had reigned for forty-four years and six months. Modern science presumes her death was caused by the lead-based foundation that she applied to her face to cover scars caused by the cowpox she caught in her youth. So it appears that, quite unwittingly, she poisoned herself.

Although acknowledged as one of the leading poets of the day, Shakespeare did not write an encomium on the death of the sovereign. Many of his friends had died in the name of the old religion to which the queen had been so adamantly opposed.

After Elizabeth's death, no more plays were presented at Richmond during Shakespeare's lifetime.

According to Raphael Holinshed, Henry VIII signed the death warrants of 72,000 people. It is estimated that Elizabeth ordered the execution of 35,000 more.

A quarter of a century earlier, Elizabeth had instructed her chief adviser, the vertically challenged Robert Cecil, to negotiate with James VI of Scotland for him to succeed her. This was undertaken in the utmost secrecy. Correspondence was conducted in code. James VI was 'No. 10', Robert Cecil was 'No. 30' and Elizabeth herself was

'No. 24'. The reason for her decision has never been satisfactorily explained, as James's wife was Catholic.

Measure for Measure was probably written about this time. The first folio of 1623 is our only textual source for this play.

23 April: The 'Sanders' portrait was executed. This is the only portrait that can be traced back to Shakespeare's lifetime and was painted in oil on an oak wood panel around this date, when the dramatist was thirty-nine. Oxford University Press has begun to use this picture in new editions of Shakespeare's plays produced for the North American market. Today the portrait is in the possession of Lloyd Sullivan of Ottawa, Ontario, who can trace his ancestry through thirteen generations to John Sanders. Radiocarbon dating and all other tests point to the portrait's authenticity. It portrays a middle-aged man wearing a black doublet with silver ornamentation. A label on the back – age-tested many times – reads:

Shakespere
Born April 23 = 1564
Died April 23 – 1616
Aged 52
This Likeness taken 1603
Age at that time 39 y

It was painted and originally owned by John Sanders, a member of the Painter-Stainers' Company, the guild officially charged with visual work for everything from coats of arms, to theatre sets. Sanders's family lived near Shakespeare's lodgings on the corner of Silver Street and Muggle Street in Cripplegate. John Sanders was the eldest son of William Sanders, who died at Coughton in 1638.

3 May: King James arrived at Greenwich from Scotland with a huge entourage. The king brought with him boon companions including Lawrence Fletcher, his favourite actor. The Scottish Kirk (Church) had tried to suppress performances by Lawrence in Edinburgh but James defied the deacons. Lawrence Fletcher was given the freedom of the City of Aberdeen.

17/18 May: Warrants for the Great Seal were written for letters patent authorising 'William Shakespeare and the rest of their associates freely to use and excercice the Arte and faculty of playinge Comedies Tragedies histories Enterludes morall pastorall Stageplaies and suche others like as theie have already studied or herafter shall use or studie as well for the recreation of our lovinge Subjectes as for our Solace and pleasure when wee shall thincke good to see them during our pleasure.' At last, the actors in Shakespeare's company were under the patronage of the king himself.

James I had such a broad Scots accent that many Englishmen had difficulty understanding him. His legs were weak and he could not walk without assistance, resulting in his lifelong love of horse riding. Sometimes, he could not go to sleep without somebody reading to him. He was mocked as 'the wisest fool in Christendom'.

James never took a great deal of interest in women and was praised for his chastity. This concealed an ambiguous side to his nature, and he had passionate friendships through the years with such men as

Robert Carr, the Earl of Somerset, Lawrence Fletcher, the Viscount Rochester and the Duke of Buckingham. 'The kings kissing them after so lascivious a mode in public, and upon the theatre, as it were, of the world, prompted many to imagine some things done in the retiring house that exceed my expressions no less than they do my experience,' to quote Sir Anthony Weldon (1583–1648) in his book, *The Court and Character of King James 1*, after which he was told that his services at court were no longer required.

May/December: Plague closed London theatres and delayed King James's coronation parade.

May 1603 to April 1604: Shakespeare rented a room from Christopher Mountjoy on the corner of Silver and Monkswell Streets. George Wilkins lodged there at the same time. An inn and brothel owner, Wilkins became a writing associate of Shakespeare.

King James was described as 'a well-informed Calvinist protestant'. Church laws were made (canons) requiring the teaching of the Catechism and the Ten Commandments to all children, servants and apprentices before Evening Prayers.

King James was born in 1566 – the only son of Mary, Queen of Scots and her second husband, Henry Stuart, Lord Darnley. When James was seven months old, his father was murdered in Edinburgh. His mother was executed twenty years later. In the interim, he had been crowned King of Scots at the age of thirteen. A succession of male tutors looked after the youthful king. Some became favourites in more ways than one. The Earl of Lennox was so close to the king that he 'went about to draw the King to carnal lust' according to the gossip of the time.

James I of England was James VI of Scotland and is not to be confused with James I of Scotland. The latter died in unfortunate circumstances in the evening of 20 February 1437. Alerted to assassins at his refuge in the Blackfriars monastery in Perth, James I of Scotland hid in a sewer tunnel but could not escape as its exit had been blocked off to prevent tennis balls floating away. Thus he was killed, trapped by the balls.

According to a Lancashire tradition, James I found a particular cut of beef, a surloine, so tasty during a meal at Hoghton Tower, that he drew his sword and knighted it, saying, 'Arise, Sir Loin.' James did like a drink or three and was capable of strange behaviour but the surloin story is a joke. The fact is, the derivation of sirloin comes from the French: 'sur' meaning 'over' and 'long' meaning 'loin'; hence, a cut of beef from above the loin.

It was suggested that King James became a heavy drinker because his wet nurse was an alcoholic and he received copious quantities of the hard stuff through her milk.

19 May: The Lord Chamberlain's Men was renamed the King's Men and a licence issued to that effect. The company of actors was billed in this order:

Lawrence Fletcher
William Shakespeare
Richard Burbage

Augustine Phillips
John Heminges
Henry Condell
William Sly
Robert Armin
Richard Cowley 'and the rest of their associates'.

It may not be too far-fetched to suppose that Shakespeare, finding himself relegated to second billing, might have been sufficiently disgruntled to consider retirement.

In the letters patent, James I entreated his players 'to perform Comedies, Tragedies, Histories, interludes, Morals, pastorals ... for the recreation of our loving subjects as for our solace and pleasure when we shall think good to see them within their now usual house called The Globe and all other towns and boroughs of the Kingdom.'

Upon the formation of the King's Men, Shakespeare, now thirty-nine, became a Groom of His Majesty's Chamber. The Master of the Great Wardrobe granted him four-and-a-half yards of scarlet cloth for his uniform.

May: Due to a virulent outbreak of the plague, the King's Men set off on tour. Their venues included Maldon, Ipswich, Coventry, Shrewsbury, Bath and Oxford.

Edmund Tilney, Master of the Revels, received a knighthood (along with about 400 other men).

July: Visitors flocked to London for the impending coronation. 'The streets were plumed with gallants, tobacconists filled up whole taverns, vintners hung out spick-and-span new ivy bushes.' Then the plague swept through the capital.

13 July: The plague orders were sent out to all parish churches.

Weekly 'Bills of Mortality' could be bought for a penny per copy. These listed the figures of the latest plague deaths parish by parish: an aide-memoire to help people know which areas of London to avoid.

Houses containing plague victims were quarantined for a month. On front doors, red crosses exactly fourteen inches in height were painted, using oil paint to prevent removal.

23 July: King James indulged in the sale of knighthoods, which he considered a nice little earner. On this day alone, he created 300 new knights in the grounds of Whitehall Palace.

25 July: By the time James was crowned in a ceremony barred to the public, 1,100 people per week were dying of the plague in London.

King James ruled a court that was soon rotten with graft and corruption, his young male favourites being granted almost unlimited licence.

James followed the precedent set by Elizabeth I, and demanded plays at court. He increased the number and frequency and paid up to £30.

ACTUS QUARTUS, SCENA PRIMA

In Shakespeare's Southwark parish more than 2,500 people died of the plague between June and Christmas.

Southwark is recorded in the 1086 Domesday Book as Sudweca. The name means 'southern defensive work' and is derived from the Old English *sūth and weorc*.

Smoking tobacco or chewing orange peel and rosemary were considered good preventatives against plague. The price of rosemary rocketed from twelve pence an armful to six shillings for a small bunch.

9 September: George Carey, second Baron Hunsdon, the Lord Chamberlain, died of mercury poisoning. The only cure for syphilis known to work consisted of sweating in hot baths whilst being rubbed vigorously with mercury ointment. Sometimes the cure was worse than the disease.

The French called syphilis 'the Neapolitan disease'. The English called it 'the French disease'. The Russians called it 'the Polish disease'. The Persians called it 'the Turkish disease'. The Turks called it 'the Christian disease'. The Tahitians called it 'the British disease'. The Indians called it 'the Portuguese disease'. The Japanese called it 'The Chinese pox'.

Venus is the goddess of love. Hence venereal disease is so called because it is a malady that develops after making love.

There was a common saying at the time: 'A night with Venus and a lifetime with mercury.' (Quoted by Richard Wiseman in *Eight Chirurgicall Treatises* [1676].)

John Heminges rented a house in Addle Street from the goldsmith, Thomas Savage, who also acted as a trustee for the Globe Theatre. Henry Condell and Shakespeare lived nearby.

Queen Anne was the second daughter of the King of Denmark. She married James I in 1589 and was described as a thoroughly stupid woman, whose chief assets were a pleasant manner and a good complexion. In court circles she was always referred to as Anna. She formed an acting company derived from the Worcester's Men, which was now called Queen Ann's Men, although the company also answered to the name of the Queen's Players.

3 October: John Heminges's ninth child was christened in the parish of St Mary's Aldermanbury, London. Shakespeare was godfather to little William Heminges, who also became a dramatist. Two of his plays are extant: *The Jews' Tragedy* (1626) and *The Fatal Contract* (1639). When John Heminges died in 1630, his son, William, inherited shares in the Globe playhouse and the Blackfriars Theatre.

John Stow in his article, *Survey of London* wrote: 'Of old time, coaches were not known to this island, but chariots or whirlicotes, then so called, and they only used of princes or great estates such as had their footmen about them ... but now of late years, the use of coaches, brought out of Germany, is taken up and made so common as there is neither distinction of time nor difference of persons observed, for the world runs on wheels with many whose parents were glad to go on foot.'

📖 Watling Street was the most famous road in Elizabethan times. It ran north from London to Chester. There were three other main roads, all in a state of disrepair, used by horsemen and messengers. These roads ran from London to Dover, from London to Bristol and London to Berwick-upon-Tweed. Travellers embarked at Chester to reach Dublin. Visitors from the continent arrived at Dover, went on horseback to Gravesend, and took a boat up the Thames to London.

📖 When James I ascended the throne, brick was becoming the fashionable building material. James said he hoped to be remembered because 'we had found our Citie ... of London of stickes, and left them of brick, being a material far more durable and safe from fire and beautiful and magnificent.' It is safe to say that nobody has yet suggested Shakespeare's plays were written by James I.

📖 I November: The first known performance of *Othello*. The plot of the play was partly based on a short story by the Italian, Giraldo Cinthio, published in 1565.

📖 Sir Walter Raleigh founded the original boozy club for 'wits' called The Mermaid Club, though it was more often referred to as the Friday Club. Ben Jonson, John Donne, John Fletcher, Francis Beaumont, Thomas Coryat, John Selden, Robert Bruce Cotton, Richard Carew, Richard Martin and William Shakespeare gathered here on the first Friday of every month. The club was situated at the Mermaid Tavern with a front entrance on Friday Street. There was also a convenient 'staggering' back entrance onto Bread Street, Cheapside.

Beaumont wrote to Jonson:

Methinks the little wit I had is lost
Since I saw you, for wit is like a rest
Held up at tennis, which men do the best
With the best gamesters: what things have we seen
Done at the Mermaid! heard words that have been
So nimble, and so full of subtile flame,
As if that every one from whence they came
Had meant to put his whole wit in a jest,
And had resolv'd to live a fool the rest
Of his dull life; then when there hath been thrown
Wit able enough to justify the town
For three days past, wit that might warrant be
For the whole city to talk foolishly
'Till that were cancell'd: and when that was gone
We left an air behind us, which alone
Was able to make the two next companies
Right witty; though but downright fools, mere wise.
(from the Beaumont letters).

William Johnson owned The Mermaid Tavern as well as being a member of its drinking club. He went on to purchase property in partnership with Shakespeare.

To digress for a moment, the tradition of boozy clubs housing the current wits of the age continue through the years. Famously, from 1919 until 1930, writers, actors and wits gathered on a fairly regular basis at the Algonquin Round Table in New York. They dubbed themselves 'The Vicious Circle' and disseminated outrageous gossip and puns across the country. Such wits as Robert Benchley, George S. Kaufman, Dorothy Parker, Robert E. Sherwood, Alexander Woollcott, Edna Ferber and Harpo Marx mingled over many a liquid lunch.

2 December: To avoid the plague raging in London, James I moved to the comparative safety of the Earl of Pembroke's house at Wilton near Salisbury. The King's Men, including William Shakespeare, travelled from Mortlake to give a performance of *As You Like It* before the king. They were paid £30 'for the paynes and expenses of himself and the rest of the company in coming from Mortelake in the countie of Surrie unto the court aforesaid and there presenting before his majestie on playe.'

20 December: Ben Jonson's tragedy play *Sejanus: His Fall* was first performed at Court with Shakespeare listed amongst the 'Principal Tragedians', billed as Will Shake-Speare, he played Tiberius.

Ben Jonson declared that during his whole lifetime he had only earned £200 from his writing.

Bear-baiting rings had been licensed to operate on Sundays since 1550. Within a few months of his reign, James, for all his love of animal sports, banned bear-baiting on the Sabbath.

1604

1 January: The King's Men performed *A Midsummer Night's Dream* at Court.

From the accession of James I until Shakespeare died in 1616, the King's Men gave more than 180 Royal Command performances.

February: The first meeting of the plotters took place at Robert Catesby's Lambeth House. They planned to blow up Parliament. These men included the best swordsman in England, John Wright, and his co-conspirator, Thomas Wintour.

15 March: King James, Queen Anne and their son, Prince Henry, made their triumphal entry through London, following its post-ponement from the previous summer due to the plague.

Sir George Home, Master of the Great Wardrobe, bestowed four yards of red cloth to each of the King's players to attend his investiture. The actors were: 'William Shakespeare, Augustine Phillipps, Lawrence Fletcher, John Hemminges, Richard Burbidge, William Slye, Robert Armin, Henry Cundell, and Richard Cowley.' Shakespeare had regained top billing.

Everyone in the royal service, even down to the basket makers, wore the scarlet livery, and Shakespeare was no exception. The English court, in conciliatory mood after so many years of war, invited the Spanish Ambassador, the Constable of Castile, to Somerset House where the king's servants attended on him. As the ambassador did not speak English, bear-baiting was provided as entertainment. The twelve actors had to stand by, smiling and bowing prettily in their red doublets and cloaks. The ambassador brought with him 234 attendants affording plenty to look at. Shakespeare and each of the grooms of the chamber were paid two shillings per day.

Shakespeare was one in a long line of 'Grooms of His Majesty's Chamber'. Geoffrey Chaucer held a similar position in the court of Richard II. Richard Tarleton, the actor, had been a Groom when appointed to the Queen's Men.

May: King James made an amendment to the 'Act for punishment of rogues, vagabonds and surly beggars'. In effect this meant that all acting companies had to be under the patronage of royalty or the nobility. The number of companies burgeoned under the banner of various royal princes and princesses.

The king's son, Prince Henry, formed a separate acting company – an offshoot of the Admiral's Men – called Prince Henry's Servants. Prince Henry was nine years old. When the Prince of Wales died in 1612, the name of the company changed again to Palgrave's Men (referring to Frederick V, later the Elector Palatine).

Theatre companies employed 'plotters' to devise new plays. The head of the plotting department for the Admiral's Men was Anthony Munday. Several writers were paid up to £2 each to develop plot outlines and add in the dialogue.

May/ September: Plague closed the playhouses again.

20 May: The first meeting took place of the conspirators in the 'Gunpowder Plot', including Guy Fawkes – using the pseudonym 'John Johnson' – together with Thomas Percy, Catesby, Wintour and Wright took place at The Duck and Drake Inn, off the Strand, where Thomas Wintour stayed when he came to London.

Guy Fawkes was a Yorkshireman. He had been born next door to the Star Inn in Stonegate, York. When he fought as a mercenary in Spain he changed his name to Guido.

The formula for the explosive used in the Gunpowder Plot was: sulphur, charcoal, saltpeter and potassium with alcohol and a little water. This was mixed then oven-dried and broken into small pieces known as 'corned powder'. It ignited at 550 degrees Fahrenheit. Apparently the chefs drew straws for oven-drying duties.

27 June: Robert Cowdray (1538–1605) wrote the dedicatory epistle to his book *A Table Alphabeticall*, the prototype of the first English dictionary, containing 2,500 words. 'A table alphabeticall conteyning and teaching the true writing, and understanding of hard vsuall English wordes, borrowed from the Hebrew, Greeke, Latine, or French, &c. With the interpretation thereof by plaine English words, gathered for the benefit & helpe of ladies, gentlewomen, or any other unskilfull persons. Whereby they may the more easilie and better vnderstand many hard English wordes, vvhich they shall heare or read in scriptures, sermons, or elswhere, and also be made able to vse the same aptly themselues.'

Shakespeare rented lodgings in London where, as far as the tax authorities were concerned, his assets never exceeded £5. Most of his income found its way back to Stratford.

Shakespeare counted the pennies. On one of his visits to Stratford he sued Philip Rogers, an apothecary, who owed him one pound, fifteen shillings and ten pence for twenty bushels of malt. William Tetherton, acting as Shakespeare's attorney, demanded full repayment plus ten shillings damages.

For a time, William Shakespeare lodged with Christopher and Mary Mountjoy (or Mountjoie) at the corner of Monkwell and Silver Street, Cripplegate, in the city of London. Mary Mountjoy supplied gloves, amongst other things, to the royal family. Shakespeare had a working knowledge of glovemaking.

October: Robert Keyes and Thomas Bates (Catesby's servant) joined the conspiracy that became known as the Gunpowder Plot.

20 October: James I started calling himself 'King of Great Britaine' and expressing the wish for a United Kingdom with the following proclamation: 'the blessed Union, or rather Reuniting of these two mightie, famous, and ancient kingdoms of England and Scotland, under one Imperiall Crowne...' He saw himself as the founder of a new dynasty and drew parallels with the first emperor of ancient Rome, Augustus.

24 October: The Public Record Office recorded a land survey of Rowington Manor: 'William Shakespeare Lykewise holdeth there one

cottage and one garden by estimation a quarter of one acre and payeth rent yearly.'

31 October: A season of seven plays by Shakespeare started to go into production including two performances of *The Merchant of Venice*.

A rumour spread throughout England that Philip II of Spain had, in a fit of jealousy, strangled his wife after growing suspicious of her infidelity when she came into the possession of a handkerchief that did not belong to her.

1 November: *Othello* was first performed at Whitehall. Richard Burbage played the lead. The account book of the Master of the Revels records this: 'On Hallamas Day, being the first of Nouembar the Kings Maiesties plaiers in King James Banketinghouse at Whit Hall Called The Moor of Venis. By Shaxberd, …' This had started life as a short story by Giraldo Cinthio (1504–73).

Originally, the company's comic actor, Robert Armin, played the character of Iago, presumably to create a figure of fun.

The word 'Moor' had a religious connotation in Tudor times. It meant Mohammadan or Muslim. Being black was not the issue.

According to Jonathan Bate in *Shakespeare: Staging the Word*: 'the latest archival research suggests there might have been 900 black Africans out of a population of 200,000 in Elizabethan London.' The majority of these black Africans were considered to be slaves. In the twenty-first century it is difficult to conceive how commonplace acceptance of slavery was among Europeans. And the complacency endured. Even two hundred years later, Horatio Nelson brought home a slave girl, Fatima, as a present for Emma Hamilton. Nelson missed his own father's funeral in order to be present at the christening of the girl as Fatima Nelson in his local church at Merton.

Literary scholars often complain about unnecessary commas in Shakespeare's plays. However, there is a tendency among actors to add commas when learning lines to indicate 'breath' marks.

4 November: *The Merry Wives of Windsor* was performed by the King's Men at Whitehall Palace, which was then called York Place.

24 December: St Stephen's Night. *Measure for Measure* was performed over Christmas at Whitehall. This is the earliest recorded performance. It was not published until the First Folio in 1623. It is adapted from a short story called 'The Story of Epitia' by the Italian writer, Giraldo Cinthio. The title, *Measure for Measure*, is a Biblical reference taken from Matthew 7:2.

26 December: *Measure for Measure* was again performed by the King's Men at Court.

28 December: *The Comedy of Errors* was performed by the King's Men at Court.

From November until the end of February 1605, the King's Men played at Court on eleven occasions, including seven plays by

Shakespeare and two by Ben Jonson. This was a substantial increase since the days they performed under Elizabeth I. The King's Men consequently enlarged the shareholding committee to include John Lowin, Alexander Cooke and Nicholas Tooley. By 1609, two more shareholders joined: John Underwood and William Ostler.

So far as is known, the first play of Shakespeare to be translated into another language was *Romeo and Juliet*. It was performed at Nördlingen in Bavaria under the title *Von Romeo undth Julitha*.

1604/1611: The New Authorised Version of the Bible was produced, known as the King James Version. James appointed forty-seven translators divided into six committees, each committee being responsible for a particular section of the Bible.

James loved animal baiting and kept a menagerie of wild and exotic animals in the Tower of London. Shakespeare used the name of a living bear called Sackerson – who was famous for his fierceness – in *The Merry Wives of Windsor*. Slender has the line: 'I have seen Sackerson loose twenty times, and have taken him be the chain.'

An anonymous poem was written that describes Richard Burbage's portrayal of the distracted *Hamlet*. Apparently, the actor sucked at a quill pen as if it were a pipe of tobacco and drank from the inkwell as if it were a bottle of ale.

In the original quarto of Hamlet, the character Polonius is called Corambis. In this early version, Hamlet actually succeeds in convincing Gertrude that Claudius was guilty of killing her first husband.

Actors look for a motivational reason to leave the stage. Until recently, it was not uncommon for actors to ask playwrights to give them 'an exit line'. Shakespeare indicated when actors were obliged to enter but often left them to their own devices as to how to get off. (A lazy habit perpetuated by dramatists to the present day, including Agatha Christie.)

James I brought graft and corruption with him into the English court. 'Franchises', 'monopolies', and 'honours' could be bought. King James created 838 new knights. A knighthood cost £30. Realising he was on to a good thing he invented the new rank of 'knight baronet': these he sold for £1,905 each. Altogether, James created three dukes, a marquess, thirty-two earls, nineteen viscounts and fifty-six barons, filling his coffers to the tune of £120,000. Shakespeare is not mentioned as a player after 1604.

1605

Stage design took on a different aspect with the presence of Inigo Jones (1573–1652). He is credited with introducing the proscenium arch to English theatre. Between 1605 and 1640, Jones was responsible for staging over 500 performances, collaborating with Ben Jonson despite a relationship fraught with competition and jealousy. For Jonson, the words were all-important and when Jones experimented with movable scenery, Jonson felt such innovation was nothing but a distraction. The two had famous arguments about whether stage design or literature was more important in theatre. Jonson ridiculed Jones in a series of his works, written over a span of two decades.

Timon of Athens was probably written at this time but there are no records of performances. It was not entered into the Stationer's Register until 1623. There is an untidiness about the play that suggests that the extant copy is based on a rough draft. Scholars believe it to be a collaboration between Shakespeare and Thomas Middleston.

1 January: *A Midsummer Night's Dream* was performed. This is the first recorded instance of a performance of the play, although it states in the first quarto edition (1600) that it had been 'sundry times publickely acted' prior to that date.

4 January: Ulrik of Denmark, Queen Anne of Denmark's brother, visited England. Sir Robert Cecil (as Viscount Cranbourne) asked Sir Walter Cope (a government official) to select a play for Anne. Cope responded to say: 'Burbage is come and says there is no new play the Queen has not seen but they have revived an old one called Love's Labours Lost which for wit and mirth he says will please her exceedingly.' It was performed at the house of Sir Robert Cecil (Lord Burghley's son).

6 January: The day after the masque on Twelfth Night, the players presented *The Comedy of Errors* in Ulrik of Holstein's honour at the house of Robert Cecil.

King James's wife, Anne, had a talent for spending money that is well demonstrated by the £3,000 she spent on the *Twelfth Night* masque before the court at Whitehall. She brought Inigo Jones and Ben Jonson together to create *The Masque of Blackness*, in which the queen participated, appearing fully 'blacked up' along with eleven of her ladies-in-waiting. She played the nymph Euphoris from the River Niger. The theme was that she was desirous to become white under the auspices of the divine King James. Foreign guests watched the spectacle goggle-eyed.

7 January: First recorded performance of *Henry V* at the Globe playhouse.

8 January: *Love's Labour's Lost* was presented at Southampton House. The Earl of Southampton entertained Queen Anne and her entourage as part of his strategy to reinstate himself in Court circles following the disgrace he suffered at the end of Elizabeth's reign. Richard Burbage and William Shakespeare were in the production. Shakespeare had dedicated his first epic poems to Southampton.

10 February: *The Merchant of Venice* was performed by the King's Men at Court for James I.

12 February: The king was so pleased with *The Merchant of Venice* that he commanded it to be performed again at Whitehall on this day. According to the Court Revels Account book, the play was written by *Shaxberd*.

25 March: Lady Day/New Year's Day. Robert Wintour, John Grant and Christopher Wright added to the conspirators of the Gunpowder Plot.

11 May: The actor, Augustine Phillips, died at Mortlake. Actors were more commonly referred to as 'players' because they were

expected to be competent enough to play at least one musical instrument. In his will, Augustine Phillips bequeathed a bass viol, a bandore, a cittern and a lute. A bandore is a long-necked plucked string-instrument and a cittern is similar to a plucked guitar.

Among other items that Augustine Phillips gifted were:
Item. a silver bowl worth £5 to each of the executors, John Heminges, Richard Burbage and William Sly.
Item. a 30-shilling gold piece each to Shakespeare, Henry Condell and Christopher Beeston, who was a former apprentice of Phillips.
Item. 20 shillings in gold each to Lawrence Fletcher, Robert Armin, Alexander Cooke, Richard Cowley and Nicholas Tooley.

24 July: Shakespeare paid £440 for the remaining thirty-one-years' lease on some of the Stratford 'tithes of corn, grain, blade and hay'. These tithes were taxes formerly collected by the Church, but in 1544 they had been rented out on a ninety-two-year lease to the Barker family, who passed them on to the Hubands. Shakespeare paid Ralph Huband for one-eighth of the entire property for the remainder of the lease. In all, Shakespeare made 10 per cent annual profit on this – from which it was estimated he would receive £60 per annum in rent.

Buying tithes, on behalf of the Church, entitled Shakespeare to be a lay preacher.

William Shakespeare's income from his shareholding in the Chamberlain's Men – later named the King's Men – varied from £150 to £200 per year.

28 July: Due to an outbreak of the plague, the opening of Parliament was postponed until 5 November (a date to remember).

August: In Christ Church Hall, Oxford, Inigo Jones used revolving screens, copied from the Italians; flats fitted onto a revolve called *machina versatilis* that turned to show different angles of an apparently solid set. For the first time he painted backcloths giving the illusion of perspective. He used a proscenium arch to frame the settings, giving them unity of location.

Three more sympathisers joined the plot to blow up Parliament, making a total of thirteen. Knowing they had over three months in which to prepare, the conspirators accumulated thirty-six barrels of gunpowder.

Plague closed playhouses from October until December.

5 November: The Gunpowder Plot was foiled.

Extract from a letter from Sir Edward Hoby – Gentleman of the Bedchamber – to Sir Thomas Edwards, Ambassador at Brussells: 'On the 5th of November we began our Parliament, to which the King should have come in person, but refrained through a practise but that morning discovered. The plot was to have blown up the King at such time as he should have been set on his Royal Throne, accompanied with all his Children, Nobility and Commoners and assisted with all Bishops, Judges and Doctors; at one instant and blast to have ruin'd the whole State and Kingdom of England. And for the effecting of this, there was placed under the Parliament House, where the King should sit, some 30 barrels of powder, with good store of wood, faggots, pieces and bars of iron.'

6 November: The king's agents captured one of the conspirators who was calling himself 'John Johnson', but whose real name was Guy Fawkes, of York. Johnson refused to talk. Torture was forbidden except by royal executive appointment. Consequently, James I wrote: 'The gentler tortours are to be first used unto him, *et sic per gradua ad ima tenditur*... [meaning "and proceeding little by little to greater ones"] ...and so God speed your good work.'

7 November: Having been tortured on the rack, 'John Johnson's' resolve was broken. His subsequent confession: that he was a participant in an English Catholic conspiracy organised by Robert Catesby to annihilate England's entire Protestant government, including King James I, resulted in the inevitable consequences. Guy (Johnson) Fawkes was sentenced along with the other surviving chief conspirators, to be hanged, drawn, and quartered on 31 January 1606. It transpired that he was destined to avoid this fate.

As a consequence of the Gunpowder Plot, the Yeoman of the Guard continue to inspect the Westminster cellars before every State Opening of Parliament up to the present day.

For the first time, Hackney carriages became commercially available for hire in the streets of London.

William and Joan Hart baptised their second child, Thomas Hart — William Shakespeare's nephew. Hart's descendants lived in Stratford until 1806.

A plaque at the Henley Street house in Stratford gives the following information:

> The property remained in the ownership of Shakespeare's direct descendants until 1670, when his granddaughter, Elizabeth Barnard, died. As she had no children, Elizabeth left the estate to her relative Thomas Hart, Shakespeare's great-nephew. Following the death of John Shakespeare in 1601 the main house became a tenanted Inn called the Maidenhead (later the Swan and Maidenhead). Members of the Hart family continued living in the small adjoining cottage throughout the century.

Nathaniel Butter published the play entitled: *The London Prodigal as it was played by the King Majesty's Servants. By William Shakespeare.*

The going rate for a finished play was between £6 and £10. The payment for the play also bought the copyright, so that it belonged to the company, not to the author. In addition, if the work was performed more than three times in a season, the playwright might expect the box-office takings of the third performance. Although William Shakespeare earned most of his income as a shareholder of the company, he would also have received an actor's fee on those occasions he performed. This became negotiable but started at a shilling per performance.

The Master of the Revels at Clerkenwell charged anything between seven shillings and one pound to give his judgment on a play. He was the ultimate censor.

1606

Between 1606 and 1616 the moors on the north side of the city walls of London were drained and laid out as public gardens.

30 January: The execution of the Gunpowder Plot conspirators began.

31 January: Guy Fawkes was the last of the conspirators to be drawn from the Tower on a wattled hurdle to the Old Palace Yard at Westminster. However, while climbing to the hanging platform he jumped from the ladder and broke his neck, dying instantly. Even so, his dead body was quartered and his body parts distributed to 'the four corners of the kingdom' as was the custom.

3 March: William Davenant was baptised with William Shakespeare present as his godfather. This was the son of Jennet Shepherd Davenant and John Davenant, proprietor of The Crown Tavern, Oxford. Later, on several occasions, William Davenant told companions that Shakespeare was his real father.

William Davenant followed Ben Jonson to become the second Poet Laureate from 1638–68.

John Aubrey recalled the following story by the satirist, Samuel Butler (1613–80):

Mr William Shakespeare was wont to go into Warwickshire once a year, and did commonly in his journey lie at this the Crown in Oxon, where he was exceedingly respected... Now Sir William Davenant would sometimes, when he was pleasant over a glass of wine with his most intimate friends ... say, that it seemed to him that he writ with the very spirit that did Shakespeare, and seemed contented enough to be thought his Son. He would tell them the story as above, in which way his mother had a very light report, whereby she was called a Whore.

As a young man, Davenant was careless in personal affairs and 'he got a terrible clap of a black handsome wench that lay in Axeyard, Westminster.'

In April, Philip Henslowe dismantled the Rose playhouse.

12 April: King James 'united' Britain with the creation of the Christian Britannia, subsequently called the Union Jack. The word 'Jack' is a shortened version of Jacobus - the Latin equivalent of James. The flag of Wales was not included in the Union Jack because it was regarded as a principality.

Until James came to the throne, Shakespeare referred to England, Scotland and Wales as individual countries. When King James called his realm 'United Britain', Shakespeare began to write the word 'Britain' into his plays instead of England and/or Scotland.

Hamnet and Judith Sadler – the godparents to Shakespeare's twins – were arraigned in church for their Catholicism.

🕮 *Macbeth* was written. The Scottish theme was specially selected for the benefit of James I.

🕮 The primary source of Shakespeare's play was Raphael Holinshed's *Chronicle of Scottish History*, which delineates the character of Lady Macbeth in a single sentence.

🕮 21 April: The first performance of *Macbeth* at court. A medal had been struck to commemorate James I's deliverance from the Gunpowder Plot. This depicted a serpent hiding in a flowerbed. Lady Macbeth has a line in the play referring to this: 'Look like the innocent flower, but be the serpent under it.'

🕮 The actor, Richard Huggett (1929–2000) alleged that King Christian of Denmark made a reference to the first performance of *Macbeth* in a letter kept in the Danish Royal Archives. According to this, immediately before the premiere, the boy actor playing Lady Macbeth – Hal Berridge – fell ill. At such short notice, the only person competent to take over in the royal presence was William Shakespeare himself, who went on to 'top and tail' the character in performance because he had no time to memorise the entire play. This may go some way to explain why the part of Lady Macbeth is quite short. Also it may have started the tradition that *Macbeth* is an unlucky play. (Noted in *The Golden Age of English Theatre* by Judith Cooke, page 207.)

🕮 Witch-hunting was a common pursuit. James I wrote a treatise laying down the signs to look for, such as extra teats on which devilish familiars were believed to suck. The genitalia of female suspects were examined to discover a 'devil's hood': a prominent clitoris was regarded as scientific proof of demonic possession.

Antony and Cleopatra was written around this time although it was not entered into the Stationers' Register until May 1608.

5 May: William's oldest daughter Susanna Shakespeare, now twenty-three, was named as a recusant and written up in the court's act book thus:

Officium domini contra
Susannum Shakespeere similitier similiter
Dismissa.

She was charged for failing to receive the Anglican Sacrament at Easter on 20 April, leaving her open to a fine of £20 to £60. She ignored the first summons and had to attend a higher court where she was discharged ('dismissa'). This episcopal record was discovered in Maidstone in 1964 (Hugh A. Hanley in TLS dated 21 May 1964).

An Act of Parliament was drawn up in May 'to Restrain the Abuses of Players'. After this date, printed plays were heavily revised to avoid paying the £10 penalty incurred for *each* breach of the Act that was likely to be described as 'profanity'. In *Othello*, for instance, the word 'tush' was removed from the very first line – just in case.

Summer: Plague again closed the playhouses. Apart from April, May and June in 1608, they were not to open their doors again for three-and-a-half years. This did not prevent plays being seasonally performed at court, at whichever palace the king happened to be.

One of Shakespeare's fellow actors, Christopher Beeston, worked with Shakespeare as a member of the Chamberlain's Men and the Queen Anne's Men. John Aubrey in *Brief Lives* (set down between the Years 1669 and 1696) wrote that Beeston's son (also named William), recounted that Shakespeare '...would not be debauched, and if invited to be, writ that he was in paine...' Perhaps this indicates that Shakespeare was one of the first people to excuse themselves from conjugal relations with 'Not tonight, dear, I've got a headache.'

20 December: Three ships carrying potential colonists left England on a mission to North America headed by Captain Christopher Newport. They first landed at the entrance to the Chesapeake Bay in April 1607 on the south shore at a place they named Cape Henry, after the Prince of Wales.

26 December: St Stephen's Night. *King Lear* was presented for the first time at Whitehall in a command performance before James I.

Scena Secunda

1607 to
the Grave

1607

The winter months of 1606–7 were among the coldest ever recorded.

6 January: Twelfth Night. The premier event of the holiday season was held in the Great Hall of Whitehall Palace. This was Lord Hay's masque, written by Thomas Campion with spectacular scenes designed by Inigo Jones. Sir James Hay (1580–1636) a Scotsman, was brought to England by James I and was the king's current 'prime favourite' and gentleman of the bedchamber, famed for his extravagance and 'double-suppers'. The masque was to celebrate Lord Hay's wedding to Honoria Denny, the daughter of Lord Denny (the first Earl of Norwich). The king had arranged the marriage in an effort to suppress widespread gossip. The newlyweds were not happy and within two years they lived separate lives. The masque was financed by the Secretary of State, the first Earl of Salisbury. When he

died, by which time he had become the Earl of Carlisle, James Hay
left debts in excess of £80,000.

Masques grew increasingly popular, with more elaborate scenery
thanks to Inigo Jones's designs. Ben Jonson, conscious of plays being
in decline, on being asked who was the greatest theatrical villain,
replied gruffly, 'Inigo.'

30 January: The Bristol Channel and Severn Estuary suffered the
worst flooding ever recorded in Britain, killing over 2,000 people.

All's Well That Ends Well was written around this period.

April: The first known performance of *Pericles, Prince of Tyre* was
witnessed by the Venetian ambassador, Zorzo Giustinian. The source
of the plot comes from Confessio Amantis (1393) by the English poet
John Gower (1330–1408).

Pericles, Prince of Tyre was printed twice in 1609 by the stationer
Henry Gosson. During his lifetime, it was one of Shakespeare's most
popular plays. *Pericles* was not included in the First Folio, though it
was one of seven plays added in the second impression of the Third
Folio in 1664.

4 May: With regard to the purchase of New Place in Stratford, in
the Final Concord, William Shakespeare was assigned 'a messuage
with two barns and two gardens.' (*uno mesuagio duobus horreis et duobu
gardinis.*) (Chambers, *William Shakespeare: A Study of Facts and Problems*,
vol. 1.) Shakespeare bought New Place off William Underhill in the

Easter Term, 39 Eliz. 1597, for £60, as appears from the foot of the fine, levied on that occasion, preserved in the Chapter House, Westminster.

14 May: The first successful English settlement on the mainland of North America, Jamestown (originally called 'James Fort'), was founded by Sir Dudley Digges, the second son of the Digges family (the man mentioned in William Shakespeare's will) in association with Captain Edward Wingfield. Near the entrance to Hampton River, the colonists seized the Native American community of Kecoughtan. This came to be known as part of Hampton, which claims to be the oldest, continuously occupied English settlement in the United States. Hampton was named for the third Earl of Southampton, a patron of the Virginia Company of London. For whom Hampton River, Hampton Roads and Southampton County were also named. Shakespeare dedicated his two narrative poems, *Venus and Adonis* and *The Rape of Lucrece* to this same Henry Wriothesley, Earl of Southampton, when he was an effete youth. The dedication to *The Rape of Lucrece* was particularly gushing: 'The love I dedicate to your lordship is without end ... What I have done is yours; what I have to do is yours; being part in all I have, devoted yours.'

Sir Dudley was on the council of the Virginia Company. His son, Edward Digges, would later become the Governor of Virginia.

5 June: William Shakespeare gave away his eldest daughter, Susanna, to John Hall, (1575–1635) in the Church of the Holy Trinity, Stratford-upon-Avon. Susanna was twenty-four. John Hall was thirty-two. He had received a B.A. in 1593 and an M.A. in 1597, after which

he went to study medicine in France. He had a Cambridge degree in 'physick' but he practised medicine without a doctorate. Some years later he was offered a knighthood, which he refused.

The vicar of Stratford (1662–81), John Ward, noted: 'Shakspear had but two daughters, one whereof Mr Hall, the physitian, married, and by her had one daughter married, to wit, the Lady Bernard of Abbingdon.' This is a reference to the offspring of Dr John Hall and Susanna Shakespeare. Shakespeare's granddaughter, Elizabeth Hall, married Sir John Barnard of Abington Park.

Mr John Hall and Susanna moved to a house (today called Hall's Croft) within walking distance of New Place.

29 June: Edmund Tilney was still involved in the offices of the Master of the Revels. He licensed for publication a piece called 'Cupid's Whirligig' by Edward Sharpham. Shortly after, Tilney retired to Leatherhead.

7 July: The first recorded instance of 'God Save the King' being sung occurred at a dinner given by 'the gentlemen and children of His Majesty's Chapel Royal' at Merchant Taylor's Hall in the presence of James I to give thanks for his escape from the Gunpowder Plot. The tune was slightly different from the version we hear today.

12 July: William Shakespeare's brother, Edmund, was registered as the father of an illegitimate son, Edward. The baby was baptised at the Church of St Leonard, Shoreditch.

18 July: Sir George Buc, who had been assisting Edmund Tilney as Master of the Revels, took administrative control.

12 August: Just a month old, Edward Shakespeare, the 'base born' son of Edmund Shakespeare and an unknown woman, was buried in St Giles, Cripplegate. Edward, an infant, is sometimes incorrectly referred to as 'Edmund Sharksbye'. The register recorded that the father (Edmund) was living in Morefilds [Moorfields] near the Curtain playhouse, where Queen Anne's company was performing.

5 September: A performance of *Hamlet* took place off the coast of Sierra Leone in West Africa aboard a ship called the Red Dragon, performed by its crew before an audience of African dignitaries who were given a running commentary in Portuguese. This is purported to be from the journal of Captain William Keeling, who commanded the ship on the East India Company's third voyage to the Far East. He led three ships on a search for cloves and nutmegs. A fragment of Keeling's diary was kept in the India Office and the pages that contain these entries of theatrical performances were for a time thought to be forgeries.

Captain Keeling discovered twenty-seven islands in the Southern Indian Ocean. Coconuts grew in abundance so he named them the Cocos-Keeling Islands.

5 September: If Shakespeare was still acting with the King's Men, on this day he was playing in Oxford.

18 October: Shakespeare attended the marriage of his nephew, Richard Hathaway, a baker, at Stratford's Holy Trinity Church.

26 November: *King Lear* was entered into the Stationers' Register as: 'A booke called Mr William Shakespeare his history of Kinge Lear'. The source material for this play came from *Holinshed's Chronicles*. The subplot concerning Gloucester, Edgar and Edmund came from *Countess of Pembroke's Arcadia* by Philip Sidney.

29 November: At St Saviour's in Southwark, John Harvard was baptised. He was the second son of Robert Harvard and his second wife, Katherine, the daughter of Thomas Rogers of Stratford-upon-Avon. After the 1594 fire that devastated Stratford, Thomas – a master butcher – rebuilt his property, now known as Harvard House. John Harvard spent seven years at Cambridge University and sailed to the New World in 1637, where he died the following year at the tragically early age of thirty-one. However, under the direction of his widow and her new husband, the Rev. Thomas Allen, his estate funded the beginnings of Harvard College, Massachusetts.

31 December: Edmund Shakespeare, aged twenty-seven (William's youngest brother) was buried inside the Church of St Saviour in the Borough of Southwark. In the church register he is referred to as 'Edmond Shakespeare, a player.' Twenty shillings was paid for a 'forenoone knell of the great bell', thus the burial did not interfere with that afternoon's theatre performance. St Saviour's was within the parish of the Globe playhouse.

1597/98: During the winter, Anne Shakespeare and her two daughters, Susannah and Judith (aged fourteen and twelve) moved into New Place, the second biggest house in Stratford.

1608

8 January: The River Thames froze over and people skated on the ice and crossed the river on foot.

Galileo patented his first telescope. This invention caused a sensation. Planets could be seen in the solar system with their own moons. 'There are more things in heaven and earth, Horatio, than are dreamt of in your philosophy' (Hamlet to Horatio).

19 February: William Shakespeare celebrated the birth of his first grandchild. Like father, like daughter; baby Elizabeth was born just eight months after Susannah's marriage to Mr John Hall.

21 February: Elizabeth was baptised at Holy Trinity Church, Stratford.

Shakespeare rented out two or three rooms of New Place, Stratford to a prosperous lawyer, Thomas Greene, who went frequently to London to work in the Middle Temple. This arrangement lasted for some years. It is believed that Greene was Shakespeare's cousin.

2 May: An entry in the Stationers' Register records a work called *A Yorkshire Tragedy* written by William Shakespeare, stating that it was played by the King's Men at the Globe. It is barely one third the length of Shakespeare's shortest play, *Macbeth*.

The original printed text of the play identifies it as '*ALL'S ONE. OR, One of the foure Plaies in one, called a York-Shire Tragedy....*' (and ...

'*not so new as lamentable and true*'). This implies that the short play (it consists of only ten scenes) is one of a quartet played in repertory. The Third Folio (1664) included *The Yorkshire Tragedy* in the *Complete works of Shakespeare*, and although the quarto version published in his lifetime also declared that the author was Shakespeare, modern scholars incline to attribute it to Thomas Middleton. The plot of the play is based on the biographical account of Walter Calverley of Calverley Hall, Yorkshire, who was executed (pressed to death in York Castle) on 5 August 1605 for murdering two of his children and stabbing his wife. At the time, it was a cause célèbre.

20 May: *Antony and Cleopatra* was entered into the Stationers' Register. The source of this play is Sir Thomas North's 1579 translation of Plutarch's *Life of Mark Antony*. Certain passages are lifted practically verbatim from North. Shakespeare used hautboys offstage in *Antony and Cleopatra* to give ghostly sound effects. The play was not published until the First Folio of 1623.

20 May: *Pericles*, *Prince of Tyre* was entered into the Stationers' Register. This play was a collaboration between Shakespeare and the man who shared his lodgings, George Wilkins. He was once arrested for kicking a pregnant woman and on another occasion he was taken in for beating a woman called Judith Walton. Later, Watkins wrote a novelisation of the play. *Pericles* was omitted from the First Folio.

George Wilkins was landlord of a Turnmill Street tavern, in the centre of a ring of brothels in Clerkenwell adjacent to what is now Farringdon Station.

Ben Jonson described *Pericles* as 'a mouldy old tale'. For all his sour grapes, it was hugely popular with the public.

Due to another outbreak of the plague, London playhouses were closed throughout the summer and did not reopen for eighteen months.

The Office of the Revels moved from St John's Gate into the former Whitefriars cloisters, already partly redesigned to accommodate try-out stage performances two years earlier.

Coriolanus was written at about this time.

9 August: Richard Burbage, in partnership with Shakespeare, bought a twenty-one-year lease on the indoor theatre at Blackfriars. Previously, this was the home of the Children of the Chapel Royal who had now disbanded. The building was 'in decay for want of reparations'. Shakespeare's company proceeded to re-equip it.

The Blackfriars Theatre was the same hall used for the papal enquiry into the marriage between Henry VIII and Katherine of Aragon.

23 August: Shakespeare's nephew (his sister Joan's son) Michael Hart was christened in Stratford.

The King's Men formed the first company ever to play in an indoor theatre within the city walls, the Blackfriars Theatre. Each of the original sharers, including Shakespeare, paid one-seventh part of the £40 annual rental. Cuthbert Burbage acted as Bursar.

The leaseholders were:

Henry Evans 1600–1608
William Sly 09/08/1608–16/08/1608
William Shakespeare 09/08/1608–1613
Richard Burbage 09/08/1608–13/03/1619
Henry Condell 09/08/1608–29/12/1627
John Heminges 09/08/1608–12/10/1630
Cuthbert Burbage 09/08/1608–17/09/1636
John Shanks 1613–27/01/1636
John Underwood

William Sly died a week after the arrangement was made; his share was divided among the remaining six partners.

A sharing partnership in the running of a playhouse between players was not new. Shakespeare, Pope, Heminges and Augustine Phillips had banded together for the Globe (with Richard and Cuthbert Burbage taking 50 per cent for themselves). Thomas Pope and John Underwood ended up as shareholders of the Curtain playhouse too, although it is not known who else was involved or when the arrangement started.

John Underwood started his career as a boy player with the Children of the Chapel. He progressed to become a major player and continued as a member of the King's Men until he died a wealthy man in 1624.

The seating capacity of the Blackfriars Theatre was 700 – barely a quarter of the size of the Globe playhouse, so prices of admission to the indoor theatre were increased dramatically. Whereas at the Globe a penny would secure a place in the pit and three pennies would guarantee a bench with a cushion, at the Blackfriars Theatre the cheapest rate of admission was sixpence. A bench in the pit cost a shilling and a stool for toffs to sit on the side of the stage was two shillings. The large sum of two shillings and sixpence (a half-crown) was charged for an exclusive box next to the stage. The gentry sitting on stage soon became a nuisance and years later, during the Restoration, this method of seating was banned.

Blackfriars Theatre became the template for subsequent artificially-lit theatres.

When plays moved indoors, performances began to shift from two or three o'clock in the afternoon. Opening time crept from four p.m. until gradually slipping into the early evening. As well as chandeliers and oil lamps, footlights were introduced. At first these consisted of twelve candles stuck onto independent saucers floating in a narrow, shallow water-trough across the front edge of the stage. These became known as 'floats' and are still referred to by that name today. It was not until 1943, with the productions of Roger and Hammerstein's *Oklahoma* and later, *South Pacific* that theatres started to dispense with footlights.

Patrons of the Blackfriars Theatre had to leave their horses and coaches by the west end of St Paul's or by the Fleet conduit and walk the rest of the way.

Lighting was by means of huge hanging candelabra that could be lowered to replace candles. The auditorium was as brightly lit as the stage.

It became necessary from time to time to halt plays so that oil lamp wicks could be trimmed and candles replaced. Accordingly, 'Intervals' were introduced in theatres for the first time. Sometimes these gaps in the action were quite arbitrary, halting the flow of a piece at a critical point. Alarmed playwrights soon decided that they themselves would prefer to decide where the intervals should occur and began to integrate acts and intervals into the scripts.

Shakespeare's works, *A Winter's Tale* and *The Tempest* (both 1611) are the first plays known to have specific 'Interval' breaks written into them.

When theatre moved from the open-air playhouses to indoor auditoria, specially composed music filled in the recently introduced 'entr'actes'.

Musician Robert Johnson was Emilia Lanier's cousin of the family of musicians brought from Venice to England by Henry VIII. Emilia topped the lists of possibilities as 'The Dark Lady of the sonnets'. Robert collaborated with Shakespeare in the music of his last plays. He wrote the settings for 'Full fathom five' in *The Tempest* and 'Where the bee sucks'. He was original musical director of *Cymbeline* and *The Winter's Tale*.

The King's Men performed at the Blackfriars Theatre during the winter and at the Globe playhouse during the summer. Shakespeare had a stake in both establishments.

17 August: In Stratford, Shakespeare opened a lawsuit against John Addenbrooke for £6, plus 24 shillings damages. This continued through the courts until 7 June 1609. The case went before a jury with Henry Walker presiding. Thomas Greene (lodging at New Place) was town clerk. Shakespeare won and was awarded damages. When Addenbrooke continued to prevaricate, an order was issued for his arrest.

9 September: Mary Shakespeare — née Arden — was buried in Stratford at the age if sixty-eight. Shakespeare attended his mother's funeral at Holy Trinity Church.

Since his father's death in 1601, Shakespeare had leased out part of the Henley Street premises to Lewis Hiccox and his wife, Alice. Following the death of Shakespeare's mother, the Hiccoxes converted the eastern half of the house into a small inn called The Maidenhead. William Shakespeare continued to take rent money. He allowed his sister, Joan Hart, and her husband, William, to remain living in the western wing of the Henley Street house.

16 October: Shakespeare was again in Holy Trinity Church, this time as godfather to William Walker. The child's father, Alderman Henry Walker, had just completed a term as High Bailiff of Stratford. The Parish Register reads: 'On Sunday October 16, 1608, Shakespeare attended the christening of the son of a prominent

Stratford citizen, the boy being named after him: William, son to Henry Walker *unus aldermannus*.'

Edmund Tilney wrote a memorandum on the function of the Office of the Revels, explaining that they '... consisteth of a wardrobe and other several [i.e. separate] rooms for artificers to work in (viz. tailors, embroiderers, property makers, painters, wire-drawers and carpenters), together with a convenient place for the rehearsals and setting forth of plays and other shows...'

There is a possibility that Shakespeare retired as an actor in the company circa 1608. Mr Collier found a letter among the papers of the Earl of Ellesmere apparently written to the Council by Henry Earl of Southampton at a time when the Mayor was trying to suppress theatre activities in London. It reads:

My verie honored Lord. The manie good offices I have received at your Lordships handes, which ought to make me backward in asking further favors, onely imbouldeneth me to require more in the same kinde. Your Lordship wilbe warned howe hereafter you graunt anie sute, seeing it draweth on more and greater demaunds. This which now presseth is to request your Lordship, in all you can, to be good to the poore players of the Blacke ffryers, who call themselves by authoritie the Servantes of his Majestie, and aske for the proteccion of their most gracious Maister and Soveraigne in this the tyme of theire troble. They are threatened by the Lord Maior and Aldermen of London, never friendly to their calling, with the distruccion of their meanes of livelihood, by the pulling downe of their plaiehouse, which is a private theatre, and hath never given ocasion of anger by anie disorders. These bearers are two of the chiefe of the companie; one of them by name Richard Burbidge, who humblie sueth for your Lordships kinde helpe, for that he is a man famous as our English Roscius, one who fitteth the action to the worde and the word to the action most admirably. By the exercise of his qualitie, industry, and good behaviour, he hath become possessed of the Blacke ffryers playhouse, which hath bene imployed for playes sithence it was builded by his ffather now nere 50 yeres agone. The other is a man no whitt lesse deserving favor, and my especial friende, till of late an actor of good account in the cumpanie, now a sharer in the same, and writer of some of our best English playes, which, as your Lordship knoweth, were most singulerly liked of Quene Elizabeth, when the cumpanie was called uppon to performe before her Majestie at Court at Christmas and Shrovetide. His most gracious Majestie King James alsoe, since his coming to the crowne, hath extended his royall favour to the companie in divers waies and at sundrie tymes. This other hath to name William Shakespeare, and they are both of one countie, and indeede allmost of one towne: both are right famous in their qualities, though it longeth not of your Lo. gravitie and wisedome to resort unto the places where they are wont to delight the publique care. Their trust and sute nowe is not to bee molested in their waye of life whereby they maintaine themselves and their wives and families (being both maried and of good reputacion) as well as the widowes and orphanes of some of their dead fellows.

Your Lo. most bounden at com. H.S.

1609

28 January: *Troilus and Cressida* was re-entered into the Stationers' Register. (It had first been registered on 7 February 1603 but never published or performed.) Richard Bonian and Henry Walley re-registered the play and later in the year issued the first quarto editions but in two 'states'. The first claims the play was acted 'by the King's Majesty's servants at the Globe.' The second edition makes no mention of a production and goes further, stating that it is 'a new play, never staled with the stage, never clapper-clawed with the palms of the vulgar.'

This implies that the original production was called off for some reason, most likely it got into censorship difficulties with the Master of the Revels.

Shakespeare's play *The Winter's Tale* was loosely adapted from the novel *Pandosto* by Robert Greene.

21 February: The baptism of Elizabeth Hall, Mary Arden Shakespeare's great granddaughter.

Plague caused the closure of London playhouses for most of 1609.

Pericles, Prince of Tyre was published in quarto by Henry Gosson, described as: 'acted by his Majesty's Servants at the Globe on the Bankside. By William Shakespeare.'

Troilus and Cressida was published in quarto.

20 May: *'Shake-speare's Sonnets — Never before Imprinted'* were published in a quarto version by Thomas Thorpe, price 5 pence, 'and are to be solde by William Ashley.'

Elizabethan and Jacobean dramatists had their share of failures. Shakespeare's flops were not published and have been conveniently forgotten. His close friend — self-publicist, Ben Jonson — has not been so lucky. His play, *Epicene or The Silent Woman* was received with such lack of response that it was nicknamed *The Silent Audience.*

It was generally believed that the sonnets had been given a public airing without Shakespeare's permission, but after the Bard's death, when Ben Jonson went on his Highland walkabout in 1618, according to conversations that took place between Jonson and the Scottish poet, William Drummond of Hawthornden (1585–1649), the sonnets were published with the author's blessing. Because of their racy nature, Shakespeare may have delayed publication until the death of his mother the previous September.

There were 154 sonnets in the original edition plus the 329 lines of *A Lover's Complaint.* Some academics doubt that the narrative poem was Shakespeare's work.

The sonnets are thought to cover a period of three or four years. In this regard, E.K. Chambers warned: 'one must not … attempt to construct a complete personality from the transient utterances of individual moods.' (Chambers, *William Shakespeare A Study of Facts and Problems.*)

Despite this caveat, subsequent scholars have never stopped mining the sonnets for glimpses of Shakespeare's soul.

The dedication to the first edition of Shakespeare's Sonnets reads 'To the only begetter of these ensuing sonnets Mr WH. All happiness and that eternity promised by our ever-living poet wisheth the well-wishing adventurer in setting forth. TT.' TT refers to Thomas Thorpe, the publisher of the piece. The identity of WH has been the subject of intense speculation for centuries. For a while, WH was thought to be Shakespeare's secret male lover. The Earls of Southampton and Pembroke also came under scrutiny because their names were Henry Wriothesley and William Herbert.

Recent research by the American archivist Geoffrey Caveney reveals that William Holme was the publishing associate of Thomas Thorpe and that they both came from Chester. Holme died in 1607 and, it is suggested, collated the material that Mr Thorpe eventually published, thus making sense of the dedication. William Holme was a colleague of the printers Adam Islip and George Eld, who also published Ben Jonson's *Every Man Out of His Humour*.

Professor Stanley Wells, considered by many to be the greatest living authority on Shakespeare, described the theory promulgating William Holme as WH as 'better than any suggestion so far.'

Fourteen years later, Heminges and Condell dedicated the First Folio to William Herbert, third Earl of Pembroke. Some academics argue that Mr WH and the Earl of Pembroke are the same man. However, would they have had the temerity to call a Lord of the Realm 'Master'?

📖 Some of the sonnets are bawdy and replete with sexual connotation to the point of pornography, with allusions to the vagina and to the rising and fall of the penis.

📖 It has been argued that the final two sonnets in the collection indicate that Shakespeare caught syphilis and took the mercury-bath cure. Once put into one's mind, this thought lingers but it has never been substantiated.

📖 The 'Dark Lady' is described in Sonnet 127:

> In the old age black was not counted fair,
> Or if it were it bore not beauty's name;
> But now is black beauty's successive heir,
> And beauty slandered with a bastard shame.

The names of several candidates have been put forward over the years, with additional possibilities added yearly. Among them are Mary Fitton, Penelope Rich and Mrs Jennet Davenant. Another pretty hat thrown into the ring belongs to 'Black Lucy', alias Luce alias Lucy Negro née Morgan, who left the queen's service to become a notorious brothel-keeper in Clerkenwell.

📖 In 1973, A.L. Rowse made a strong case for Emilia Lanier alias Amelia Lanyear (née Bassano), the illegitimate daughter of Baptista Bassano and his common-law wife, Margaret Johnson, a Venetian court musician (Rowse, *Shakespeare the Man*).

The Bassano coat of arms displays three silkworm moths and a mulberry tree, which suggests they were Jewish, since the Jews introduced silk farming into Italy.

In his plays, Shakespeare's Jews come from Venice and are associated with a character named Bassanio. The Bassanos were described as having a swarthy appearance.

Emilia became pregnant in 1592 and was hastily married to the hapless Alphonso Lanier. The child was christened Henry Lanier. The name Henry was after his father (Lord Hunsdon) and also his grandfather (Henry VIII).

It is alleged that Shakespeare dedicated sonnet 145 to his wife, Anne Hathaway.

Shakespeare's gradual withdrawal from theatre life left a void that Beaumont and Fletcher did their best to fill. In July they wrote their first play together called *Philaster*.

7 June: Meanwhile, in Stratford, Shakespeare's pursuit of the merchant Addenbrooke for the return of a £6 loan was in its tenth month. Earlier, Addenbrooke was arrested and imprisoned for his recalcitrance. A local taphouse owner, Thomas Hornby, stood 'surety' for the defendant and bailed him, at which point Addenbrooke promptly disappeared. Shakespeare decided that Hornby, as bondsman, should pay and asked the court to enforce him to do so. The court found in Shakespeare's favour, awarding him the original £6, plus 24 shillings for damages. It is unknown whether Hornby ever paid up.

24 July: The London Company's flagship, *The Sea Venture*, on an expedition to America, was wrecked in a hurricane off Bermuda. Most passengers survived but later the wife and child of John Rolfe died on the island. Rolfe went on to be one of the original founders of Virginia's tobacco plantations. He married Chief Powhatan's daughter Matoaka (Pocahontas) on 5 April 1614. Some survivors returned to England in September and regaled London with their story. William Strachey wrote an account of the shipwreck that became the source notes of Shakespeare's play, *The Tempest*.

26 July: Thomas Harriot was the first man to make a drawing of the moon as seen through a telescope, beating Galileo by four months. Two years later, Harriot developed a lens with a magnification of 32x and discovered sunspots.

Cymbeline may have been written for the investiture of Henry, the Prince of Wales.

9 September: The lawyer Thomas Greene and his wife, Lettice, while lodging at New Place in Stratford, noted in his diary that his own nearby home was undergoing renovation and that he had a deadline to leave New Place by the end of March 1610. From this, scholars interpolate that Shakespeare intended to retire to Stratford in the spring of 1610.

23 September: Joan Hart's son, Michael Hart, William Shakespeare's nephew, was christened. The line of the Hart family tree continued unbroken until 1800.

8 October: The Stationers' Company registered John Davies's book *Scourge of Folly* in which the play *Philaster or Love Lies Bleeding* by Beaumont and Fletcher is first mentioned. The play was published in 1620 by Thomas Walkley.

December: At the Whitefriars Theatre, the Children of the Queen's Revels, a group of boy players, premiered *Epicoene, or The Silent Woman* by Ben Jonson. One of the themes of this play was borrowed by Billy Wilder for the film, *Some Like It Hot*. Initially, the play was a flop. On its revival after the Restoration, it found great success with Charles II.

The Whitefriars Theatre, with an audience capacity of about 500, was leased to Thomas Woodford, an early entrepreneur. Beaumont and Fletcher's *Cupid's Revenge* and Ben Jonson's *Epicoene, or The Silent Woman* were premiered at this theatre. However, local residents in the parish to the west of the River Fleet complained that the theatre was not 'fitting nor tolerable'. The Puritan movement was gaining ground. The theatre reverted to being a venue for the Children of the Queen's Revels but full-time production slowed to a standstill when the lease ran out in 1614.

1610

6 January: Ben Jonson wrote masques and jousting entertainments in the weeks leading up to Prince's Henry's investiture ceremony. As in Henry VIII's time, these displays celebrated the future king in an idealising, myth-making way.

20 April: Saturday. Dr Simon Forman (1552–1611) recorded in his diary that he saw *Macbeth* at the Globe playhouse. It was written some time after 1604 since there is an allusion to the union of England and Scotland under James I. It was not published until the First Folio version of 1623. The storyline is taken from Holinshed's *Chronicles of England, Scotland and Ireland* (1577).

4 June: Shakespeare's *Pericles, Prince of Tyre* was presented as part of the celebration for the creation of the Prince of Wales, a ceremony that would in future become known as an investiture. Henry Stuart was sixteen and had the reputation for being somewhat priggish. He treated his younger brother scornfully. However, Henry Stuart died two years later and his brother Charles went on to become the unfortunate Charles I.

20 August: Edmund Tilney died in Leatherhead. He had been Master of the Revels for over thirty years. Plays would be permitted only if the manuscript had the signature of the Master. Any offender could be imprisoned by Tilney's orders. Sir George Buck, who had been an envoy to Queen Elizabeth, had become Tilney's assistant in 1606 when the regulations added new laws against blasphemy. This required a re-evaluation of all plays being revived for court performance. Buck was thus responsible for censoring Shakespeare's later plays, and for supervising performances of any earlier Shakespeare plays, which he had to re-censor, due to the new blasphemy laws. In April 1622, Sir George Buck was declared insane and removed from office.

🕮 *The Tempest* was written in the autumn of this year. The play is set on a remote island based on Bermuda. Some of Prospero's speeches are copied word-for-word from Medea's dialogue in Ovid's poem *Metamorphoses*. It was not registered into the Stationers' Register until 8 November 1623, when Edward Blount entered sixteen of Shakespeare's plays in one day. The wreck of the *Sea Venture* on the shores of Bermuda in 1609 reported as 'A True Reportory of the Wracke and Redemption of Sir Thomas Gates, Knight' by William Strachey is considered a prime source for the story. The character Caliban was a crude anagram of cannibal.

🕮 Another source book for *The Tempest* is *A Discovery of the Bermudas, otherwise called the Ile of Divels* by Silvester Jourdain.

🕮 In Act 1 Scene 2 of *The Tempest*, Shakespeare gave Ariel the lines:

Safely in harbour
Is the King's ship. In the deep nook, where once
Thou call'dst me up at midnight to fetch dew
From the still-vex'd Bermoothes, there she's hid...

The above indicates that the Bermudas were in Shakespeare's mind. In another scene, less than an hour after the wrecking of the ship, the rest of the fleet are said to be upon the Meditarranean 'bound sadly home for Naples'. Perhaps Shakespeare intended for Ariel to have the facility of Puck to put girdles round the earth in record time.

🕮 In *The Tempest*, Shakespeare obeys the Greek unities, the whole taking place within twenty-four hours. This manuscript is dated 15

July 1610. It is thought to be Shakespeare's last play and contains the line: 'We are such stuff as dreams are made on, and our little life is rounded with a sleep.'

It is believed that *The Tempest* was specifically written for an indoor theatre, where the storm effects could be displayed more convincingly. The most likely venue was the Blackfriars Theatre.

The original Blackfriars Theatre was demolished in 1655. In September 2001, a faithful replica of the Blackfriars Theatre opened its doors in Staunton, Virginia, USA. It has since achieved greatness and growing public acclaim.

The Tempest includes some of Shakespeare's most detailed stage directions. For example: 'Enter Ariel like a harpy; claps his wings upon the table; and, with a quaint device, the banquet vanishes.'

5 October: John Combe was buried at Warwick. On 1 May 1602, Shakespeare had bought property from him. The testator's heir, William Combe (1586–1667), was the eldest son of the testator's nephew of the half blood, Thomas Combe (d.1609), and brother of Thomas Combe (1589–1657), to whom William Shakespeare of Stratford left a sword in his will.

1611

Amelia Lanier published a volume of her own poems entitled *Salve Deus Rex Judaeorum*. The Bassano family was brought over from Italy by Henry VIII in 1533. By 1538 Anthony Bassano was appointed 'maker of diverse musical instruments to the court'. Emilia had been the mistress of the Lord Chamberlain, Lord Hunsdon, and had a child by him.

In Italy, table forks were first mentioned. In England they were a foreign curiosity and considered unmanly. They became fashionable only after Thomas Coryat (1577–1617) published his book, *Coryat's Curdities Hastily gobbled up in Five Months Travels in France, Savoy, Italy, &c*. Even then, he was mocked about promoting the use of forks and called 'Furcifer', meaning fork-bearer.

20 April: Dr Simon Forman was the first to try to describe the psychology behind the character of Lady Macbeth. A keen theatregoer, he recorded that he had seen *Macbeth* at the Globe playhouse. A few days later he noted that he had also seen *Cymbeline*.

The character of Imogen in *Cymbeline* is described as having a mole below her throat. Emilia Lanier, thought to be Shakespeare's mistress, had a mole in the same place.

Mary Frith (also known as Moll) was the daughter of a shoemaker who grew up to be a cross-dressing tomboy. A bisexual, she smoked a pipe, was branded as a thief on at least four occasions, and had a play written about her called *The Roaring Girl* by Middleton and Dekker. Mary was to make a personal appearance in the afterpiece of the play, announced in the epilogue:

The Roaring Girl herself, some few days hence,
Shall on this stage give larger recompense.

On the day that she duly appeared 'in mans apparell & in her bootes & with a sworde by her syde', the Fortune playhouse had an audience of 2,340. She announced unashamedly, 'that she thought that many of them were of opinion that she was a man, but if any of them would come to her lodging, they should finde that she is a woman.' It was illegal for women to appear on stage and subsequently she was indicted by the authorities. Her declaration from the stage was classified by the ecclesiastical judges as 'immodest & lascivious speaches that she also vsed at that time.'

September: Mary Frith was committed to Bridewell prison, though not for long. Years later, during the Civil War, she acted as a spy for the Royalists. She eventually died of dropsy in her Fleet Street home opposite the Globe Tavern on 26 July 1659.

30 April: Dr Simon Forman saw *Richard II* at The Globe playhouse.

11 May: Forman recorded that he saw *The Winter's Tale* at the Globe, and painted a vivid verbal portrait of Autolycus.

Dr Forman was an astrologer and occulist. He was notable for his sexual conquests. Ben Jonson characterised him as an evil magician in league with the Devil. One of his patients was Mrs Webb, who had been the mistress of Kit Marlowe's old lover, Thomas Walsingham. In his notebook Forman wrote, 'Haleked Martha Webb 15 March at ten past two p.m. plene and volunteer' (fully and freely). 'Haleked' is an obsolete word meaning to have had sexual intercourse.

8 September: Foreman accurately predicted his own death. He told his wife that he would die the following Thursday night. Another astrologer, William Lilly, picked up the story, saying:

> Wednesday came, and still he was well; with which his impertinent wife, Tronco, did much twit him in his teeth. Thursday came, and dinner was ended, he very well: he went down to the water-side, and took a pair of oars to go to some buildings he was in hand with in Puddle-dock. Being in the middle of the Thames, he presently fell down, only saying, 'An impost, an impost,' and so died.

One of Forman's patients was the Lord Chamberlain's mistress, the musician and poet Emilia Lanier, whose candidacy as Shakespeare's 'Dark Lady' was given strong support by the historian A.L. Rowse. Another patient was Mrs Mountjoy, Shakespeare's landlady. Forman left his papers to his astrological protégé, Richard Napier. In the seventeenth century, Elias Ashmole collected sixty-four volumes of Forman's manuscripts that are now held in the Bodleian Library, Oxford.

May/June: During Trinity term Shakespeare bought twenty more acres of pasture land from the Combes in Stratford and had a special document drawn up to confirm his title to his purchase of land from the Combes nine years previously, ensuring that there could be no question of his legal ownership. When it came to financial matters, Shakespeare was an astute man.

11 September: Shakespeare's name appears in the margin of a list of petitioners supporting 'the Charge of prosedtynnge a Bill in

parliament for the better Repayre of the highe waies and amendinge divers defectes in the Statues alredy made.' In other words, highway improvement. Shakespeare travelled a lot.

1 November: All Hallows' Day. *The Tempest* was performed at Whitehall for James I. Intervals were written into the structure. It was constructed in strict conformity with 'the Greek unities' – the action taking place within twenty-four hours. This was the last complete play that Shakespeare wrote.

5 November: *The Winter's Tale* was performed at Court for James I. Intervals were written into the structure and henceforth became commonplace.

11 November: *The Winter's Tale* was performed again at Court. James and his entourage loved plays. The King's Men had to work hard to keep up with demand.

Lutenist Robert Johnson (1583–1634) joined the household of Sir George Carey, second Baron Hunsdon, as an apprentice in 1596. Hunsdon became Lord Chamberlain a year later and was patron of the acting company in which Shakespeare had a share. *The Tempest* was staged at the Blackfriars Theatre, where Johnson wrote the original settings for 'Where the Bee Sucks' and 'Full Fathom Five'. It is sometimes whimsically suggested that The Tempest was the very first musical.

Robert Johnson also wrote incidental music for *King Lear* and *Antony and Cleopatra*. Some of his most popular work has survived such as 'Hark, hark, the lark' in *Cymbeline* and all six songs in *A Winter's Tale*. He said his ambition was to 'marry the words and notes well together', which seems a laudable idea in any age. He contributed music for *Cardenio*, *Henry VIII* and *The Two Noble Kinsmen*.

Robert Johnson's aunt, Margaret Johnson, had married one of the Bassano brothers. Margaret was Emilia Lanier's mother. Emilia published her own books of verse a few months after Shakespeare's sonnets were published.

Christmas: William Shakespeare, now forty-seven, left London and returned to Stratford. He gave up acting but as a writer he still collaborated with others. He seems to have become what today we might call the 'editor-in-chief'.

There was reportedly a sequel to *Love's Labour's Lost* called *Love's Labour's Won* but it has been lost. Recently the Royal Shakespeare Company presented *Much Ado About Nothing* under the title *Love's Labour's Won*. However, another school of thought believes that *The Taming of the Shrew* might be the lost play.

The new enclosed, artificially-lit theatres such as Blackfriars, offered greater comfort than the playhouses. However, though the most expensive seats were nearest the stage, patrons still had to relieve themselves in conveniently situated 'slop buckets', also known as 'jordans'.

1612

7 February: The Puritans with their strict moral and religious beliefs were gaining ground rapidly. In Stratford-upon-Avon, the penalty

for putting on plays was ten shillings. Now the town council got tough with their ten-year-old embargo against putting on plays by announcing that the fine was going up: 'the sufferance of them [plays] against the orders heretofore made and against the example of other well-governed cities and boroughs.' The council was therefore 'content that the penalty of ten shillings imposed on players heretofore should be ten pounds henceforward.' Ten years later the King's Players were bribed to get out of town without performing. (From Sir Sidney Lee's *A Life of William Shakespeare*, 1898, page 269, n.1.)

12 January: On Sunday and the following day, the Queen Anne's Men joined forces with the King's Men company to give performances of two plays: *The Rape of Lucrece* and *The Silver Age* by Thomas Heywood. The casts were huge. *The Silver Age* required thirteen extra actors just to play planets and centaurs.

2 February: Gilbert Shakespeare, aged forty-five, two years younger than William, was buried at the Holy Trinity Church in Stratford. He had been a haberdasher in St Bride's parish, selling cloth and cotton. In May of 1602, he returned to Stratford as his brother William's representative in taking delivery of the deed to 107 acres of farmland in Old Stratford, which William had bought from John and William Combe for £320. Gilbert was named in a bill of complaint on 21 November 1609 instigated by Joan Bromley, a Stratford widow, but the details of the suit are unknown.

During the six months to April 1612, the King's Men produced twenty-two plays at Court including *The Tempest* and *The Winter's Tale*.

11 May: Shakespeare was summoned as a witness in a court case. More is known about Shakespeare's court appearances than about his stage performances. Seven years prior to the case, Shakespeare had been living in lodgings on the corner of Silver Street and Monkswell Street in the Cripplegate area of London. His landlords were Christopher and Marie Mountjoy, Huguenot tiremakers – 'tire' being the shortened form of 'attire' meaning 'head attire'. They were, in fact, hatters.

The first known signature of Shakespeare is on a deposition in the Belott v. Mountjoy case. A marriage was arranged between the Mountjoys' daughter and their apprentice, Stephen Belott. A substantial dowry of £60 was promised to Stephen in order for him to set up as a hatter on his own recognisance. The marriage took place in the form of a handfasting ceremony at which William Shakespeare was the chief witness. However, the dowry was never paid and now, seven years later, Stephen Belott took his father-in-law to court. William Shakespeare was summoned as a witness. In his deposition, Shakespeare claimed to remember nothing of the details of the marriage agreement. He signed this statement: 'Willm Shaksp'.

19 June: A second hearing was called in the Belott v. Mountjoy case but Shakespeare did not turn up. The judge referred it to arbitration by the church fathers of the French Church in London, who eventually awarded Belott a mere 20 nobles in settlement (£6 14s 4d).

The printer William Jaggard issued an expanded edition of *The Passionate Pilgrim*, an anthology of poems with additions by Thomas

Heywood and William Shakespeare. Heywood objected to this publication, accusing Jaggard of piracy and complaining of the 'manifest injury' that had been caused, adding that Shakespeare was 'much offended with M. Jaggard (that altogether unknown to him) presumed to make so bold with his name.' Jaggard immediately withdrew the publication and removed Shakespeare's name from future editions.

1 October: The Middlesex Court General banned 'Jigs, Rhymes and Dances' at the end of plays because complaints had been made of their lewdness.

6 November: Henry, Prince of Wales died of typhoid, aged eighteen.

Christmas: First recorded performance of *Sir John Falstaffe* performed for the court at Whitehall. This was the name sometimes given to *Henry IV, Part 2*.

1612/13: Throughout the winter months, Court festivities were held celebrating the marriage of King James's daughter Princess Elizabeth to Frederick, Elector Palatine.

The King's Men gave twenty performances, including seven plays by Shakespeare (including *Much Ado About Nothing* twice) one by Jonson, and four by Francis Beaumont and John Fletcher, reflecting their growing popularity with audiences and dominance in the King's Men's repertoire. *Cardenio*, allegedly by Shakespeare and Fletcher, was also performed.

24 December 1612 to 20 May 1613: The King's Men presented fourteen plays at Court in honour of the marriage of James I's daughter, Elizabeth. The company was rewarded with one hundred-and-fifty-three pounds, six shillings and eightpence.

1613

4 February: Little is known about William's brother, Richard Shakespeare, who died at the age of thirty-nine. He was the seventh child of John and Mary Shakespeare and was born when his father's social standing in Stratford was declining and his debts were mounting. It is possible that Richard did not attend school. There is no record of a signature or a business dealing anywhere. He never married. He probably remained in Stratford helping his father. He was buried in Stratford.

14 February: First recorded performance of *Much Ado About Nothing* performed before the court at Whitehall as part of the celebrations surrounding the marriage of Princess Elizabeth Stuart (James I's daughter) and Frederick V, Elector Palatine, on St Valentine's Day. They were both sixteen years old. They were to become King and Queen of Bohemia for a short time in 1619 and Frederick was known as the Winter King. In the interim, he took over as patron of the theatre company formerly known as Prince Henry's Men and renamed it Palgrave's Men.

According to Frankie Rubinstein in her book *A Dictionary of Shakespeare's Puns and Their Significance*, in Jacobean times the word 'nothing' was a pun on copulation. It is 'a pun on "noting" so music in which the notes are pricked is called a prick-song. *Much Ado about Nothing* is much ado over (sexual) pricking.'

10 March: The second known signature of Shakespeare follows his first London acquisition: the gatehouse of the old monastery of Black Friars, bought for £140 from Henry Walker. The signature reads:

William Shakespē

The address was in Ireland Yard adjoining Blackfriars Lane, wherein was the Playhouse Yard. He made a down payment of £80 and took out a mortgage of £60 guaranteed by John Heminges, John Jackson (a City merchant) and William Johnson, who happened to be the landlord of the Mermaid Tavern. Thomas Pope also declared his willingness to be a guarantor. The Royal Court kept the property under observation, as it had been used as a Catholic safe house. Within its structure there was a warren of tunnels. The place was bought to let out. In his will, Shakespeare bequeathed this house to John Robinson. However, according to information in the National Archives, on Shakespeare's death the trustees sold the property on behalf of his family with the profit going to them.

11 March: Shakespeare's third known signature is extant on a parchment mortgage document. It reads:

Wm Shakspē

Three other signatures exist on each page of his will.

A favourite touring venue for the Chamberlain's Men was the town of Bristol, which opened the third free public library in

England. (The first was Norwich in 1608 followed by Ipswich in 1612.)

24 March: An extravagant tournament was arranged to celebrate the anniversary of the king's accession. The participating knights wore paper shields on which were representations of each knight's current circumstance painted in a jocular cartoon style, such as a Venus for a man in love, or a Sisyphean figure pushing a rock up a hill for a man seeking advancement and so on. A close friend of the Earl of Southampton, the sixth Earl of Rutland was especially keen to gain plaudits from a cleverly drawn shield. Shakespeare and Richard Burbage were each paid four pounds and eight shillings to design the shield. It is noted in the earl's accounts that they were paid in gold. The drawing was executed by Burbage and Shakespeare wrote the caption. Burbage was an accomplished painter. The likeness we most associate with him is a self-portrait. Unfortunately, the painting on the shield and the accompanying words are lost to history. Also, Lord Rutland lost the tournament.

23 April: After his forty-ninth birthday Shakespeare cut down his writing output to virtually nothing, though he may have contributed the odd stanza to works such as *Two Noble Kinsmen*. He retired from acting too and spent much of his time in the great garden of New Place in Stratford-upon-Avon where the mulberries he had planted were yet young. His original tree became so well known that by the 1750s the then resident of New Place, the Rev Francis Gastrell, grew tired of visitors making constant requests to see it. Gastrell chopped down the tree. Spotting an entrepreneurial opportunity, Thomas Sharpe who was an assistant of the local tour guide, John Jordan,

bought the wood, from which he carved a casket that was presented to David Garrick in 1769, containing the freedom of the town. Rather like the holy cross, so many objects claimed to have been made from Shakespeare's mulberry trees that New Place must have been a veritable forest. The disagreeable Reverend Gastrell demolished New Place in 1759 and fled the town forever.

8 June: *Cardenio* was performed at the Court in Whitehall before the ambassador from Savoy. It was also performed at The Globe playhouse. This was one of Shakespeare's last projects with which he collaborated with Fletcher. They based it on the first volume of Cervantes's *Don Quixote*, that had recently been published in London. The manuscript has been lost but academics are optimistic that a copy may yet turn up in one of the great private libraries. *The History of Cardenio* was not entered into the Stationers' Register until 1653.

John Downes was a prompter at the Drury Lane Theatre in the early eighteenth century and it is claimed that a copy of *Cardenio* was in his possession. He gave the manuscript to Shakespearian scholar, Lewis Theobald (1688–1744), who adapted the play under the title *Double Falsehood* and produced it in 1727 under Colley Cibber's management. The London run was successful. The play is thought to have been destroyed in the Covent Garden theatre fire in 1808, but experts are re-evaluating the play and its provenance. It is a puzzle as to where John Downes obtained the scripts. He claimed he had inherited them from the actor, Thomas Betterton who, in turn, claimed to have been given them by Shakespeare's illegitimate daughter. Nobody has so far traced this 'bastard'.

June: Susanna Hall, Shakespeare's eldest daughter, was accused of adultery with Rafe Smith, a thirty-five-year-old haberdasher. The accusation by John Lane Jr, twenty-three, was that Susannah Hall: '... had the running of the reins and had been naughty with Rafe Smith at John Palmer's.' He also accused Susanna of catching a venereal disease. Dr John Hall and Susanna, supported by the vicar, Thomas Wilson, brought a charge of slander against John Lane. It has been suggested that Lane made his claims for some political reason, but since he was later named in court as a persistent drunkard, there may be no more to it than alcoholism.

29 June: *Henry VIII*, one of the last plays to be written by Shakespeare (again with John Fletcher) had its third performance at the Globe. To mark the grand, theatrical entrance of Henry VIII, a cannon was fired. In those days, the effects were real. Unfortunately the red-hot cannonball landed on the south side of the thatched roof and ignited the wooden beams. The playhouse burnt down within two hours. Luckily everyone managed to get out safely through the two exits.

A story circulated at the time that only one injury was sustained. A spectator's jerkin caught alight on his backside and an enterprising bystander quenched the flames by spraying a bottle of ale on his buttocks.

Henry VIII was produced in painstaking detail. Kings and queens and courtiers and bishops and judges were clothed in exact replicas of the real robes of office down to the last coronet and insignia. The play was presented under its original title, *All Is True*.

15 July: John Lane failed to appear at the Consistory Court in Worcester. Lane was found guilty of slander against Susanna Hall and he was excommunicated. Robert Whatcott, who would later witness Shakespeare's will, testified for the Halls.

Thomas Greene and his wife, Lettice, resided with Ann Shakespeare in New Place on the corner of Chapel Street and Dead Lane. Greene referred to Shakespeare as his cousin.

29 August: A building contract was signed by Philip Henslowe. This was to construct the Hope playhouse to the same design as the Swan, but it was to be built as a dual-purpose venue. It would also serve as an animal-baiting arena. Having learnt their lesson from the Globe inferno, the roof was covered with tiles instead of thatch. Roof tiling was a recent innovation and considered state-of-the-art at the beginning of the seventeenth century.

The baiting place called The Bear Garden was demolished and Gilbert Katherens, carpenter, undertook for the sum of £360 to build 'one other game place or plaiehouse fitt and convenient in all thinges bothe for players to plaie in and for the game of Beares and bulls to be bayted in the same, and also a fitt and convenient tyre house and a stage to be carryed or taken awaie and to stand uppon tressels' the whole to be 'of suche large compasse, fforme, widenes and height as the plaie housse called the Swan in the libertie of Parris garden.' The new playhouse, the Hope, was more substantial than the Rose, as part of it was of brick, the brickwork being put in by a sub-contractor, John Browne, bricklayer, at a cost of £80. The contract with Gilbert Katherens was made in August and it seems likely that Henslowe seized the opportunity given him by the destruction of the Globe Playhouse by fire, to establish another playhouse on Bankside.

Having completed some scenes in the play *The Two Noble Kinsman* Shakespeare returned to Stratford. His place in the London company was taken by twenty-nine-year-old Nathan Field (1587–1620) who, by all accounts, was something of a ladies' man. The Countess of Argyll was alleged to have had an illegitimate child by him. Field played important roles in *Volpone* and *The Alchemist*. As a playwright he wrote *Amends for Ladies* and *The Fatal Dowry* (with Philip Massinger).

Work was completed on a New River. Welsh born Hugh Myddleton – goldsmith, banker and friend of Sir Walter Raleigh – undertook to supply London with fresh water. It took four-and-a-half years to construct a canal 40 miles long, 3 metres wide and 1 metre deep. The source of this canal, which became known as the New River, was a series of springs near Ware in Hertfordshire. From here, it followed the contours of the terrain to a reservoir in Clerkenwell, North London, known as New River Head. By 1670, two thirds of London's houses had running water thanks to this new source. Today, it is mostly covered over and peters out at Stoke Newington.

1614

26 January: James I banned duelling. It was rumoured that the reason why the king was afraid of knives was because, while he was still unborn, his mother had seen his father stab her lover to death.

2 May–7 June: James I's parliament was deemed so ineffective it acquired the sobriquet of 'the Addled Parliament'.

30 June: One year and one day after fire had destroyed the playhouse, the Globe reopened with a tiled roof 'in a far fairer manner than before.'

July: There was a huge fire in Stratford, destroying fifty-four houses, barns and outhouses to the tune of £8,000. Shakespeare was in residence at New Place at the time but his house was unaffected.

5 September: The Town Clerk of Stratford Council, Thomas Greene, drew up a document showing that Shakespeare headed the list of 'Auncient ffreeholders in the ffieldes of Oldstratford and Welcombe' due to his ownership of a large proportion of Stratford tithes. Enclosure meant consolidating the yardlands – these were bundles of acre or half-acre strips in an open field – into larger units bounded by fences or hedges. If the Welcombe fields were enclosed then the arable tracts would be converted into sheep pasture-land, which yielded less income per square acre than when it was used for growing grain and hay. Property holders were concerned by this so called 'enclosure', as it reduced employment and forced up the price of grain. In Thomas Geene's diary of 1614, he refers to Shakespeare as 'cousin' and there are four references to William Shakespeare's involvement in the Welcombe enclosures between 1614 and 1615. 'Shakspeare' is listed as holding '4 yard land.'

23 September: Thomas Greene voiced his anxieties to a council meeting about the land enclosures threatened by William Combe and

Arthur Mainwaring. The council voted unanimously to oppose enclosure. Meanwhile Shakespeare prudently entered into a covenant with Mainwaring's cousin.

28 October: The Public Record Office contains a document recording a covenant with William Replingham, who was the attorney acting as Mainwaring's agent, which undertook to compensate 'William Shackespeare or his heirs or assigns for all such losse detriment & hinderance' with respect to the annual value of his tithes, 'by reason of anie Inclosure or decaye of Tyllage there ment and intended by the said William Replingham.' The enclosure process did not conclude until two years after Shakespeare's death.

The first production in the rebuilt venue was a new play, described thus: 'The Two Noble Kinsmen, written by Mr John Fletcher and Mr William Shakespeare, Gentleman.'

Towards the end of Shakespeare's career the Puritans grew more vocal in their condemnation of frivolous amusements, such as card-playing and theatre-going. Puritan pamphlets declared that theatres were 'sinks of pride and prodigality, villainy and blasphemy'.

The Hathaway family in Stratford-upon-Avon tended toward Puritan values, which may go some way to explain why William's wife, Anne Hathaway, never appeared to join him in London.

Shakespeare and his son-in-law travelled together to London on occasions. Dr John Hall became a leading Puritan.

The Puritan movement grew to the point where Oxford and Cambridge universities forbade their students from attending professional theatre shows.

Three years after the reopening of the Globe in London, the Puritans of Stratford were powerful enough to persuade the local council to pass a decree forbidding touring companies from performing in their town. Shakespeare was in Stratford but it seems he did nothing to protest aginst the decision.

31 October: Philip Henslowe and Jacob Meade, a waterman, organised Lady Elizabeth's Men under the leadership of Nathan Field, to present the inaugural production of Ben Jonson's *Bartholomew Fair* at the Hope playhouse on the Bankside in Southwark. The Hope had taken longer to build than estimated, as the nearby Globe was being rebuilt at the same time. Philip Henslowe's brief for the new venue was two-fold. It called for a '...Plaiehouse fitt & convenient in all thinges, bothe for players to playe in, and for the game of Beares and Bulls to be bayted in the same, and also a fitt and convenient Tyre house and a stage to be carryed and taken awaie, and to stande vppon tressels...'

Once the Hope playhouse had opened it was still sometimes referred to as 'the Beargarden' because it was used for animal baiting on Tuesdays and Thursdays. Plays were shown on Mondays, Wednesday, Fridays and Saturdays.

Bear-baiting did not become illegal until 1642, when theatres were closed by the Puritans. The last seven captive bears were shot dead by Commonwealth soldiers in 1656. Cocks and fighting dogs were also destroyed. Officially, that was the end of animal baiting. Yet Samuel Pepys records a visit to the Beargarden in August 1666. Cockfighting and dogfights continue behind closed doors to this day.

Early November: Shakespeare was in Stratford protecting his land from enclosure by a rival landowner called William Combe. The town clerk, Thomas Greene, drew up a note of sundry interests: 'Master Shakespeare, four yardland, no common nor ground beyond Gospel Busy, nor ground in Sandfield, nor none in Sloe Hill Field beyond Bishopton, nor one in the enclosure of Bishopston.'

17 November: Greene wrote in his journal: 'My cousin Shakespeare, coming to town, I went to see him how he did. He told me that they had assured him they meant to enclose no further than to the Field, to the gate in Clopton hedge and take in Salisbury's piece; and that they mean in April to survey the land and then give satisfaction and not before. And he and Master Hall say they think will be nothing done at all.'

In the end, William Combe agreed to compensate Shakespeare for any loss of tithes consequent to wrongly enclosed land.

Sir Arthur Mainwaring continued attempting to enclose lands at Welcombe near Stratford-upon-Avon, but his endeavours were defeated by local resistance, which had Shakespeare's support.

It is presumed that Shakespeare remained in London over the Christmas season, as the King's Men performed at court on eight occasions.

ACTUS QUARTUS, SCENA SECUNDA

🕮 The King's relationship with George Villiers became so intimate that he referred to George as 'my sweet child and wife'. Villiers was eventually rewarded. He fell to his knees and rapidly rose through the ranks of nobility – baron, viscount, earl, marquess – becoming a Gentleman of the Bedchamber before clambering back to his feet as the Duke of Buckingham.

🕮 James I addressed the Privy Council justifying his bisexuality, finishing his statement with: '...I wish to speak in my own behalf and not to have it thought to be a defect, for Jesus Christ did the same, and therefore I cannot be blamed. Christ had John, and I have George' (i.e. the first Duke of Buckingham, 1592–1628).

🕮 1615

26 April: A court record in the Public Records Office under 'Bendishe, et al. v. Bacon' states: 'Bill of Complaint entered in the Court of Chancery by Shakespere and others to obtain possession of documents relating to the Blackfriars property.' Shakespeare was also involved in litigation regarding unauthorised improvements to the Blackfriars building. He issued a bill of complaint against Matthew Bacon of Gray's Inn.

🕮 5 May: Answer to Bill of Complaint in Bendishe et al. v. Bacon: 'Willyam Shakespere'. (Referenced in E.K.Chambers, *William Shakespeare: A Study of the Facts and Problems*, 1930, page 161.) Resorting to litigation was more common then. Shakespeare's close friend, John Heminges, was sued by his own daughter over family property.

9 October: The Public Record Office records Thomasina Ostler's court plea with a list of shareholders for the Globe playhouse and the Blackfriars property that included Shakespeare's name. It states: 'From Plea of Thomasina Ostler in suit of Ostler v. Heminges, Coram Rege Roll 1454. Court plea of Thomasina Ostler listing Shakespeare as shareholder in the Globe and Blackfriars property.'

It is said that Shakespeare spent the last year of his life in retirement in Stratford.

Scholars inform us that Shakespeare wrote 884,647 words spread over 118,406 lines. It is likely that at least as much again has been lost.

The new writing team of Beaumont and Fletcher evolved. Their collaboration was so close they allegedly shared their clothes, their mistress and their bed.

30 November: In the Registers of St Botolph's in Aldgate the burial is recorded of Robert Armin (1563–1615). Armin was one of Shakespeare's longest known associates in the Chamberlain Men's company. He created Feste in *Twelfth Night*, the Fool in *King Lear*, the Porter in *Macbeth*, Autolycus in *The Winter's Tale* and Touchstone in *As You Like It*. It is thought that he retired in about 1610.

1616

6 January: Philip Henslowe, impresario and theatre owner, died at the age of sixty-six. Edward Alleyn, leading actor in the Admiral's Men, had married Henslowe's stepdaughter Joan in 1592, and they

worked in partnership. In 1584, Henslowe purchased the Little Rose property in Southwark and converted it into the Rose – the third permanent playhouse in London. In 1598, he had founded the Fortune playhouse north of the Thames. This resulted in the Watermen's Company presenting a petition to the Crown. Their fear was the anticipated loss of business in transporting theatre patrons across the Thames to the south bank. An astute businessman, Henslowe kept a diary that has proved to be an invaluable source of theatrical information for the period. It is written on the reverse pages of his account books and is now held by Dulwich College – founded and funded by Edward Alleyn.

January: Following Henslowe's funeral, William Shakespeare summoned his lawyer, Francis Collins, to draft his own will.

10 February: At Holy Trinity Church, Stratford, Shakespeare's youngest daughter, Judith, thirty-one, married Thomas Quiney, twenty-six. The assistant vicar, Richard Watts, who later married Quiney's sister Mary, probably officiated. (Thomas's father Richard Quiney died in 1602 after a tavern brawl with the henchmen of the Lord of the Manor, Sir Edward Greville.) This wedding happened to take place during the church's Lenten season (23 January to 7 April), when marriages were not permitted without a special licence. In Stratford, the proper authority to grant such a licence was the Bishop of Worcester. However, Quiney never bothered to present himself at the consistory court in Worcester to collect it. The consequences for his tardiness were dire.

12 March: Thomas Quiney was excommunicated.

15 March: Thomas Quiney was summoned before the Bawdy Court to answer charges of 'carnal copulation' with a Margaret Wheeler, who died in childbirth.

Judith and Thomas had three children: Shakespeare, Richard, and Thomas. Shakespeare Quiney died at six months of age, and neither Richard nor Thomas lived past twenty-one.

Shakespeare's will is kept at the National Archives at Kew. It is written on three pieces of parchment, each of unequal size.

William Shakespeare redrafted his will because he was not best pleased with Thomas Quiney. In the Will, the words 'sonne-in-L[aw]' were scratched out and that item of the bequest was redirected for the sole benefit of his daughter, 'Judyth'.

An extract from his will, dated 25 (*vicesimo quinto*) March reads:

Item, I Gyve and bequeath unto my ~~sonne in Law and~~ Daughter Judyth One Hundred and fyftie pounds of lawfull English money to be paied unto her in manner and forme following That ys to saye One Hundred Poundes in discharge of her marriage porcion within one yeare after my deceas with consideracion after the Rate of twoe shillinges in the pound for soe long tyme as the same shalbe unpaid unto her after my deceas & the fyftie pounds.

(Shakespeare's will, in its entirety, can be seen in Appendix D.)

🕮 26 March: Thomas Quiney appeared before the Bawdy Court, which dealt with 'carnal copulation'. Quiney confessed to '*fassus est se carnalem copulacionem habuisse cum dicta Wheeler*' (having had carnal copulation with the said Wheeler) and as a penance was commanded to appear for three successive Sundays wearing a white sheet in church. His father-in-law, William Shakespeare, presumably watched this penance on Sunday, 27 March. Fortuitously, he was spared from witnessing the humiliation repeated on 3 and 10 April, because the Bawdy Court commuted Quiney's sentence to a small fine.

🕮 As a vintner, Thomas Quiney sampled his stock too lavishly. After marrying Judith Shakespeare, he took charge of a tavern called The Cage on the corner of High Street and Bridge Street, Stratford. He slid into debt and, according to rumour, he left for London in 1625 and was never again seen in Stratford.

🕮 17 April: William Hart, Shakespeare's brother-in-law was buried in Stratford.

🕮 22 April: Miguel de Cervantes died.

🕮 23 April: Saturday. William Shakespeare died, coinciding with his birthday. However, John Ward (1629–81), the vicar of Stratford since 1662, wrote that William Shakespeare died after over-indulging at his fifty-second birthday party held at New Place, Stratford, saying: '… Shakespeare, Drayton and Ben Jonson had a merry meeting and it seems drank too hard for Shakespeare died of a feavour there contracted.' From other references in his journal, it is inferred that he received this information at an earlier date from Judith Quiney, Shakespeare's daughter. This suggests that the true date of William's birthday was likely to have been a day or two earlier than generally accepted, i.e. 21 or 22 April 1564.

A local tradition claims that the fatal birthday party took place at the Bell Inn at Welford-on-Avon. It exists on the Binton Road to this day and the *Good Pub Guide* has voted it the Best Dining Pub in Warwickshire on several occasions.

25 April: Monday. William Shakespeare was buried, recorded in the Stratford Parish Register as 'Will Shakspeare gent'. His tomb is buried seventeen feet beneath the floor of Holy Trinity Church, Stratford-upon-Avon, and inscribed on it are these words allegedly written by the poet himself:

Good friend for Jesus' sake forbear
To dig the dust enclosed here!
Blest be the man that spares these stones
And curst be he that moves my bones.

Mark Twain pointed out that these are the only words that can be definitely ascribed to Shakespeare.

The standard depth of a grave was six feet, so the reason to be buried seventeen feet deep may indicate that Shakespeare died of the plague or some other communicable disease.

There was no spire on Holy Trinity Church, Stratford, in Shakespeare's time. A wooden spire was added to the church in 1675 and replaced with the current stone one in 1763.

Shakespeare left bequests to the value of £350 and an estate worth £1,200 at a time when the average annual wage for a schoolmaster was little more than £20.

The Kesselstadt death mask of Shakespeare was discovered by Dr Ludwig Becker, librarian, at the ducal palace at Darmstadt, in a rag-shop at Mainz in 1849. Darmstadt is a city in the state of Hesse in Germany, where the mask is kept. Stanley Wells, the Shakespearian expert, is sceptical about the claim and suggests it is more likely to be the death mask of Ben Jonson.

It is sometimes remarked that Shakespeare and Miguel de Cervantes died within a day of each other. However, Spain was using the Gregorian calendar while England persisted with the older Julian calendar. So in fact Cervantes died ten days before Shakespeare.

John Rogers, who was at the time the vicar of Stratford, officiated at Shakespeare's funeral. He lived in Chapel Quad.

The first two Latin lines on the plaque of the Stratford monument translate to: 'In judgment a Pylian, in genius a Socrates, in art a Maro, the earth covers him, the people mourn him, Olympus possesses him.'

22 June: William Shakespeare's will was proved at the Archbishop's Prerogative Court at Canterbury. One of the executors was Francis Collins, a landowner from Alderminster, five miles south of Stratford. The other was Thomas Russell. Shakespeare's will stated: '...And I doe intreat and Appoint the saied Thomas Russell Esquier and ffrauncis Collins gent to be overseers herof And doe Revoke All former wills and publishe this to be my last will and testament.'

In the will, Shakespeare bequeathed £5 to Francis Collins, who went on to marry a wealthy widow, Ann Digges. Seven years later, her son, Leonard Digges, was to write a dedication in the First Folio (1623).

Sir John Davies, a contemporary of William Shakespeare, wrote: 'our English Terence, Master William Shakespeare – thou hast no railing but a reigning wit.' (Chute, *Shakespeare of London*.)

During Shakespeare's lifetime, more than seventy editions of his works were issued.

In his book *Is Shakespeare Dead?*, Mark Twain declared his incredulity that Shakespeare's will mentioned: '... not a single book. Books were more precious than swords and silver-gilt bowls and second-best beds in those days, and when a departing person owned one he gave it a high place in his will.' Twain continues: 'The will mentioned not a play, not a poem, not an unfinished literary work, not a scrap of manuscript of any kind... Many poets have died poor, but this is the only one in history that had died this poor; the others all left literary remains behind. Also a book. Maybe two.'

It is believed that Shakespeare's daughter and her husband Dr Hall commissioned the effigy of Shakespeare's monument in the church at Stratford. The quill in his right hand writing on a sheet of paper was added later. A printed image of the memorial engraved in 1656 shows Shakespeare holding what appears to be a woolsack.

It might be said that a fitting epitaph is found in one of Shakespeare's noblest sonnets, 146:

> Poor soul, the centre of my sinful earth,
> My sins these rebel powers that thee array,
> Why dost thou pine within and suffer dearth,
> Painting thy outward walls so costly gay?
> Why so large cost, having so short a lease,
> Dost thou upon thy fading mansion spend?
> Shall worms, inheritors of this excess,
> Eat up thy charge? Is this thy body's end?
> Then, soul, live thou upon thy servant's loss,
> And let that pine to aggravate thy store;
> Buy terms divine with selling hours of dross
> Within be fed, without be rich no more:
> So shalt thou feed on Death, that feeds on men,
> And Death once dead, there's no more dying then.

Reference to the Stratford bust was made by Leonard Digges in the First Folio:

> And time dissolves thy Stratford Monument
> Here we alive shall view thee soon.

This book, when brass and marble fade
Shall make thee look Fresh to all ages.

This indicates that the memorial bust was erected some time between 1616 and 1623.

The question has been asked, particularly by Mark Twain, 'What happened to Shakespeare's library?' Over the years many books have turned up purporting to bear Shakespeare's signature, but most of them are almost certainly forgeries. Two books which scholars cautiously suspect might have belonged to Shakespeare include a translation of Montaigne of 1603 and a translated version of Plutarch dated 1612.

Richard Davies (Archdeacon of Lichfield from 26 July 1703 until his death in 1708) wrote that according to Stratford oral tradition, a priest was fetched when Shakespeare lay dying and that he received the last rites of a Catholic. This claim prompts some scholars to ask, 'Was Shakespeare a left-footed bard?' (Left-footer was a derogatory term applied to Roman Catholics, referring to the rural population of Gaelic Ireland, who dug with a one-sided spade, using 'the wrong foot').

9 August: John Best, Cockmaster to the Prince of Wales, leased a derelict cockpit to the leading actor of the Queen's Men, Christopher Beeston who, after years of sharing the Red Bull playhouse in Clerkenwell, wanted his company to have a more identifiable base. The Phoenix became the second indoor theatre to be built in London, tucked a few yards to the left of Drury Lane.

Drury Lane is named after Sir Robert Drury, a Suffolk barrister, who, in 1500, built a mansion in the grounds of St Giles Leper Hospital on the border of Aldwych Close. This was known as Drury House and the lane beside it running down from High Holborn to the Strand on the edge of the Thames became known as Drury Lane. By the start of the seventeenth century, the building had been converted into a pub called The Queen of Bohemia, and the tone of the area was that of a place crammed with brothels, gin palaces, and cockpits.

Most indoor theatres were situated on the first floors of existing buildings. The Phoenix Theatre (considered to be the forerunner of modern 'West End theatres'), built in Cockpit Lane behind Drury Lane, was an exception.

October: The benchers of Lincoln's Inn – only five hundred yards away – lodged a complaint about 'the convertinge of the Cock Pytte in the fieldes into a playe house.'

23 November: William Shakespeare's grandson was born and given the name of Shakespeare Quiney. It was fortunate that by this time Thomas Quiney's excommunication had been rescinded, allowing Shakespeare Quiney to be baptised.

E. K. Chambers quoted Francis Beaumont's homage to Shakespeare:

Here I would let slip,
If I had any in me, scholarship,
And from all learning keep these lines as clear,

315

As Shakespeare's best are, which our heirs shall hear
Preachers apt to their auditors to show
How far sometimes a mortal man may go
By the dim light of Nature.
(From Chambers, *William Shakespeare: A Study of Facts and Problems*, vol. 1.)

Why would his close contemporary have written these lines if Shakespeare had been merely a front-man for another writer?

Actus Quintus

Scena Prima

Post Mortem

One of William Shakespeare's last projects was to collaborate with John Fletcher (1579–1625) to write a play called *Cardenio* based on the first volume of the comic novel, *Don Quixote* (published 16 January 1605). Irish-born Thomas Shelton's English translation appeared in 1612. Shakespeare's playscript has been lost but academics are optimistic that a copy may be hidden away in one of the great private libraries and that it may one day turn up.

It was not necessary to have more than two people to witness a will and yet John Robinson must have been a valued friend to be trusted as a third witness. Robinson's signature on Shakespeare's will indicates that he was an educated man:

Witnesses to the publishing hereof:
Fra: Collins [Francis Collins was Shakespeare's lawyer]

Julyus Shawe
John Robinson
Hamnet Sadler
Robert Whattcott

It seems likely that the first draft of the will was drawn up in January 2016. When Collins revised the document on 25 March, he or his clerk inadvertently wrote January instead of March when copying the unrevised details from the earlier document. It appears that Collins never had time to make a fair copy of the will.

After her father's death, Susannah rented out rooms in New Place, Stratford-upon-Avon. One of her tenants was John Robinson, who stayed on and off for some years. When he was in London, Robinson rented rooms at Shakespeare's Gatehouse property in Blackfriars. The Henley Street property was taken by Lewis Hiccox on a long lease, although Joan Hart retained three rooms there.

1617

4 March: Shrove Tuesday. There was a riot, described as below, from Julian Bowsher, *Shakespeare's London Theatre* (2012):

Many disordered persons of sundry kinds, amongst whom were very many young boys and lads, that assembled themselves in Lincolns Inn Field, Finsbury Field, in Ratcliffe and Stepney Field, where in riotous manner they did beat down the walls and windows of many victualling houses and of all other houses which they suspected to be bawdy houses. And that afternoon they spoiled a new playhouse, and did likewise more hurt in diverse other places.

Following this riot, Christopher Beeston, now leader of the Queen's Men, renovated the damaged playhouse building and christened it 'The Phoenix Theatre'. It was just outside the jurisdiction of the City of London, situated off Drury Lane and had been in use as a staging area for cockfights since 1609. Forty years later, in 1656, Wenceslaus Hollar drew the 'Great Map' of central London in which the Phoenix Theatre is portrayed as a three-gabled building with three storeys. The Phoenix fell into disuse around 1663 and was demolished in 1721.

8 May: Shakespeare's grandson, Shakespeare Quiney, was buried. He was five-and-a-half months old.

William Davenant knew Shakespeare and declared himself to be Shakespeare's illegitimate child. In later life he became the Poet Laureate. At the age of twelve, soon after Shakespeare's death, he wrote the following poem:

Beware, delighted poets, when you sing,
To welcome nature in the early spring,
Your numerous feet not tread
The banks of Avon, for each flower
(As it ne'er knew a sun or shower)
Hangs there the pensive head.

Each Tree, whose thick, and spreading growth hath made,

Rather a Night beneath the Boughs, than Shade,
(Unwilling now to grow)
Looks like the Plume a Captive wears,
Whose rifled Falls are steeped i'th tears
Which from his last rage flow.

The piteous River wept itself away
Long since (Alas!) to such a swift decay;
That reach the Map; and look
If you a River there can spy;
And for a River your mock'd Eye,
Will find a shallow Brook.

1618

9 February: Richard Quiney, the second of Judith Shakespeare's sons, was baptised.

Shakespeare's Blackfriars property came into the possession of Matthew Morrys of Stratford and John Greene of Clement's Inn.

Walter Raleigh had been sent to Venezuela on a quest for gold (to El Dorado) along the Orinoco River. He failed to find treasure and his son died. In grief and frustration, he attacked the Spanish outpost of Santo Tome de Guyana. However, Spain and England were no longer at war. Therefore, Walter was in deep trouble on his return to England. James I was keen to remain at peace with the Spanish, who insisted that the man that sank so many of their ships should be put to death. This was their condition to allow James's son, Prince Charles, to marry their Spanish princess. James acquiesced to the demands of the Spanish ambassador and Raleigh was sacrificed.

29 October: Sir Walter Raleigh, England's national hero, was beheaded in the Old Palace Yard at the Palace of Westminster. It was for nothing. The marriage between the princess and Charles never took place. Raleigh asked to see the axe that was about to behead him. Allegedly, his last words were: 'This is sharp medicine but it is a remedy for all diseases and miseries.'

1619

2 March: Queen Anne died. National mourning was called for.

13 March: Monday. William Shakespeare's close acting friend, Richard Burbage, died at the age of fifty-one. Shakespeare had written great dramatic roles for Burbage: Henry V, Richard III, Duke Vincentio, Othello, Lear, Macbeth, Timon, Antony, Coriolanus and, of course, Hamlet. Burbage's funeral caused disruption to the city with mournful fans turning up to pay their respects. This was of great embarrassment to the Court, because Queen Anne had died only the previous week and Burbage's death threatened to overshadow the official mourning for her. He was buried in St Leonard's Churchyard at Shoreditch, Hackney.

Richard Burbage painted in his spare time. The picture most generally associated with him is thought to be a self-portrait. There is a school of thought that claims the 'Felton' portrait of Shakespeare could be attributed to Burbage. Dulwich College possesses several portraits of women painted by him.

Ben Jonson decided to go on a great walkabout to Scotland. He had been engaged in friendly rivalry with Shakespeare since 1595. In conversations with the Scottish poet William Drummond, he summed up his thoughts on his old friend thus: 'I remember the Players have often mentioned it as an honour to Shakespeare that in his writing, whatsoever he penned, he never blotted out a line. My answer hath been; would he have blotted a thousand. Which they thought a malevolent speech.' Jonson's conversations with Drummond were discovered in the Advocates' Library, Edinburgh in 1842, and contain many anecdotes of historic interest.

Oxford University awarded Ben Jonson an honorary M.A. degree for literature.

1620

23 January: Thomas Quiney (junior) was born. This was Shakespeare's third grandson born to his daughter Judith, the wife of Thomas Quiney, senior. The infant, Shakespeare Quiney, was already dead and neither of the remaining two grandsons, Richard and Thomas, survived beyond the age of twenty-one.

1621

The Rose playhouse, situated on Golden Lane, Cripplegate, burnt down in two hours. However, the ground rent was so high, the Admiral's Men had abandoned the building some years before. Most of their work was produced at the Fortune playhouse. It is quite possible that much of the usable wood had been removed from the building before the fire.

1622

The Curtain playhouse closed and for a while became a venue for fencing displays. It fell into disuse by 1627. A plaque marks the site of the venue at 18, Hewett Street, off Curtain Road.

5 April: Jennet Davenant died and was buried at St Martin's Church, Oxford.

The antiquarian, Thomas Hearne (1678–1735) stated of Jennet's second son, William Davenant, that 'it was an Oxford tradition that Mr Shakespear was his father and gave him his name.' Alexander Pope repeated the legend independently.

23 April: John Davenant followed his wife to the grave. Davenant Road in North Oxford is named after him.

1623

8 May: *Timon of Athens* was entered into the Stationers' Register.

3/4 August: Anne (Hathaway) Shakespeare died aged sixty-seven. She missed the publication of the First Folio of Shakespeare's Works by a few weeks.

6 August: Anne Shakespeare was buried in the chancel of Holy Trinity Church, Stratford, next to her husband William.

8 November: *Coriolanus* was entered into the Stationers' Register.

5 December: The First Folio was published with 154 Sonnets, thirty-seven plays and two epic poems and consisted of 900 pages. Shakespeare's affectionate rival and sometime drinking companion, Ben Jonson, wrote in his introduction: 'He had small Latin and less Greek.' A few lines later he added, 'He was not of an age but for all time.'

The original intention was to publish the First Folio in 1622 but undisclosed financial difficulties delayed publication for a year. Some copies are extant with the 1622 publication date. Only copper-engravings of pictures could be printed at this time.

Ralph Crane was the name of the scribe assigned the task of producing fair copies for the printers of the First Folio. The word 'folio' indicates the size of the printer's page of paper. When folded once, making four sides, it is called folio. When folded twice, making eight sides, it is called quarto.

Five hundred copies of the 'First Folio' were printed at the price of £1 per copy. Today, 239 copies are known to exist, eighty-three of which are held by the Folger Library in Washington (at the last count).

The 'paging' (page numbering) of the three sections of the First Folio is appalling. In *Hamlet*, page 156 leaps to page 257 and carries on from there. Even so, a second edition was required within a decade.

The engraving of Shakespeare on the frontispiece of the First Folio is by Martin Droeshout, and until recently it was considered to be the work of a young man born in 1601 who, had he ever met

Shakespeare, would have been barely fifteen. Recent research has revealed that this young engraver had an uncle, also called Martin Droeshout (1560–1642) a member of the Worshipful Company of Painter-Stainers, and who may well have made an original drawing of Shakespeare from life.

There are 160 songs and musical interludes in the works of Shakespeare.

Shakespeare gave lines to 1,378 separate characters.

Sir Edward Dering adapted both Parts of *Henry IV* and truncated the script for a private performance at his home, Surrenden Manor. He paid the local rector to write out the play and invested seventeen shillings and eightpence 'for heads of hair and beards'. The handwritten manuscript of this version is held in the Folger Library in Washington.

5 December: Sir Edward Dering is the first person known to have bought a copy of the First Folio from John Smethwick's shop situated 'under the dial' in St Dunstan's Churchyard on Fleet Street. In fact, according to his account book, he bought two copies at the same time for £2.00, plus a volume of Ben Jonson's plays for nine shillings. The Folio had been listed in a catalogue at the Frankfurt Book Fair in the previous year, but the first impression did not roll off the press until February 1623.

1624

The Mermaid Club (sometimes called The Friday Club because one of its entrances was in Friday Street) had been started by Walter

Raleigh to encourage witty dinner conversation. Following the demise of most of its members, Ben Jonson decided to start it up again. He founded the Apollo Club at The Devil and St Dunstan Tavern in Fleet Street. Gastronomes with resilient livers were encouraged to dine, drink and tell witty stories. No music was allowed. It was rather similar to today's Useless Information Society.

1625

29 August: The playwright, John Fletcher, died of the plague and was buried in St Saviour's Church, Southwark. Fletcher worked mostly for the King's Company and for ten years he wrote plays with Francis Beaumont. He had been a close collaborator with William Shakespeare in his later years (working with him on *Henry VIII, The Two Noble Kinsmen* and *Cardenio*). For a while, his popularity rivalled Shakespeare's.

King Charles I owned a copy of Shakespeare's works. In the Index of Contents, *Twelfth Night* is crossed out and the word *Malvolio* substituted, suggesting that the comedy sub-plot was more popular in court circles than the love stories.

In his mid-twenties, William Davenant was successfully cured of syphilis though not before his nose was permanently disfigured, as can be seen in later portraits.

The so-called 'Chandos' portrait of Shakespeare (the one with the earring in his left ear) can be traced back to Davenant. This makes its candidacy as an authentic likeness credible. Davenant claimed he sold the portrait to Thomas Betterton, who sold it on to his lawyer, Robert Keck. The artist is unknown. Two likely suspects are Richard Burbage (who was a tolerable painter) and John Taylor. (See the year 1856.)

21 November: The actor and theatre manager, Edward Alleyn, died, aged sixty, leaving £10,000 to endow Dulwich College, preparations for which had begun in 1605. By 1614, he had invested £35,000 to buy up the land suitable for his proposed college. In letters patent dated 21 June 1619, Alleyn finally won through and founded the College of God's Gift at Dulwich. Not bad going for the son of a Bishopsgate innkeeper. *The Alleyn Papers* published in 1843 give us a unique insight into theatrical life at that time. Much of the source material for this era comes by courtesy of Edward Alleyn.

1626

22 April: Shakespeare's granddaughter, Elizabeth, aged seventeen, married Thomas Nash of Lincoln's Inn.

1627

29 December: Henry Condell (or Cundell, as Shakespeare spells the name in his will) died in Fulham. He was buried at St Mary Aldermanbury. A direct descendant, Pamela Cundell, an actress who was married to actor Bill Fraser, died in 2015.

1629

30 January: Following the beheading of King Charles I, theatres were closed and eventually abandoned during the period of the Puritan

Commonwealth. Many actors joined the army and some reverted to their former trades.

📖 Ben Jonson's library, containing many precious copies of play-scripts, including some by Shakespeare, was destroyed in a fire.

📖 **1630**

10 October: John Heminges died in Southwark and was buried at the parish church of St Mary Aldermanbury two days later. He had owned an alehouse abutting the Globe playhouse and had been one of Shakespeare's trustees when he purchased a house in Blackfriars in 1613.

📖 **1632**

According to the antiquary, Anthony Wood (1632–95): 'Shakespeare often baited at The Crown Inn or Tavern in Oxford, in his journey to and from London. The landlady was a woman of great beauty and sprightly wit: and her husband, Mr John Davenant (afterwards mayor of that city), a grave, melancholy man who as well as his wife used much to delight in Shakespeare's pleasant company.' (From James Halliwell-Phillipps, *A Life of William Shakespeare*, 1848.)

📖 **1634**

8 April: *The Two Noble Kinsmen* was entered into the Stationers' Register. Shortly afterwards it was published in quarto by the bookseller, John Waterston. The title page declares: 'presented at the Blackfriars by the King's Majesty servants, with great applause. Written by the memorable worthies of their time: Mr John Fletcher

and Mr William Shakespeare. Gent.' The plot derives from Chaucer's *The Knight's Tale*.

1637

6 August: After a series of strokes, Ben Jonson, who had grown fat, died at the age of sixty-five. He had finished the first two acts of a new play, *The Sad Shepherd*. From a discreet distance, Charles I had taken care of him, continuing to pay the allowance granted by his father, James I. Ben Jonson squeezed by on an annual pension of one hundred pounds plus a 'tierce' of wine (one sixth of a tun). He declared that during his whole lifetime he had only earned £200 from his writing.

Ben Jonson was buried in the North Aisle of Westminster Abbey. He had joked with the Dean that he could not afford a full-size burial plot alongside his fellow poets. He requested just two square feet. Consequently, his cheap coffin was buried upright instead of horizontally.

1639

28 January: Thomas Quiney – aged twenty-one – one of William Shakespeare's grandsons, was buried.

6 February: Richard Quiney – aged nineteen – another of William Shakespeare's grandsons, was buried.

1640

The second edition of *The Complete Works of Shakespeare* was published. This was not only re-edited but contained additions. The engraving on the frontispiece was adapted by William Marshall and shows a subtly different version of William Shakespeare, viewed from a different angle to the Martin Droeshout engraving. This edition was published by John Benson, which happens to be an inversion of the name Ben Jonson. The First Folio's signatory was B.I. That of the second folio is signed I.B. (The letters J and I were interchangeable and the initials most often used by Ben Jonson were B. I.)

The opening lines read:

> This Shadow is renowned Shakespear's? Soul of th' age
> The applause? Delight? The wonder of the Stage.
> Nature her selfe, was proud of his designs
> And joy'd to weare the dressing of his lines,
> The learned will confess his works as such
> As neither man, nor Muse can praise to much
> For ever live they fame, the world to tell,
> Thy like, no age, shall ever parallel.

1641

Timber; or, Discoveries Made upon Men and Matter by Ben Jonson was published, being one of the first attempts to appraise Shakespeare's work.

1643

Summer: Henrietta Maria, wife of Charles I, travelled to Stratford-upon-Avon and stayed for three weeks with her courtiers at New Place (then called The Great House).

Following his exploits on the royalist side during the siege of Gloucester, William Davenant was knighted by King Charles. After the demise of Ben Jonson the role of Poet Laureate was up for grabs, and Davenant became the first to be given royal approval.

1644

15 April: The Globe playhouse was demolished.

1645

Emilia Lanier died at the age of seventy-six and was buried at Clerkenwell, on 3 April. A.L. Rowse has put a strong case forward nominating her as the 'Dark Lady of the Sonnets'. At the age of forty-two, in 1611, Lanier published her volume of poetry, *Salve Deus Rex Judaeorum*. Shakespeare was then forty-seven. Lanier was the first woman in England to declare herself a poet. Her work is regarded as being the first flowering of feminism.

1646

4 November: Joan Shakespeare was buried. Joan was Shakespeare's younger sister, named after her parents' deceased first-born child. She married a hatter, William Hart with whom she had four children: William (1600–39), Mary (1603–7), Thomas (1605–61), and Michael (1608–18). Her other descendants via Thomas lived in Stratford until 1806.

In Tewkesbury Abbey cemetery, an inscription on the gravestone of John Hart (1755–1800) identified him as 'the 6th descendant of the poet Shakespeare'. Other descendants continue to the present day.

1647

There are signatures extant on documents in Susanna Shakespeare's hand involving New Place and other properties dated not only on 27 May 1639 but also 2 June 1647, whereas her sister, Judith, signed a deed of bargain and sale with only her mark on 4 December 1611.

Humphrey Robinson and Humphrey Moseley were foremost publishers at this time. Robinson based his shop at the Sign of the Three Pigeons in St Paul's Churchyard. In 1647 they published the first folio of Beaumont and Fletcher plays. After Moseley's death, Robinson started a news service that was the forerunner of newspapers.

22 October: All theatres were shut down and plays were banned for the next thirteen years. The Red Bull in Clerkenwell occasionally defied the ban but paid the penalty of being invaded by the militia.

1649

11 July: Susanna Hall (née Shakespeare) died aged sixty-six, and, being buried beside her husband on the sixteenth, 'made his tomb complete'. Tradition has it that Elizabeth Nash, Shakespeare's grandchild, composed her mother's epitaph inscribed on her tomb:

> Here lyeth the body of Susanna, wife of John Hall, gent., the daughter of William Shakespeare, gent. She deceased the 11 day of July, Anno 1649, aged 66.

> Witty above her sex, but that's not all,
> Wise to Salvation was good Mistress Hall,

Something of Shakespeare was in that, but this
Wholly of him with whom she's now in blisse.
Then, passenger, hast nere a tear
To weep with her that wept with all
That wept, yet set herself to chere
Them up with comforts cordiall?
Her love shall live, her mercy spread
When thou hast nere a tear to shed.

5 June: Elizabeth Nash married Mr John Barnard, of Abington, Northamptonshire, at Billesley, a village four miles from Stratford.

Susannah's death limited Shakespeare's lineal descendants to two – Judith Quiney, daughter, and Elizabeth Barnard, granddaughter. A fine was levied on New Place in 1650, in which John Barnard and Henry Smith were made trustees to the settlement of 1647, instead of Richard Lane and William Smith. In 1652 a new settlement was made, passing the property on to John Barnard and his wife, and then to the heirs of the body of Elizabeth, failing whom to any persons she might name. A fine was again levied on this settlement.

17 August: Judith Combe died. She was the betrothed of Richard Combe, who chose marble for the monument and whose alabaster bust appears hand-in-hand with hers in the double-headed recess to the right of Shakespeare's memorial bust.

Judith's death, at the age of seventy-seven, left Lady Elizabeth Barnard as William Shakespeare's sole survivor. She had no children by her second marriage, and there is no mention of her husband's previous family in Lady Barnard's will. She did not leave her husband as executor. The will was drawn up on 29 January 1669–70, and she died at Abington in February, records stating: 'Madam Elizabeth Bernard, wife of Sir John Bernard, Knight, was buried 17th Feb., 1669–70.' No sepulchral monument was raised in memory of the granddaughter and heir of Shakespeare, but she probably lay in the same tomb as her husband, who died in 1674. A memorial slab to him still remains in Abington Church, but the place of his burial is unknown, and the vault below this stone is used by another family.

By his death, his wife's will came into force, written while she was still 'in perfect memory – blessed be God! – and mindful of mortality.' She recounted the settlement of 18 April 1653, to which the trustees were Henry Smith, of Stratford, gent., and Job Dighton, of the Middle Temple, London, Esquire. Henry Smith, her surviving trustee, or his heirs, six months after the death of her husband, Sir John Barnard, was to sell New Place, giving the first offer to her loving cousin, Edward Nash, and the money was to be used in legacies. She made her 'loving kinsman Edward Bagley' executor, 'in witness of which I set my hand and seal.' It may be seen that she retained absolute power of her grandfather's purchases, but justly left his inheritance from his father John to his sister's descendants.

Tenements were built on the grounds of the Globe playhouse during the Commonwealth period. Most of the other London theatres were left derelict and were eventually demolished.

1652

After thirteen years, the legal dispute between Susanna and Judith regarding their inheritance from William Shakespeare was finally resolved. The deaths of all Judith's children resulted in legal consequences. The entail on her father's inheritance led Susanna, along with her daughter and son-in-law, to make a settlement using an elaborate legal device for the inheritance of her own branch of the family.

1653

Plays were suppressed entirely during the term of office that Oliver Cromwell became First Lord Protector of the Commonwealth of England, Scotland and Ireland (from 25 December 1653 until 3 September 1658), together with the nine months' succession of his son, Richard.

Puritanism did not stand in the way of Oliver Cromwell's marital life. He had at least nine children. His successor, Richard Cromwell, whose sole contribution to the Commonwealth seems to be the invention of the chequebook, was held in such low esteem that the people called him Tumbledown Dick. Royalists nicknamed him Queen Dick.

Sir William Dugdale (1605–86), a herald and antiquarian, published a book called *Antiquities of Warwickshire*. In it, he sketched the Stratford Memorial bust of Shakespeare. This differs in several ways from the monument we see today. Originally there was no quill pen on show and the bard's hands rested on a woolsack.

1655

6 August: The Blackfriars Theatre was demolished.

October: A rough census reckoned there were only 150 Jews living in England. An eminent Rabbi, Manasseh ben Israel, came from Holland and in December he made a written plea for the readmission of Jews into England. Cromwell granted the request.

1656

25 March: The seven remaining captive bears in Southwark kept for animal-baiting were shot to death by a company of soldiers.

In the autumn, William Davenant was credited with introducing to the stage England's first known singer/actress, Mrs Edward Coleman, who sang the role of the heroine Ianthe in a production of Davenant's 'opera' *The Siege of Rhodes*, co-written with Charles Colemam in a private performance at Rutland House. She was not highly regarded in her profession and in the 1660s she was superseded by Mary Saunderson Betterton. (See 8 December 1660.)

Davenant, hinting in his cups that he was Shakespeare's illegitimate son, went on to adapt several of Shakespeare's plays to suit the tastes of Restoration audiences.

1660

With the death of Cromwell, theatres started to reopen. Samuel Pepys was an habitual playgoer and recorded seeing forty-one performances of Shakespeare's plays in his 351 theatre visits. He wrote in his diary that he thought most of the Shakespearian productions he saw were 'insipid', and others 'ridiculous'.

ACTUS QUINTUS, SCENA PRIMA

December: Charles II, the Merry Monarch, had been recalled to England in May. The interim government, called the Convention Parliament, was dissolved and Charles became king. This restoration of his monarchical rights was marred by the deaths of his younger siblings, Henry and Mary, who both died of smallpox.

When Charles II returned from exile in France he brought with him ideas from the French theatres, including a front curtain across the proscenium arch.

Charles issued patents for two theatre companies in London to stage, as the Act puts it, 'legitimate drama'. William Davenant and Thomas Killigrew (1612–83) presented plays at various sites across the city before they set up permanent theatres in Drury Lane and Covent Garden.

8 December: Margaret Hughes (1630–1719) is credited with becoming the first 'paid' actress to appear on an English stage at the Tennis Court Theatre in Vere Street. She played Desdemona in *Othello*, which was produced by Thomas Killigrew's new King's Company. Anne Marshall (1631–82) took over the role in later performances. Katherine Corey (1635–92) became the third woman to earn her living as a professional actress. In the 'humble petition of Katherine Corey' she stated that she 'was the first and is the last of all the actresses that were constituted by King Charles the Second at his Restauration.' She began under her maiden name of Mitchell but changed it to Mrs Corey in 1663. She was 'a big woman with a gift for comedy' according to Pepys.

After Charles II was restored to the throne, and Shakespeare's plays began to be staged again, they were not considered untouchable gems, and were invariably rewritten to fit the less oppressive and more optimistic age. For example, under the quill of men like Nahum Tate, the tragic characters Romeo and Juliet woke up and recovered as the final curtain fell. Even *King Lear* acquired a happy ending.

Nahum Tate wrote the lyrics of 'While Shepherds Watched Their Flocks by Night' (misquoted by every successive generation of children as 'While Shepherds washed their socks by night').

1661

Elizabeth Hall's second husband, the staunch Royalist John Barnard (1604–74), was knighted by Charles II. With him being made a baronet, this meant that Elizabeth was now Lady Barnard.

1662

9 February: Judith Quiney, née Shakespeare, was buried in the grounds of Holy Trinity Church, Stratford-upon-Avon. The Stratford Register of 1661–62 records the death of Elizabeth's aunt, Judith, thus: 'uxor Thomas Quiney, gent., Feb. 9th, 1661–2.' The use of the word 'uxor' is no certain proof that he was alive at the time.

When Samuel Pepys saw a production of *Romeo and Juliet* in 1662 he wrote: 'It is a play of itself the worst that I ever heard in my life.'

Charles II was concerned that there had been a history of 'embarrassing incidents' occurring amongst male actors playing female roles leading to what was described as 'unnatural vice'. He issued a royal warrant declaring that all female roles should be played only by female actresses.

Thomes Fuller, in his *The History of the Worthies of England*, 1662, wrote of Shakespeare thus:

> Many were the wit-combats betwixt him and Ben Jonson, which two I behold like a Spanish great galleon and an English man of war; Master Jonson (like the former) was built far higher in learning, solid but slow in his performances. Shakespeare, with the Englishman of war, lesser in bulk, but lighter in sailing, could turn with all tides, tack about, and take advantage of all winds by the quickness of his wit and invention.

Dr John Donne (1572–1631) is held responsible for a story attesting to the amicable relations between Shakespeare and Jonson. He is alleged to have told a Member of Parliament that:

> Shakespeare was godfather to one of Ben Jonson's children, and after the christening, being in a deep study, Jonson came to cheer him up and asked him why he was so melancholy. 'No, faith, Ben,' says he, 'not I, but I have been considering a great while what should be the fittest gift for me to bestow upon my godchild, and I have resolv'd at last.'
>
> 'I pr'ythee, what?' sayes he.
>
> 'I' faith, Ben, I'll e'en give him a dozen good Lattin spoons, and thou shalt translate them.

This was a poor pun, but a Shakespearian one, referring to metal spoons plated with lattin, an alloy of copper and zinc. 'Apostle spoons' (with an image of an apostle or saint on them) were traditionally given by godfathers at baptisms and christenings.

If Shakespeare was godfather to one of Ben Jonson's children, it may have been the third child (and the last). Ben had a daughter who died in infancy, a son called Benjamin who died at the age of seven, followed by another son, also called Benjamin, who lived until the 1630s.

1663

7 May: The Theatre Royal, Drury Lane, opened. To begin with, it was sometimes referred to as 'the King's Playhouse'. The building was a three-tiered wooden structure, 112 feet (34m) long and 59 feet (18m) wide; its seating capacity was 700.

1664

A ballad by Thomas Jordan called 'The Forfeiture' included the following verse describing Shylock:

His beard was red; his face was made
Not much unlike a witches.
His habit was a Jewish gown
That would defend all weather;
His chin turned up, his nose hung down,
And both ends met together.

A Third Folio edition of Shakespeare's works was printed, re-edited by Philip Chetwinde. This included plays previously excluded, namely: *A Yorkshire Tragedy* (first printed in 1608 by R.B. for Thomas Pavier), *Pericles* (first printed in 1609 by Henry Gosson), *Sir John Oldcastle* (first printed in 1600 by William Jaggard for Thomas Pavier), *The London Prodigal* (first printed in 1605 printed by T.C. for Nathaniel Butter), *Thomas Lord Cromwell* (first printed in 1602 by William Jones and sold at the signe of the Gunne neere Holburne conduict), *The Puritan Widdow of Watling-streete* (first printed in 1607 by G. Eld), and *The Lamentable Tragedy of Locrine* (first printed in 1595 by Thomas Creede). Later editors in the eighteenth century removed these additions and reverted to the original canon.

Charles II owned his own bound collection of Shakespeare's plays. Volume One included *The Merry Devil of Edmonton* (first printed in 1608), *Fair Em* (the love story of William the Conqueror), and *Mucedorus* (the old story of a prince disguising himself as a shepherd to court a beautiful woman). Scholars have disputed authorship of these scripts ever since.

1666

2–5 September: The Mermaid Tavern was destroyed in the Great Fire of London. The fire started in a baker's shop in the appropriately named Pudding Lane. The Lord Mayor of London was summoned when it began. Thinking the blaze was of little consequence, he departed saying, 'a woman might piss it out.'

Shakespeare's Blackfriars tenement was reduced to ashes in the Great Fire. The rights of anything remaining on its site was bequeathed

343

by Lady Elizabeth Barnard, Shakespeare's sole lineal survivor, to Edward Bagley, 'citizen of London', who she had made her executor and residuary legatee, who proved her will on 4 March 1669. However, this is contentious because in the *Dictionary of National Biography*, it states that the property was sold.

Edward Nash declined to purchase New Place. it was bought by Sir Edward Walker, who was at one time Secretary of War to Charles I. Halliwell-Phillipps states it was sold by the 'surviving trustee'. Thus, the property Shakespeare had put together became dispersed shortly after his family became extinct, and New Place came full circle back to the heirs of the Cloptons, from whom it had been purchased. It is therefore clear that the whole period covered by Shakespeare's life and that of his descendants was 105 years, i.e., from 1564 to 1669, and 'that no lineal descendants can survive'.

1668

John Dryden (1631–1700) and William Davenant adapted *The Tempest* into an opera.

7 April: William Davenant died aged sixty-two. He had been born at The Crown Inn at Oxford, where Shakespeare frequently stayed on his journeys to and from Stratford. His eldest son, Charles Davenant (possibly Shakespeare's grandson), became Tory MP for St Ives.

1670

17 February: Elizabeth, Lady Barnard, died aged sixty-one. Elizabeth, (formerly Elizabeth Nash, née Elizabeth Hall) was

the poet's granddaughter and last direct descendant. When her mother, Susanna, died, Elizabeth inherited all the Shakespeare property in Stratford together with the mementoes that had been handed down. She married for a second time in 1661, to Sir John Barnard, MP for Huntingdon and soon afterwards they moved from Stratford to Abington.

📖 The family home of John and Lady Barnard is now Abington Park Museum, in the environs of Northampton.

📖 The Henley Street lease held by Lewis and Alicia Hiccox reverted at last to the Hart family. The sons and grandsons of Joan Hart had taken up trades such as tailoring, plumbing and eventually chair-making (John Hart 1753–1800). (See the year 1806 below.)

📖 1686

17 December: William Cartwright died aged about eighty. He was an actor who, after the Restoration, had played many character parts in the re-opening of the theatres. His father had also been an actor, William Cartwright senior (1598–1636). From him the son inherited artworks that formed the basis of his own collection. At his death he had accumulated 239 portraits, together with drawings, books and manuscripts. He bequeathed the whole lot to Dulwich College. The portraits included Mary, Queen of Scots, and a self-portrait of Richard Burbage that still hangs on the West Wall of the Dulwich Picture Gallery (near to and founded by Dulwich College).

📖 1693

A visitor to Stratford-upon-Avon was reported as saying, 'The clerk who showed me this church is above eighty years old and recalls how the young Shakespeare went to London and there was received into the playhouse as a serviture', i.e. a subordinate performing menial duties. (quoted from J.O. Halliwell-Phillips, *Outlines of the life of Shakespeare*, vol. 2, 1883, page 288)

As a historian, James Halliwell-Phillipps (1820–89) cannot always be trusted. He stole ancient manuscripts from Trinity College, Cambridge and a 1603 quarto of *Hamlet* from his prospective father-in-law, Thomas Phillipps (whose surname James Halliwell added to his own). He had a habit of cutting up seventeenth-century books and pasting parts he liked into scrapbooks. Altogether he destroyed up to 1,000 ancient volumes of books and plays.

1697

Pursuant of a Parliamentary Statute, the London Stock Exchange limited the number of participating Jews to twelve.

1701

Shylock was still being played for comedy. The leading 'low comedian' of the day, Dublin-born Thomas Doggett (1670–1721) played Shylock in a major London revival of *The Merchant of Venice*. A plaque outside St John's Church in Eltham High Street where he is buried, has the inscription that Doggett 'died a pauper'.

1709

The first attempt at a biography of William Shakespeare was a forty-page effort by Nicholas Rowe, the dramatist who was appointed Poet Laureate in 1715.

1721

John Warburton (1682–1759) was the Herald of Somerset, an antiquary, and an indefatigable collector of many rarities in print and in manuscript. He was not noted for his abstemiousness, and after a rather heavy day, he visited his own kitchen one evening in search of a 'libation of alcoholic nature'. Whether or not he found the intoxicating substance is lost to history, as is the pile of fifty-five rare Elizabethan and Jacobean plays that he left piled up on the kitchen table. Some months later, when he remembered where he had mislaid them, he went back to the kitchen to retrieve them. His cook, the impressively named Betsy Baker, had 'unluckily burnd or put them under pye bottoms', assuming her master had kindly left the paper there for that purpose. He rescued three priceless manuscripts. The rest had gone up in smoke, including at least three by William Shakespeare: *Duke Humphrey, Henry I*, plus another previously unknown play, the name of which he could not remember.

1727

Lewis Theobald (1688–1744), the scholar who cleared up Alexander Pope's mishmash to establish fair texts of Shakespeare's works, produced a play called *Double Falsehood* or *The Distrest Lovers* which he claimed was based on the adaptation of Don Quixote entitled *The History of Cardenio*, by Shakespeare and John Fletcher. It was first acted at the Theatre Royal, Drury Lane on 13 December. Shakespeare's original manuscript remains lost.

In the early twenty-first century, scientists at the University of Texas, Austin, subjected Lewis Theobald's work to sophisticated analysis and concluded that the various linguistic tropes point the finger to it being truly based on a Shakespearian original.

🕱 1740

The Palladian-style architect, William Kent, designed a statue of William Shakespeare to stand in Poets' Corner, Westminster Abbey. Executed by Peter Scheemakers, Shakespeare poses elegantly with cloak swirling, leaning on his elbow, his legs crossed. His left hand is indicating a scroll on which are some of Prospero's lines in Latin: 'The cloud capt Tow'rs, The Gorgeous Palaces, The Solemn Temples, The Great Globe itself, Yea all which it Inherit, Shall Dissolve; And like the baseless Fabrick of a Vision, Leave not a wreck behind.' The inscription above the statue translates as: 'William Shakespeare 124 years after death by public esteem'. The carved heads on the pedestal are believed to be of Elizabeth I, Henry V and Richard III.

🕱 1741

14 February: Charles Macklin (1699–1797) a noted Irish playwright and actor, presented a characterisation of Shylock at Drury Lane that astounded the audience. He dispensed with the usual red fright wig and wore instead a red skullcap. Rather than being portrayed as a buffoon, Macklin acted him realistically, underscoring his malice and revengefulness. In other words he created a not very funny monster, but this approach proved popular with audiences for the rest of the century. In 1814, attitudes to Shylock were to change again.

🕱 1746

9 September: Tuesday. Beginning at 6.00 p.m. in the Town Hall of Stratford-upon-Avon, John Ward's touring company presented

Othello to raise funds to restore the Shakespeare monument in Holy Trinity Church. This was the first Shakespearian play to be presented in Stratford for over a hundred years. John Ward was the grandfather of Sarah Siddons. The production raised £17.

1752

Subsequent to Charles II's royal patents that allowed drama to be performed at only Drury Lane and Covent Garden Opera House, a new act was passed permitting local magistrates to license theatres all over the city at their own discretion. There was as usual a proviso. The locally licensed entertainments had to be classified as musical plays or 'burlettas'. This resulted in theatrical travesties. For example, performances of *Othello* were accompanied by a piano playing a single note at frequent intervals to qualify as a burletta within the meaning of the act. (A burletta is a musical term denoting a brief Italian opera.)

1757

The *Jesuit Testamenta* (by Cardinal Borromeo) and signed by John Shakespeare, dated 1581, was found hidden in the loft of the Henley Street house in Stratford. Written on a standardised form attesting to Shakespeare's obedience to 'the Catholicke, Romaine and Apostolicke Church' it was probably provided to him by the underground priest Edmund Campion, who was canonised in 1970.

1759

Vicar Francis Gastrell of Frodsham, who had taken possession of New Place in Stratford, grew so tired of sightseers constantly flocking to see where Shakespeare had lived, that he tore down the house.

In London, the first signs of doubt regarding the authorship of Shakespeare appeared in a farce called *High Life Below Stairs* (by David Garrick) in which a Miss Kitty asks, 'Who wrote Shakespeare?' A Duke replies, 'Ben Jonson.' Lady Bab intercedes saying, 'Oh, no. Shakespeare was written by Mr Finis, for I saw his name at the end of the book.' This turned out to be a bad joke that started a bad ball rolling.

1769

David Garrick led the way, with Dr Arne and Boswell, in strong support for a Shakespearian revival in Stratford-upon-Avon when he produced the bicentenary commemoration of the birth of Shakespeare – albeit five years behind schedule. Thomas Arne (1710–78) provided the musical settings. This gave a kick-start to the Stratford tourist industry.

Herbert Lawrence promulgated the theory that Shakespeare was not the author of the works attributed to him because he lacked the background and culture capable of producing these plays. In his short book, *The Life and Adventures of Common Sense: An Historical Allegory*, Lawrence, as narrator, portrays Shakespeare as a thief who stole a commonplace book containing 'an infinite variety of Modes and Forms to express all the different sentiments of the human mind' from his father, 'Wit' and his half-brother, 'Humour'. He also stole a magical glass created by 'Genius', which allowed him to 'penetrate into the deep recesses of the Soul of Man'.

1775

Sarah Siddons, sister of the actor John Kemble, was the first woman to play *Hamlet*.

1780

John Jordan, a Stratford householder, produced the last will and testament of John Shakespeare, William's father. He put together collections of papers pertaining to Shakespeare under two titles. 1) *Original Collections on Shakespeare and Stratford-upon-Avon* and 2) *Original Memoirs and Historical Accounts of the Families of Shakespeare and Hart*. The will of John Shakespeare proved to be a forgery. The other papers can only be regarded with suspicion. Nonetheless, the gnawed cuticles of countless academics testify to the fact that there may be grains of truth amongst Jordan's jottings.

1786

In 1786, Catherine the Great of Russia translated *The Merry Wives of Windsor*, giving it the title of *What It Is to Have Linen and Buck-Baskets*. Having replaced Peter the Great's Winter Palace in St Petersburg with her own new Hermitage Theatre, she staged her adaptation there: the first Russian play to admit Shakespeare's influence. Catherine also translated *Timon of Athens*.

1790

The monument to Shakespeare in the Holy Trinity Church chancel in Stratford is known to have been painted white in 1790, and only returned to a more natural colour scheme in the nineteenth century.

1796

A book was produced by Samuel Ireland called *Miscellaneous Papers and Legal Instruments under the Hand and Seal of William Shakespeare*, including the tragedy of 'King Lear' and a small fragment of 'Hamlet' from *the original MSS in the possession of Samuel Ireland.* The Irelands (father Samuel and son William Henry) also claimed to have come into the possession of a hitherto unknown Shakespeare play called *Vortigern*, which was produced by Kemble at the Drury Lane Theatre on 2 April. After much investigation, it was proved that all the discoveries by Samuel Ireland were scams, forged by his son William, and the latter published his *Confessions* in 1805. William Henry Ireland had mastered Shakespeare's handwriting style from studying the extant and genuine signatures. He added notes and marginalia in many sixteenth-century books in the same feigned style. When these came into unsuspecting hands, they caused confusion amongst academics. It is assumed that his father was unaware of this trickery, and was indeed the 'chief victim'.

1797–1810

Between 1797 and 1810, the works of Shakespeare were translated into German (August W. Schelegal with Ludig Tiekin, *Shakespeares DramatischeWerke*). These were so skillfully done that they have become masterpieces in their own right.

1800

It was claimed at the beginning of the nineteenth century that a number of new plays by Shakespeare had been discovered. Included among these fresh gems were the following titles:

Locrine

Thomas Lord Cromwell

Schlegal

The Puritan

Arden of Faversham

Edmund Ironside

Sir Thomas More

Thomas of Woodstock

A Knack to Know a Knave

Vortigern and Rowena

1804

The mural scripture stories whitewashed by John Shakespeare in 1564 were uncovered and revealed a partial semblance of their religious significance in Holy Trinity Church, Stratford.

1806

The descendants of Shakespeare's sister Joan finally sold Henley Street. The incumbent, a chairmaker, recalled that William Shakespeare Hart was in financial difficulties. The £210 he received for the sale of the property wiped away his debts. W.S. Hart married Hannah Potter and had six children. There are no lineal descendants of Shakespeare himself but people descending from Joan are alive today. The most likely surnames are either Hart or Ashley, some of whom now live in New Zealand and others in America.

1807

The first edition of the Bowdlers' *The Family Shakspeare* (*sic*) was published, containing twenty-four plays cutting out anything considered to be racy. The word 'Heavens!' was substituted for 'God'. Lady Macbeth's line 'Out, damned spot' was replaced by 'Out, crimson spot.'

Thomas Bowdler (1754–1825) put his name to his sister Henrietta's work. The latter's intention was to make Shakespeare's texts more appropriate for the sensitivities of nineteenth-century women and children. She stated that: 'My great objects in this undertaking are to remove from the writings of Shakspeare, some defects which diminish their value…' Hence, we have the word 'bowdlerise' meaning 'emasculate' or 'textual expurgation'.

1814

26 January: When Edmund Kean played Shylock with a black beard and a black wig he caused a theatrical sensation. Kean's motivation was to discover the human tragedy within the man. It was considered a dramatic departure from the standard presentation of the Jewish character. Up to this opening night, Drury Lane had sustained 135 evenings of consecutive losses. The management realised that *The Merchant of Venice* was a make or break production. The twenty-seven-year old Kean barely reached the end of his first scene before the sparse audience of fifty gave a burst of applause. This interpretation of Shylock was the first to evoke sympathy as opposed to hilarity or loathing. Coleridge described Kean's acting as 'reading Shakespeare by flashes of lightning'. Whether or not this was praise or criticism, it was evidently sensational enough to save the theatre.

1818

March: A signet ring with the initials W.S. was found in ground next to Holy Trinity Church in Stratford-upon-Avon. Although there was no absolute proof that this was a lost ring belonging to Shakespeare, the Romantic poet John Keats drew himself up to his full height of five feet and demanded an impression of it.

1820

The Irish scholar Edmond Malone was responsible for a famous edition of Shakespeare's plays. He gave this account of Shakespeare's entry into the theatre world: 'There is a stage tradition that his first office in the theatre was that of Call-boy or prompter's attendant; whose employment it is to give the performers notice to be ready to enter.' (From Chambers, *William Shakespeare: A Study of Facts and Problems*, vol. 2, page 296.) Malone was responsible for exposing William Ireland as a forger of Shakespearian documents, so his word carries significant weight; however, the allegation is controversial.

1835

John Payne Collier went about forging historical documents relating to Shakespeare in a wholesale way. He wrote *Collier's History of English Dramatic Poetry* in 1831, *Collier's New Facts Regarding the Life of Shakespeare* in 1835, and *Collier's Life of Shakespeare* in 1858, et cetera. These books contain spurious information that at the time was believed. Consequently, some of Collier's inventions have come down to us in the form of tradition and rumour. In fact, they have no foundation whatsoever.

1836

3 October: The first public demonstration of 'limelight' (an early form of stage lighting) was given outdoors over Herne Bay Pier in Kent. It accompanied an act by the magician Ching Lau Lauro. Sir Goldsworthy Gurney (1793–1875) developed the oxy-hydrogen blowpipe that produced intense white light. In a small laboratory in Cornwall, he improved upon his idea and invented what was known as the 'Bude light', created by a flaming jet of oxygen and hydrogen

gas directed onto a cylinder of calcium carbonate (quicklime). Theatres adapted this invention and lighting devices were placed into spotlights, called limes. With the use of mirrors and prisms, light beams were projected onto the stage. The stream of light was intense and could be manoeuvred to illuminate any chosen performer. Hence, the word 'limelight' came into theatrical use. In 1852, Gurney fitted Bude lights into the House of Commons. Three of his lights replaced 280 candles and lasted for sixty years until they were replaced by electricity.

1837

Limelight was first used for indoor stage illumination in the Covent Garden Theatre and soon spread to theatres throughout the world. Such theatre lighting was in universal use until the development of arc-lamps in the 1880s.

1848

December: Shakespeare's birthplace was purchased for the nation. Charles Dickens produced *The Merry Wives of Windsor* to commemorate the occasion, playing Justice Shallow himself.

1851

William Lassell established the practice of naming planets' satellites after Shakespeare's characters although Titania and Oberon had been named as far back as 1787. Ariel, Miranda, Puck, Cordelia, Ophelia, Bianca, Cressida, Desdemona, Juliet, Portia, Rosalind, Belinda, Caliban, Sycorax (Caliban's mother), Prospero, Setebos, Stephano, Trinculo, Cordelia, Cupid (from a sonnet), Perdita, Mab, Francisco (a lord in The Tempest), Margaret (a maid in Much Ado About Nothing),

Stetobos (worshipped by Sycorax in The Tempest) and Ferdinand (son of Alonso in The Tempest) are included among the moons and heavenly bodies named since.

This year marked the first recorded performance of the Folio text of *Timon of Athens* at Sadler's Wells, London by Samuel Phelps and Company.

1856

The 'Chandos' portrait of Shakespeare is 22 inches high and 18 inches wide. It is named after the Dukes of Chandos, who formerly owned the painting. It was discovered at an auction by Christie's in 1848 and purchased for 355 guineas by the Earl of Ellesmere, who donated it to the National Portrait Gallery in 1856 as its founding work. Following the death of the lawyer, Robert Keck, in 1719, it found its way into the possession of John Nichol, whose daughter, Margaret married James Brydges, third Duke of Chandos. (See the year 1625.)

By the year 1900, the National Portrait Gallery had been offered at least sixty more portraits purporting to be of William Shakespeare. However, few of them achieved even dubious provenance. Portraits probably did exist in Shakespeare's lifetime because of a reference in an anonymous Cambridge university play of 1601 called *Return from Parnassus* in which there is this line: 'Oh, sweet Master Shakespeare! I'll have his picture in my study at the court.'

Henry Irving, still calling himself Johnnie Brodribb when he started his career as an eighteen-year-old actor with Samuel Phelps at £2.00 per week, visited a theatrical costumiers in Long Acre and bought wigs, buckles, lace, rings, costume jewellery and three swords. This was because actors had to supply their own properties and accoutrements. Without them, there was no chance of playing the larger parts. As late as the 1960s, Equity's Esher Standard contract had a clause to ensure the actor supplied his own clothes for modern parts (evening dress, modern suit and a sports jacket and flannels). Ladies had to provide their own clothes appropriately.

1857

William Henry Smith suggested that Francis Bacon was the most likely person to have written the works of Shakespeare. Cryptograms were all the rage at the time. These are puzzles that consist of encrypted text. In 1887 Ignatius Donelly produced *The Great Cryptogram*, which claimed to show that Bacon had disguised his authorship by concealing pointers to his identity by means of cryptograms in the plays. Sir Edwin Durning-Lawrence supported this view. There remain some Baconians to this day. The argument has spread its net wider and other names have entered the fray as being the real authors of the works of Shakespeare. At least eighty more candidates have been proposed: the seventeenth Earl of Oxford, Christopher Marlowe, and the sixth Earl of Derby being in the top bracket.

Delia Bacon (1811–59) promoted the theory that Shakespeare's plays had been written by a group of men including Sir Francis Bacon, Sir Walter Raleigh and Edmund Spenser. Born in Ohio, Delia became a schoolteacher. In 1832 she beat Edgar Allan Poe in a short story competition. She never explained why someone of Sir Francis Bacon's stature would bother to write plays for the 'penny market' under a pseudonym. Her unorthodox views eventually earned her enduring contempt. She died in Connecticut, allegedly out of her mind. However, she started a trend that led to a spate of suggestions for alternative sixteenth-century scribes seeking anonymity including: the Earl of Oxford, Sir Edward Dyer, the fifth Earl of Rutland, the sixth Earl of Derby and the Countess of Pembroke. It seems that many academic snobs rate someone of noble birth more highly than the son of a glover.

1864

23 April to 4 May: The Shakespeare tercentenary festival was held at Stratford and organised by the local brewer, Edward Flower, using the grounds of his house, 'The Hill', as the venue.

To celebrate the three hundredth anniversary of Shakespeare's birth, John Quincy Adams Ward dedicated a Shakespearian statue at the southern end of Central Park, New York. This area became known as 'Literary Walk' when, ten years later, representations of other literary figures were added, including Fitz-Green Halleck, Sir Walter Scott and Robert Burns.

1872

23 May: The American sculptor, John Quincy Adams Ward, unveiled a full-size statue of Shakespeare on Literary Walk, Central Park, New York. There has been a Shakespeare Festival held in the park every year since 1962.

1874

A copy of the Scheemaker statue standing in Westminster Abbey was sculpted by Giovanni Fontana and unveiled in Leicester Square Gardens, London. It stands on a pedestal at the centre of a fountain surrounded by dolphins. Shakespeare holds a scroll on which is written a quotation from *Twelfth Night*: 'There is no darkness but ignorance' (Act 4, Sc. 2).

1875

Edward Flower had founded Flower's Brewery in Stratford-on-Avon as far back as 1831, and he used a version of the Droeshout engraving of William Shakespeare as the logo on the bottles and barrels. Edward Flower served four terms as Mayor of Stratford. In 1875, Edward's oldest son, Charles Flower, donated the building site for a new theatre. His radical suggestion was that it should have a permanent subsidised ensemble company of actors.

By the end of the nineteenth century, Flower's Brewery had become Stratford's largest employer.

1879

Thanks to Flower's brewery, the first theatre to be built in honour of Shakespeare opened in Stratford-upon-Avon. Most of this building was destroyed by fire in 1926, but it was rebuilt and re-opened in 1932.

1888

The sculptor Lord Ronald Sutherland-Leveson-Gower, youngest son of the second Duke of Sutherland, presented a memorial to Stratford where it stands in Bancroft Gardens. Shakespeare is seated and flanked by Lady Macbeth, Prince Hal, Hamlet, Henry V and Falstaff, representing Philosophy, Tragedy, History and Comedy. This is known as the Gower Memorial.

1896

Henry Irving, the theatrical hero of his age adapted *Cymbeline* into what had become known as 'an acting version' of the play. These adaptations removed great passages of verse to accommodate the particular attributes of the star actors. George Bernard Shaw loathed it. He wrote:

> In a true republic of art, Sir Henry Irving would ere this have expiated his acting versions on the scaffold. He does not merely cut plays; he disembowels them. In *Cymbeline* he has quite surpassed himself by extirpating the antiphonal third verse of the famous dirge. A man who would do that would do anything – cut the coda out of the first movement of Beethoven's Ninth Symphony, or shorten one of Velázquez's Philips into a kitkat to make it fit over his drawing room mantelpiece.
>
> (A kitkat – properly, kit-cat – is a portrait of a specific size, like those of the members of the Kit-Cat Club founded at the end of the seventeenth century.)

1897

William Poel (1852–1934) made a maquette of the Globe playhouse scaled 1:24, hoping for a full-scale reconstruction to arise but this did not materialise.

1899

20 September: The first film of a Shakespeare play was shown. *King John* was produced by the Biograph Company. It starred Herbert Beerbohm Tree to coincide with his stage production

at Her Majesty's Theatre in the Haymarket. Most of the movie is lost but it is thought to have been about fifteen minutes in duration.

Scena Secunda

Twentieth Century

1900

Henry V ran for fifty-four performances on Broadway, starring Richard Mansfield, making it the longest-running production of the play in Broadway history.

1902

The London Shakespeare League aspired to found a Shakespeare National Theatre to coincide with the impending 1916 tercentenary of Shakespeare's death. George Bernard Shaw's opinion of Shakespeare was not high, but for the campaign even he wrote a short play called *The Dark Lady of the Sonnets*. The venture foundered due to the First World War. In Stratford, the modern Shakespeare Memorial Theatre opened on the bard's birthday in 1932. The National Theatre in London followed in 1976 after years of preparation at The Old Vic.

1906

The Grafton portrait, as it is now known, is in the possession of the John Rylands University Library, Manchester. It was discovered in Darlington, dated 1588 when Shakespeare was twenty-four. The sitter appears to be about the same age and bears a striking resemblance to a younger version of the Martin Droeshout engraving. Underneath the painting was a much earlier religious picture. It was allegedly an heirloom of the Dukes of Grafton, whose country-seat is less than 150 miles south of Abington, where Shakespeare's granddaughter died. The dukedom was created in 1675 for one of Charles II's many illegitimate sons.

1910–11

1 September–8 April 1911: *Henry VIII* ran for 254 consecutive performances at His Majesty's Theatre. Herbert Beerbohm Tree's spectacular productions of Shakespeare plays overturned the prevailing notion that presenting Shakespeare was not financially viable.

1911

Herbert Beerbohm Tree produced *A Midsummer Night's Dream* at His Majesty's Theatre with live rabbits in the show. A junior member of the ensemble was Nellie Carter, an actress who became a tutor at the Royal Academy of Dramatic Art and whose classes your chronicler attended.

1916

A 1603 painting known as 'The Chess Players', attributed to Karel van Mander (1548–1606) was claimed by Sir Sidney Lee and Dr Paul

Wislicensus to be of Ben Jonson and Shakespeare playing chess. In recent years this view has gained ground following the research of Jeffrey Netto.

1912

Edwin Lutyens (1869–1944) built a temporary full-size Globe playhouse for the Earl's Court Exhibition called 'Shakespeare's England'.

1920

The aptly named John Thomas Looney (1870–1944) published his theory that Edward de Vere, seventeenth Earl of Oxford (1550–1604) was the true author of Shakespeare's plays. The book was called *Shakespeare Identified*. Looney's theories were purely circumstantial and yet, surprisingly, he acquired a volume of support for his theories, notably from Sigmund Freud, who convinced himself that Edward de Vere's career and personal experience could be mapped onto the action of the plays. Freud's position was influential. He re-charged the 'alternative authorship' theories that persist to this day.

1924

John Barrymore, the American film idol, came to the Haymarket Theatre in London to give his *Hamlet*. This was not received with universal acclaim. George Bernard Shaw wrote the following letter to Barrymore:

> Shakespeare, with all his shortcomings, was a very great
> playwright, and the actor who undertakes to improve his plays

undertakes thereby to excel to an extraordinary degree in two professions, in both of which the highest success is rare. Shakespeare, himself, though by no means a modest man, did not pretend to be able to play as well as write it. He was content to do a recitation in the dark as the Ghost. But you have ventured not only to act Hamlet but to discard about a third of Shakespeare's script, and substitute stuff of your own, and that too, without the help of dialogue.

1925

At Stratford-upon-Avon, the first ever 'modern dress' interpretation of *Hamlet* was presented by Barry Jackson (1879–1962). Years later, after he was knighted, Sir Barry gave your chronicler his first job.

1926

6 March: In Stratford-upon-Avon, the Shakespeare Memorial Theatre, created by Benson and Charles Flower, was burnt to the ground. The fire started after lunchtime and continued until late evening. George Bernard Shaw wrote to the devastated chairman, Archibald Flower: 'Congratulations. It will be a tremendous advantage to have a proper modern building. There are a number of other theatres I should like to see burned down.'

23 April: *William Shakespeare's Birthday Night Celebration* was presented at the Old Vic Theatre (Royal Victorian Hall) in London with Robert Atkins, Baliol Holloway, Ernest Milton, Sir Ben Greet, Dame Margaret Rutherford, Esmond Knight, Ion Swinley, Frank Vosper, Wilfrid Walter, Marie Ney, Lady Benson, Horace Sequeira,

Beatrice Wilson, Dame Edith Evans, and Constance Willis in the cast. Andrew Leigh was director.

1928

The Shakespeare Memorial Theatre at Stratford was the first important public building in Britain to be designed by a female architect. After the Shakespeare Memorial Theatre was destroyed by fire, Elisabeth Whitworth Scott (1898–1972) won an international competition to rebuild the theatre. Scott's selection and her decision to employ, where possible, women architects to assist her on the Stratford design, was instrumental in opening up the profession to women.

January: George Bernard Shaw commented that Whitworth Scott's design was the only one that showed any theatre sense. Her modernist plans for an Art Deco structure came under fire from many directions but construction continued on the new building for four years.

1929

23 April: *Shakespeare's Birthday Festival* was presented at the Old Vic Theatre with Robert Atkins, Ben Greet, Ernest Milton, Frank Vosper, Russell Thorndike, Eric Portman, Ion Swinley, Esmé Church, Beatrice Wilson, Horace Sequeira, John Laurie, Barbara Everest, Marie Ney, Hay Petrie, Joan Cross, and Adele Dixon in the cast. Andrew Leigh was director. Ninette de Valois was choreographer.

1930

23 April: *Shakespeare's Birthday Festival* took place at the Old Vic Theatre. It was presented with Robert Atkins, John Gielgud, Harcourt Williams, Edith Evans, Donald Wolfit, Adele Dixon, Martita Hunt, Esmé Church, Beatrice Wilson, Andrew Leigh, Margaret Webster, Gyles Isham, Barbara Everest, Winifred Oughton, Constance Willis, Brember Wills, Dorothy Massingham, Baliol Holloway, John Laurie, and John Garside in the cast. Harcourt Williams was director.

1932

23 April: Stratford's Memorial Theatre, designed by Elizabeth Whitworth Scott, opened triumphantly on Shakespeare's birthday.

1934

A full-scale reconstruction of the Globe playhouse was built by Thomas Wood Stevens at the Chicago World Fair. This was followed swiftly by similar projects in San Diego, Cleveland, Dallas and elsewhere across the world.

1939–45

Stratford continued production during the Second World War under the direction of Dulwich-born Robert Atkins (1886–1972). Atkins was succeeded by Sir Barry Jackson in 1945. After 1948, Anthony Quayle and Michael Benthall were appointed.

Robert Atkins's language was notoriously fruity. Somewhat peeved because he had never been asked to read the lesson in Stratford's Holy Trinity Church to celebrate Shakespeare's birthday, he confronted one of the Flower's brewery directors and was overheard to ask, 'Since I have been running this theatre for five years, can you give me one cogent fucking reason why I can't read the fucking lesson?'

In Regent's Park Open Air Theatre during a production of *A Midsummer Night's Dream* one of the ladies playing a fairy sat in the wings cross-legged with a script on her knee. Robert Atkins happened to pass by and commented, 'It's no good looking up your entrance, dear. You've missed it.'

1954

The Flower's company that had been sponsor of the Stratford Theatre for many years was acquired in 1954 by J.W. Green and the name was slightly changed to 'Flower's Breweries'. In 1961 the brewery fell under the mighty arm of the Whitbread Brewery, which brought operations to a close within six years. Thereafter, Whitbread's Cheltenham brewery took over production of the Flower's brands and the personal touch was lost forever.

1959

As a student at the Royal Academy of Dramatic Art, the maverick actor/director Ken Campbell was a term or two below your chronicler. Ken was given to making outrageous statements that struck such resounding chords they sometimes became legend. For instance, he declared it was a long-established tradition that if an actor forgot his lines in a Shakespearian play, he would indicate to fellow performers on stage that he had dried by using the word 'nub', then ad-lib a few flamboyant words and end his gaff with the words 'Milford Haven'. He claimed that Donald Wolfit, the last great actor-manager, nubbed along these lines: 'List, I sense a nubbing in far glens, where minnows swoop the pikey deep which is unpiked less pikey be, cross-bolted in their crispy muffs and choose the trammelled way . . . Oh freeze my soul in fitful sleep lest wind-filled sprites bequim the air and take us singly or in threes in mad agog or lumpsome nub, aghast to Milford Haven.' The author has heard many an actor lose his way and listened in admiration to thespian reflexology when, usually, iambic pentameters are easy to compile on the hoof. However, he has never heard 'Milford Haven' as a cue for help. Sir John Gielgud claimed that there were long chunks of Shakespeare that had no meaning for him but he had perfected the art of making up similar passages in a poetic vein so that few punters spotted the difference.

1961

The Shakespeare Memorial Theatre Company was renamed the Royal Shakespeare Company – the RSC.

1964

23 April: BBC Wales transmitted a programme on TV called *Twilight at the Globe* to celebrate the quatercentenary of Shakespeare's birth. The company consisted of William Abney, Bruce Montague, Christopher Godwin, Peter Penry-Jones, Gillian Bowen, Charmian Eyre, with Richard Valentine on guitar and the bass-baritone singer Bryan Johnson. The actors performed in an anthology of Shakespeare's works. It was produced and directed by David J. Thomas and Warren Jenkins.

1974

The Royal Shakespeare Company in Stratford acquired a theatre space in Southern Lane for experimental work. This 'corrugated hut' was given the name of 'The Other Place' – a phrase from *Hamlet*. This intimate theatre survived for fifteen years as a 'brief, shining moment in the long history of the RSC'.

1980

June: The Royal Shakespeare Company opened an acclaimed adaptation of *Nicholas Nickleby*. Other adaptations of Charles Dickens novels were being considered. Ken Campbell, then the current enfant terrible, suggested the theatre should be renamed the Royal Dickens Company.

Ralph Richardson was quoted as saying that if Francis Bacon were proved to be the writer of the plays attributed to Shakespeare then the Royal Shakespeare Company should restage *Hamlet* and consider changing its name to the Danish Bacon Company.

1986

Laurence Olivier wrote a book called *On Acting* in which he wrote of *King Lear*: 'When you've the strength for it, you're too young. When you've the age, you're too old. It's a bugger, isn't it?'

By the 1990s The Other Place had transmuted into The Courtyard Theatre but in the year 2015 there are plans to bring back The Other Place as part of a new theatre complex in Stratford-upon-Avon.

🕱 1993

Kenneth Branagh directed a film version of *Much Ado About Nothing*. The budget was $8,000,000. The box office returns were $60,000,000, making it one of the most successful Shakespearian adaptations of all time.

🕱 1996

July: A 400-year-old debt was paid off. The Mayor of Stratford-upon-Avon, Councillor Charles Bates, collected £21 from Councillor Derick Smithers, Mayor of Marlborough in Wiltshire. The debt had been incurred in 1599 by a wool-dealer, John Walford. He failed to make the payment of £21 for twenty-one tods of wool (588 pounds weight) that had been sold to him by John Shakespeare, who sued Walford for the outstanding sum, presumably to establish himself as a debtor should Walford declare bankruptcy. The people of Marlborough paid £21 to Stratford Council as a token of honour. No interest was added. Councillor Bates said, 'Maybe if this debt had been settled on time, John Shakespeare would not have been thrown out of the council as he was.'

🕱 1997

Sam Wanamaker's conception of a replica Globe playhouse constructed on its original site was finally realised on the South Bank of the Thames in London. Unfortunately, Sam did not live to see it. He died on 18 December 1993.

Scena Tertia

Twenty-First Century

1989–2010

Archeologists rediscovered the sites of the original Rose and Globe playhouses. Three-quarters of the Bankside Rose playhouse was revealed.

2001

The *South African Journal of Science* published their research following analysis of various clay smoking-pipes discovered in the garden of Shakespeare's Henley Steet house. The results showed that cannabis residue was traced in the pipes. Professor Stanley Wells expressed dubiety, saying, 'I think it's trying to suggest that Shakespeare was not a great genius, but somebody who produced his writings under an artificial influence. There are about eight million cannabis takers in this country at the present time. Are they producing anything comparable to Shakespeare's sonnets? I ask myself. I doubt it.'

2004–5

On being told that hitherto classical actor Ian McKellen was to appear in *Aladdin*, Tom Baker, who had played Doctor Who, remarked, 'I'm not surprised. I saw Ian's *Hamlet* and I thought I detected a Widow Twankey hiding in there somewhere.'

2008

During excavations for an extension of the London underground railway system, the original foundations of The Theatre playhouse were found. Examination continues at the time of writing but only a small segment of the north-east corner has come to light.

2015

The University of Witwatersrand made a fresh study of the 400-year-old smoking pipes found in Shakespeare's garden in 2001. Using a scientific technique known as gas chromatography, this confirmed the earlier findings that cannabis had been used in the pipes. The new study does not claim that Shakespeare smoked dope. The active ingredients of the cannabis plant differ from those of the tobacco plant. However, according to the *BMJ* (formerly the *British Medical Journal*), of the 4,000 chemicals produced by each plant, most of them are identical.

In Stratford the RSC currently performs in the Courtyard Theatre, opened in July 2006. As a working prototype for the new auditorium of the Royal Shakespeare Theatre it has a thrust stage and stacked tiered seating on three sides for 1,000 people. Other venues available for productions are:

1. 'The Royal Shakespeare Theatre: a large proscenium arch theatre
2. The Swan Theatre: an indoor version of an Elizabethan theatre (temporarily closed)
3. The Other Place: a small black box theatre (temporarily closed)

During the winter months, Stratford-upon-Avon's Civic Hall on Rother Street provides the RSC with a temporary theatre.

The most performed plays at Stratford over the last 135 years are: *Hamlet*, *Twelfth Night*, *As You Like It*, *The Taming of the Shrew*, *A Midsummer Night's Dream*, *Much Ado About Nothing*, *The Merchant of Venice*, *Macbeth*, *The Merry Wives of Windsor*, and *Romeo and Juliet*.

In the Manuscript Collection of the British Library is a handwritten manuscript of a play called *Edmund Ironside*. Some scholars assert this is written in Shakespeare's own hand and that it borrows from a legal text entitled *Archaionomia* (1568 – a treatise on Anglo-Saxon law) by William Lambarde, a copy of which has been found with, allegedly, Shakespeare's signature. A note in the margin by an unknown hand reads, 'Mr Wm. Shakespeare lived at No. 1, Little Crown Street, Westminster.' This is impossible to verify but if there is any truth here, it must refer to a time in the 1580s. The book is in the Folger Library and the debate remains unresolved.

The 1997 replica of William Shakespeare's theatre, The Globe, is making over forty of its period plays available for DVD rental or to download. The artistic director in 2015 (Dominic Dromgoole) declared that his aim was to 'astonish as many people as possible... We are delighted to be the first theatre with its own dedicated video-on-demand platform.'

It is estimated that 3,000 plays were staged during Shakespeare's lifetime, of which no more than 250 survive, including the thirty-eight by William Shakespeare.

William Shakespeare is an anagram of 'I am a weakish speller'. As if to prove it, he varied the spelling of his own name: Shakespe; Shakspe; Shakspere and Shakespear. In fact, he never spelt it 'Shakespeare'.

The moons of Uranus were originally named in 1852 after magical spirits from English literature. The International Astronomy Union subsequently developed the convention to name all further moons of Uranus (of which there are twenty-seven) after characters in Shakespeare's plays.

Among the eighty languages into which Shakespeare's works have been translated, the most obscure must be the artificial language of *Star Trek*'s: Klingon.

Hamlet and *Much Ado About Nothing* have both been translated as part of the Klingon Shakespeare Restoration Project.

Soon after the Second World War, two scholars – Alan Keen and Roger Lubbock – came across a copy of Hall's *Chronicles* that were heavily annotated. Shakespeare used the *Chronicles* as one of his sources for the history plays. This newly discovered volume was once in Thomas Hoghton's library. A graphologist claims there is a strong possibility that the annotations are in Shakespeare's hand. Ivor Brown in *How Shakespeare Spent the Day* regrets that there is no way this can be proved.

When the Polish musician, André Tchaikowsky (born Robert Andrzej Krauthammer, 1935–82), died of colon cancer he left his body to medical research, and donated his skull to the Royal Shakespeare Company, hoping that it would be displayed as the skull of Yorick in productions of Hamlet. Sometimes it was used as a prop during rehearsals but nobody felt comfortable handling a real skull in performance until 2008, when David Tennant, as Hamlet, used it at the Courtyard Theatre, Stratford-upon-Avon.

Later, the skull made an appearance in a television adaptation on BBC 2. Director Gregory Doran said, 'Andre Tchaikowsky's skull was a very important part of our production of *Hamlet*, and despite all the hype about him, he meant a great deal to the company.'

In 2015 on 2 February, *The Times* reported that Geoffrey Caveney, whose research was published in the academic journal *Notes and Queries*, claimed to have discovered the real identity of Mr WH to whom the first edition of the Sonnets was dedicated in 1609. Mr William Holme was also a publisher who had died in 1607. He happened to be the late associate of Mr Thorpe, who actually published the poems. Professor Stanley Wells, currently our leading authority on Shakespeare, described the new theory as 'better than any other suggestions so far.'

Scena Quarta

Some Dissatisfied Customers

'I have tried lately to read Shakespeare, and found it so intolerably dull that it nauseated me.' (Charles Darwin, 1809–82, from his *Autobiography*.)

'We can say of Shakespeare, that never has a man turned so little knowledge to such great account.' (T.S. Eliot, 1888–1965. From his *The Classics and the Man of Letters*.)

'Shakespeare never had six lines together without a fault. Perhaps you may find seven, but this does not refute my general assertion.' (Samuel Johnson, 1709–84, From Boswell's *Life of Johnson*, vol. 2.)

'With the single exception of Homer, there is no eminent writer, not even Sir Walter Scott, whom I can despise so entirely as I despise Shakespeare when I measure my mind against his... It would positively be a relief to me to dig him up and throw stones at him.' (George

Bernard Shaw, 1856–1950. From his *Dramatic Opinions and Essays*, vol.. 2).

'One of the greatest geniuses that ever existed, Shakespeare, undoubtedly wanted taste.' (Horace Walpole, 1717–97. From his letter to Sir Christopher Wren, dated 9 August 1764.)

'New Place, the house where Shakespeare died, was pulled down in the middle of the eighteenth century. For one museum the less let us be duly thankful.' ... 'Legends are a stupid man's excuse for his want of understanding. They are not evidence. Setting aside the legends, the lies, the surmises and the imputations, several uninteresting things are certainly known about him.' (John Masefield 1878–1967. From *William Shakespeare*, William & Norgate series.)

Scena Quinta

Philosophy in Poetry

🕱 Does Shakespeare's written philosophy reflect his true beliefs? Here are a few examples.

🕱 'I would there were no age between ten and three and twenty, or that youth would sleep out the rest; for there is nothing in the between but getting wenches with child, wronging the ancientry, stealing, fighting.' (*The Winter's Tale*. Act 3 Sc 3)

🕱 'And so, from hour to hour, we ripe and ripe: and then, from hour to hour, we rot and rot. And thereby hangs a tale.' (*As You Like It*. Act 2 Sc 7)

🕱 'All the world's a stage, and all the men and women merely players. They have their exits and their entrances. And one man in his time plays many parts. His acts being seven ages.' (*As You Like It*. Act 2 Sc 7)

'Life's but a walking shadow, a poor player, that struts and frets his hour upon the stage, and then is heard no more. It is a tale told by an idiot; signifying nothing.' (*Macbeth*. Act 5 Sc 5)

'Most friendship is feigning. Most loving mere folly.' (*As You Like It*. Act 2 Sc 7)

'He that wants money, means, and content, is without three good friends.' (*As You Like It*. Act 3 Sc 2)

'I do desire we may be better strangers.' (*As You Like It*. Act 3 Sc 2)

'The truest poetry is the most feigning.' (*As You Like It*. Act 3 Sc 3)

'Men have died from time to time and worms have eaten them, but not for love.' (*As You Like It*. Act 4 Sc 1)

Fear no more the heat o' the sun
Nor the furious winter's rages;
Thou thy worldly task hast done
Home art gone, and ta'en thy wages.
Golden lads and girls all must,
As chimney-sweepers, come to dust.

(A reference to dandelions in *Cymbeline*. Act 4 Sc 2: When in full bloom dandelions were called 'golden lads' – when turned to seed they were called 'chimney-sweeps'.)

382

'To be honest, as this world goes, is to be one man pick'd out of ten thousand.' (*Hamlet*. Act 2 Sc 2)

'Is it not strange that desire should so many years outlive performance?' (*Henry IV* Pt 2. Act 2 Sc 4)

'Men of few words are the best men.' (*Henry V*. Act 3 Sc 2)

'Cowards die many times before their deaths. The valiant never taste of death but once.' (*Julius Caesar*. Act 2 Sc 2)

'Life is as tedious as a twice-told tale; vexing the dull ear of a drowsy man.' (*King John*. Act 3 Sc 4)

'When we are born, we cry that we are come to this great stage of fools.' (*King Lear*. Act 4 Sc 6)

'But love is blind, and lovers cannot see the pretty follies that themselves commit.' (*The Merchant of Venice*. Act 2 Sc 6)

'How far that little candle throws his beams: so shines a good deed in a naughty world.' (*The Merchant of Venice*. Act 5 Sc 1)

'Oh, what a world of vile, ill-favoured faults looks handsome in three hundred pounds a year!' (*The Merry Wives of Windsor*. Act 3 Sc 4)

'Love looks not with the eyes but with the mind, and therefore is wing'd Cupid painted blind.' (*A Midsummer Night's Dream*. Act 1 Sc 1)

'How beauteous mankind is! Oh, brave new world that has such people in't!' (*The Tempest*. Act 5 Sc 1)

'Though I am not naturally honest, I am so sometimes by chance.' (*The Winter's Tale*. Act 4 Sc 3)

'Though authority be a stubborn bear, yet he is oft led by the nose with gold.' (*The Winter's Tale*. Act 4 Sc 3)

'A woman's face, with Nature's own hand painted,
Hast thou, the Master Mistress of my passion.' (Sonnet 20)

'Like as the waves make towards the pebbled shore
So do our minutes hasten to their end.' (Sonnet 60)

'For sweetest things turn sourest by their deeds;
Lilies that fester smell far worse than weeds.' (Sonnet 94)

Scena Sexta

Coined Words Cost Nothing

📖 Thanks to Shakespeare we have the following words:

📖 **Accused** (as a noun). *Richard II*, Act 1, Scene 1

'Face to face / And frowning brow to brow / The accuser and the accused freely speak.' – Richard

📖 **Addiction**: *Othello*, Act II, Scene II

'It is Othello's pleasure, our noble and valiant general, that, upon certain tidings now arrived, importing the mere perdition of the Turkish fleet, every man put himself into triumph; some to dance, some to make bonfires, each man to what sport and revels his addiction leads him.' – Herald

📖 **Aerial** (as an adjective) *Othello*, Act 2, Scene 1

'Even till we make the main and th'aerial blue / An indistinct regard.'
– Montano

Amazement *King John*, Act 5, Scene 1
'wild amazement hurries up and down / The little number of your doubtful friends.' – Bastard

Arch-villain: *Timon of Athens*, Act V, Scene I
'You that way and you this, but two in company; each man apart, all single and alone, yet an arch-villain keeps him company.' – Timon

Assassination: *Macbeth*, Act I, Scene VII
'If it were done when 'tis done, then 'twere well it were done quickly: if the assassination could trammel up the consequence, and catch with his surcease success.' – Macbeth

Be-all-and-end-all: *Macbeth*, Act 1 Scene 7
'that but this blow / Might be the be-all-and the end-all' – Macbeth

Bedazzled: *The Taming of the Shrew*, Act IV, Scene V
'Pardon, old father, my mistaking eyes, that have been so bedazzled with the sun that everything I look on seemeth green.' – Katherina

Belongings: *Measure for Measure*, Act I, Scene I
'Thyself and thy belongings are not thine own so proper as to waste thyself upon thy virtues, they on thee.' – Duke Vincentio

Bloodstained: *Titus Andronicus*, Act 2, Scene 3
'this unhallowed and bloodstained hole.' – Martius

Blushing: *Venus and Adonis*, lines 589-590
'a sudden pale / Like lawn being spread upon the blushing rose.'

Cold-blooded: *King John*, Act III, Scene I
'Thou cold-blooded slave, hast thou not spoke like thunder on my side, been sworn my soldier, bidding me depend upon thy stars, thy fortune and thy strength, and dost thou now fall over to my fores?' – Constance

Consanguineous: *Twelfth Night*, Act 2, Scene 3
'Am I not consanguineous? Am I not of her blood?' – Sir Toby

Dishearten: *Henry V*, Act IV, Scene I
'Therefore when he sees reason of fears, as we do, his fears, out of doubt, be of the same relish as ours are: yet, in reason, no man should possess him with any appearance of fear, lest he, by showing it, should dishearten his army.' – King Henry V

Disgraceful: *Henry VI, Part 1*, Act 1, Scene 1
'I'll fight for France / Away with these disgraceful wailing robes.' – Bedford

Dwindle: *Henry IV, Part 1*, Act 3, Scene 3
'Do I not dwindle?' – Falstaff

Embrace: *Henry VI, Part 1*, Act 3, Scene 3
'Forgive me, country, and sweet countrymen / And lords, accept this hearty kind embrace.' – Burgundy

Eventful: *As You Like It*, Act II, Scene VII

'Last scene of all, that ends this strange eventful history, is second childishness and mere oblivion, sans teeth, sans eyes, sans taste, sans everything.' – Jaques

Excitement: *Hamlet*, Act 4, Scene 4

'A father killed, a mother stain'd / Excitements of my reason and my blood.' – Hamlet

Eyeball: *The Tempest*, Act I, Scene II

'Go make thyself like a nymph o' the sea: be subject to no sight but thine and mine, invisible to every eyeball else.' – Prospero

Fashionable: *Troilus and Cressida*, Act III, Scene III

'For time is like a fashionable host that slightly shakes his parting guest by the hand, and with his arms outstretch'd, as he would fly, grasps in the comer: welcome ever smiles, and farewell goes out sighing.' – Ulysses

Frugal: *The Merry Wives of Windsor*, Act 2, Scene 1

'Why, he hath not been thrice in my company! What should I say to him? I was then frugal of my mirth.' – Mistress Page

Full-grown (adjective): *Pericles*, Act 4

'And in this kind hath our Cleon / One daughter and a wench full-grown.' – Chorus

Generous (adjective): *Love's Labour's Lost*, Act 5, Scene 1

'Most generous sir.' – Holofernes

Green-eyed: *The Merchant of Venice*, Act 3, Scene 2
'Doubtful thoughts, and rash-embrac'd despair / And shuddering fear, and green-eyed jealousy.' – Portia

Half-blooded/hot-blooded: *King Lear*, Act V, Scene III/ Act III, Scene III
'Half-blooded fellow, yes.' – Albany
'Why, the hot-blooded France, that dowerless took our youngest born, I could as well be brought to knee his throne, and, squire-like; pension beg to keep base life afoot.' – Lear

High-pitched: *Lucrece*, Lines 40–1
'Disdainfully did sting / His high-pitch'd thoughts.'

Hobnob (verb): *Twelfth Night*, Act 3, Scene 4
'Hob, nob is his word; give't or take't' – Sir Toby

Importantly (adverb): *Cymbeline*, Act 4, Scene 4
'have both their eyes / and ears so cloy'd importantly as now.' – Arviragus

Inaudible: *All's Well That Ends Well*, Act V, Scene III
'Let's take the instant by the forward top; for we are old, and on our quick'st decrees the inaudible and noiseless foot of Time steals ere we can effect them.' – King of France

Instinctively: *The Tempest*, Act 1, Scene 2
'the very rats / Instinctively have quit it.' – Prospero

Judgement Day: *Henry VI, Part 1*, Act I, Scene 1
'Unto the French the dreadful Judgement Day / So dreadful will not be as was his sight.' – Winchester

Ladybird: *Romeo and Juliet*, Act I, Scene III
'What, lamb! What, ladybird! God forbid! Where's this girl? What, Juliet!' – Nurse

Lacklustre: *As You Like It*, Act 2, Scene 7
'And looking on it, with lack-lustre eye / Says very wisely, 'It is ten o'clock'.' – Jacques

Lonely: *Coriolanus*, Act 4, Scene 1
'I go alone like to a lonely dragon' – Coriolanus

Love letter (noun): *The Two Gentlemen of Verona*, Act 3, Scene 1
'Why didst not tell me sooner? 'Pox of your love-letters.' – Speed

Madcap: *The Taming of the Shrew*, Act 2, Scene 1
'To wish me wed top one half lunatic / A madcap ruffian and a swearing Jack.' – Kate

Manager: *A Midsummer Night's Dream*, Act V, Scene I
'Where is our usual manager of mirth? What revels are in hand? Is there no play to ease the anguish of a torturing hour?' – King Theseus

Misgiving: *Julius Caesar*, Act 3, Scene 1
'Yet I have a mind / That fears him much, and my misgiving still / Falls shrewdly to the purpose.' – Cassius

Multitudinous: *Macbeth*, Act II, Scene II

'No, this my hand will rather the multitudinous seas in incarnadine, making the green one red.' – Macbeth

Negotiate: *Much Ado About Nothing*, Act 2, Scene 1

'All hearts in love use their own tongues / Let every eye negotiate for itself.' – Claudio

New-fangled: *Love's Labour's Lost*, Act I, Scene I

'At Christmas I no more desire a rose than wish a snow in May's new-fangled mirth.' – Biron

Nervy: *Coriolanus*, Act 2, Scene 1

'Death, that dark spirit, in's nervy arm doth lie / Which being advanced, declines, and then men die.' – Volumnia

Obscene: *Love's Labour's Lost*, Act 1, Scene 1

'I did encounter that obscene and most preposterous event.' – King

Obsequiously: *Richard III*, Act 1, Scene 2

'Obsequiously lament / Th'untimely fall of virtuous Lancaster.' – Anne

Pageantry: *Pericles, Prince of Tyre*, Act V, Scene II

'This, my last boon, give me, for such kindness must relieve me, that you aptly will suppose what pageantry, what feats, what shows, what minstrelsy, and pretty din, the regent made in Mytilene to greet the king.' – Gower

Pander: *Hamlet*, Act 3, Scene 4
'Reason panders will.' – Hamlet

Premeditated: *Henry VI, Part 1*, Act 3, Scene 1
'Com'st thou with deep premeditated lines?' – Winchester

Quarrelsome: *The Taming of the Shrew*, Act 1, Scene 2
'My master is grown quarrelsome.' – Grumio

Questioning: *As You Like It*, Act 5, Scene 4
'Feed yourselves with questioning. / The reason may diminish / How thus we met, and these things finish.' – Hymen

Rancorous: *The Comedy of Errors*, Act 1, Scene 1
'The enmity and discord which of late / Sprung from the rancorous outrage of your Duke / To merchants, our well-dealing countrymen.' – Duke

Rant: *Hamlet*, Act 5, Scene 1
'I'll rant as well as thou' – Hamlet

Sanctimonious: *Measure for Measure*, Act 1, Scene 2
'Thou conclud'st like the sanctimonious pirate, that went to sea with the Ten Commandments, but scrap'd one under the table.' – Lucio

Savagery: *King John*, Act 4, Scene 3
'this is the bloodiest shame / The wildest savagery, the vilest stroke / That ever wall-eyed wrath or staring rage / Presented to the tears of soft remorse.' – Salisbury

Scuffle: *Antony and Cleopatra*, Act I, Scene I
'His captain's heart, which in the scuffles of great fights hath burst the buckles on his breast, reneges all temper, and is become the bellows and the fan to cool a gipsy's lust.' – Philo

Swagger: *Henry V*, Act II, Scene IV / *A Midsummer Night's Dream*, Act III, Scene I
'An't please your majesty, a rascal that swaggered with me last night.' – Williams
'What hempen home-spuns have we swaggering here, so near the cradle of the fairy queen?' – Puck

Tardiness: *King Lear*, Act 1, Scene 1
'Is it no more but this? – a tardiness of nature, / Which often leaves the history unspoken / That it intends to do?' – France

Tranquil: *Othello*, Act 3, Scene 3
'Farewell the tranquil mind, farewell content!' – Othello

Uncomfortable: *Romeo and Juliet*, Act IV, Scene V
'Despised, distressed, hated, martyr'd, kill'd! Uncomfortable time, why camest thou now to murder, murder our solemnity?' – Capulet

Undress: *The Taming of the Shrew*, Induction, Scene 2
'Madam, undress you and come now to bed?' – Sly

Varied: *Titus Andronicus*, Act 3, Scene 1
'torn from forth that pretty hallow cage / Where, like a sweet melodious bird it sung.' – Marcus

Well-behaved: *The Merry Wives of Windsor*, Act 2, Scene 1
'gave such orderly and well-behaved reproof to all uncomeliness.' –
Mistress Ford.

Yelping: *King Henry VI, Part 1*, Act 4, Scene 2
'A little herd of England's timorous deer / Mazed with a yelping
kennel of French curs.' – Talbot

Yoking: *Venus and Adonis*, lines 591-592
'She trembles at his tale / And on his neck her yoking arms she
throws.'

Zany: *Love's Labour's Lost*, Act 5, Scene 2
'Some carry-tale, some please-man, some slightly zany.' – Berowne

In addition to the above, Shakespeare coined more than seventeen
hundred other words including: puking, obscene, skim-milk,
wormhole, eyesore, as well as 'to gossip'.

Scena Septima

Plays Chronology

Academics beg to differ when trying to place the plays in the sequence that Shakespeare wrote them. The following list is as good a guess as any. Fresh documentary evidence may contradict it.

1592, 3 March: *Henry VI, Part 1*. First printed 1594

1592–3: *Henry VI, Part 2*. First printed 1594

1592–3: *Henry VI, Part 3*. First printed 1623

1594, 24 January: *Titus Andronicus*. First printed 1594

1594, 28 December: *The Comedy of Errors*. First printed 1623

1593–4: *Taming of the Shrew*. First printed 1623

1594–5: *Two Gentlemen of Verona*. First printed 1623

1594–5: *Love's Labour's Lost*. First printed 1598

1594–5: *Romeo and Juliet*. First printed 1597

1595–7: *Richard II*. Registered 29 August 1597

1595–6: *A Midsummer Night's Dream*. First printed 1600

1596–7: *The Merchant of Venice*. First printed 1600

1597–8: *Henry IV, Part 1*. First printed 1598

1597–8: *Henry IV, Part 2*. First printed 1600

1598: *King John*. Notice by Meres 7 September 1598

1598–9: *Much Ado About Nothing*. First printed 1600

1598–9: *Henry V*. First printed 1600

1599–1600: *As You Like It*. First printed 1623

1600–1: *Julius Caesar*. First printed 1623

1601, 7 February: *Richard II*. First printed 1597

1600–1: *Richard III*. First printed 1597

1600–1: *Hamlet*. First printed 1603

1600–1: *The Merry Wives of Windsor*. First printed 1602

1602, 2 February: *Twelfth Night*. First printed 1623

1602–3: *All's Well That Ends Well*. First printed 1623

1604, 7 February: *Troilus and Cressida*. First printed 1609

1604, 26 December: *Measure for Measure*. First printed 1623

1604–5: *Othello*. First printed 1622

1606, 26 December: *King Lear*. First printed 1608

1605–6: *Macbeth*. First printed 1623

1606–7: *Antony and Cleopatra*. First printed 1623

1607–8: *Coriolanus*. First printed 1623

1607–8: *Timon of Athens*. First printed 1623

1608–9: *Pericles*. First printed 1609

1611, 1 November: *The Tempest*. First printed 1623

1611–12: *Cymbeline*. First printed 1623

1611–12: *The Winter's Tale*. First printed 1623

1612–13: *Henry VIII*. First printed 1623

1612–13: *The Two Noble Kinsmen*. First printed 1634

CURTAIN

Scena Octavia
Epilogue

The late Keith Waterhouse created the concept of the 'useless information' books. In the early sixties he wrote a series of light-hearted paperbacks with titles such as *How to Avoid Matrimony*, *How to Avoid Income Tax* and so on. His writing partner was a larger-than-life Hungarian actor called Guy Deghy and it was through Guy that I first met Keith when they co-wrote *Café Royal: Ninety Years of Bohemia*.

The Useless Information Society was founded by accident. It started out as an occasional liquid lunch after which the survivors told amusing stories that could be of use to neither man nor beast. Whoever told the most pointless story had his share of the bill paid by the others – if they were still compos mentis. The Beagle (undertaken in full regalia by the musician, Kenny Clayton) allowed just fifty-nine seconds per story before banging his halberd on the floor and moving on to the next speaker.

Members included John Blake, Joseph Connelly, Richard Littlejohn, The Rev. Michael Seed, Struan Rodger, Michael Dillon, and the late Noel Botham. Others, like myself, were invited on an ad hoc basis.

It was an era when pubs shut at 14.55 and did not reopen until 18.30. As with speakeasies during American Prohibition, officious restrictions created a need for afternoon oases. All over London, watering holes sprang up in their hundreds. Opposite the little Arts Theatre off Leicester Square, in the bowels of the earth hewn out of an abandoned tube train siding, was The Kismet Club. Parched alcoholics, oblivious to the sticky, threadbare carpet, descended to an unventilated, ill-lit, seventh circle of Hell. The story goes that on his first visit, Lionel Bart asked, 'What's that awful smell?' His companion, Frank Norman, rejoined, 'That, mate, is the sweet smell of failure.'

This did not deter thirsty thespians from wasting many an afternoon there.

Another famous watering hole was The Colony Room Club in Dean Street, known to its habitués as 'Muriel's' after the lady who ran it. Muriel Belcher used language that 'Can only be described as Fruity', with an emphasis on the C and the F. Artists who frequented this seedy upstairs bar included Francis Bacon, Lucian Freud, Dan Farson, Malcolm Arnold, Sandy Fawkes, Tony Hancock, John le Mesurier, John Hurt and last, but by no means least, Keith Waterhouse.

Keith rose at dawn and worked at home like a beaver on his ancient typewriter. When computers were in their infancy, he was given one and within a fortnight he had thrown it out of the window. As soon as the sun rose above the yardarm, he broke off for a spot of lunch. Frequently, this continued until midnight. I hazily remember sharing the odd egg and bacon with Keith in the early hours at some all-night café off Old Compton Street.

Sometimes I supplied him with useless information but, as they say in the movies, my input often went uncredited. The only useless information I remember delivering at the end of an evening was with reference to the origin of the theatrical phrase 'the ghost walks' on the last night of a season. The phrase means that the manager is on his way round the dressing rooms with the actors' wages. Legend has it that Shakespeare, as a part owner of the Jacobean theatres, had the responsibility to apportion the share of receipts. Traditionally, Shakespeare played the Ghost in *Hamlet*, and after completing his scene at the beginning of the play, he had plenty of time to do his rounds as paymaster. Far-fetched, you may well think. However, this story has been recounted by actors for hundreds of years, making it typically useless information.

I hope you found some equally useless stuff in this book.

B.M. 2016

Scena Nona

Appendixes

APPENDIX A
LONDON'S GATES

The Great Wall built to surround the Roman city of London was constructed from 85,000 tons of hard grey limestone, called ragstone, shipped from the appropriately named town of Maidstone in Kent. The wall was 6 feet wide, 20 feet high and two miles long, enclosing an area of 330 acres.

The Romans used London as a garrison, placing gates in strategic places along their wall. Originally, there were seven gates:

1) Aldgate – leading to Colchester and Essex.
2) Bishopsgate – leading to Shoreditch, Spitalfields and thence towards Cambridge.

3) Moorgate – it was probably used an emergency exit in Roman times and only became a gate in 1415. This led to a marshy area in the north called Moorfields.

4) Cripplegate – leading to the village of Islington.

5) Aldersgate – leading north-westwards towards St Bartholomew's Abbey and Smithfield Market.

6) Newgate – leading towards Oxford.

7) Ludgate – leading towards Bath and the South West.

By order of William the Conqueror, the Tower of London was constructed on the south-east corner of the wall. Work started in 1078 and was completed in 1100. This added a pedestrian-only gate, known as Tower Gate.

Newgate acquired a fearsome reputation because of the public executions that took place there. Today, the Old Bailey stands on the site of Newgate prison.

During Shakespeare's lifetime, three of the gates were rebuilt in Renaissance style: Ludgate (1586), Aldgate (1608) and Aldersgate (1610).

APPENDIX B
SUPERSTITIONS

Today, actors say off-handedly, 'See you on the green' or 'I'll be in the green room' without giving the expressions much thought. In Shakespeare's day, actors changed behind the stage in the 'tiring house', which was usually painted green. When performing tragedy in particular, English playhouses borrowed the French idea and covered the stage with a green cloth. This may have been a throwback to the days when touring plays and masques 'played on the village green'. Peter Quince, in *A Midsummer Night's Dream* (Act 3, Scene 1) mentions this to his troupe when rehearsing in the woods. 'Pat, pat; and here's a marvellous convenient place for our rehearsal. This green plot shall be our stage, this hawthorn-brake our tiring-house; and we will do it in action as we will do it before the duke.'

Max Wall, the comedian, declared that 'green' was short for 'greengage' which rhymed with stage, and in Cockney rhyming slang, one would say, 'see you on the green' meaning stage. A good theory, but the expression was in use centuries before rhyming slang came into common usage.

There are two explanations for saying 'break a leg' before a performance instead of 'good luck', which is considered to bring bad luck on to the production. First, at the end of a play in olden days, if the response was enthusiastic, the leading players would kneel on one knee and pray for the safety of the sovereign. So, by saying 'break a leg' the hope was that the show would receive a favourable reception.

Secondly, in the nineteenth century, in the early days of vaudeville, acts vied for the manager's permission to get on stage and do their performance. If they succeeded, they had to make an entrance from the side of the stage through 'the legs' – the vertical border curtains – and this meant that they then had their chance to wow the audience.

As for why *Macbeth* is considered an unlucky word to say in a theatre, legend has it that when the play was first staged, the actor playing Lady Macbeth was taken ill and Shakespeare himself had to take over. There is a lot of fighting in the play and over time many actors were injured. The witches' curses were too close to the truth for comfort and King James I, who studied witchcraft and wrote a book on the subject, developed an aversion to the play *Macbeth*.

Live flowers are never used on stage because if, during a performance, they droop and drop their petals, it is feared the play will die with them.

Real peacock feathers are not allowed on stage, as the feathers are alleged to possess the 'evil eye' the malevolence of which can put a curse on the show.

Whistling in the theatre is considered bad luck. Until the twentieth century, stage-hands were often recruited from the docklands. Seamen were good at hauling ropes and responded to instructions by means of whistled commands. (Theatrical rigging was developed from sailing-ship rigging.) Therefore extraneous whistling sometimes caused scenery to fly in or out at the wrong time. Actors caught whistling in dressing rooms pay a penalty, usually to leave the room, spin round three times, spit and wipe their lips before knocking on the dressing room door to be allowed back inside.

There is a convention in theatres to have one light above the stage permanently illuminating downstage centre. This is known as 'the ghost light', presumably in order to ward away ghosts. However, it has been known to come in useful when, as sometimes happens, a member of the company finds him or herself accidentally locked into the theatre overnight. This is not an adventure your chronicler recommends. He still has uneasy memories of a sleepless night spent in the Grand Theatre, Blackpool, in the early 1960s.

APPENDIX C
WILLIAM SHAKESPEARE'S WILL

Vicesimo Quinto die ~~Januarii~~ Martii Anno Regni Domini nostri Jacobi nucn Regis Angliae etc decimo quarto & Scotie xlixo Annoque Domini 1616

Testamentum Willemi Shackspeare Registretur

In the name of god Amen I William Shackspeare of Stratford-upon-Avon in the countrie of Warr' gent in perfect health and memorie god by praysed doe make and Ordayne this my last will and testament in manner and forme followeing that ys to saye first I Comend my Soule into the hands of god my Creator hoping and assuredlie beleeving through the onelie merittes of Jesus Christe my Saviour to be made partaker of lyfe everlastinge And my bodye to the Earthe whereof yt ys made.

Item. I Gyve and bequeath unto my ~~sonne in Law and~~ Daughter Judyth One Hundred and fyftie pounds of lawfull English money to be paied unto her in manner and forme following That ys to saye One Hundred Poundes in discharge of her marriage porcion within one yeare after my deceas with consideracion after the Rate of twoe shillinges in the pound for soe long tyme as the same shal be unpaid unto her after my deceas & the fyftie pounds Residewe therof upon her surrendering of or gyving of such sufficient securitie as the overseers of this my will shall like of to Surrender or graunte All her estate and Right that shall discend or come unto her after my deceas or that she nowe hath of in or to one Copiehold tenemente with theappertenances lyeing & being in Stratford-upon-Avon aforesaied in the saide countie of warr' being parcell or holden of the mannor of Rowington unto my daughter Susanna Hall and her heires for ever.

Item. I gyve and bequeath unto my saied Daughter Judyth One Hundred and ffyftie Poundes more if shee or Anie issue of her bodie Lyvinge att thend of three yeares next ensueing the daie of the date of this my will during which tyme my executors to paie her consideracion from my deceas according to the Rate afore saied. And if she dye within the saied terme without issue of her bodye then my will ys and so I doe gyve and bequeath One Hundred Poundes therof to my Neece Eliabeth Hall and ffiftie Poundes to be sett fourth by my executors during the lief of my Sister Johane Harte and the use and proffitt therof cominge shal be payed to my saied Sister Jone and after her deceas the saied L li [£50] shall Remaine Amongst the childredn of my saied Sister Equallie to be devided Amongst them. But if my saied daughter Judith be lyving att the end of the saeid three yeares or anie issue of her bodye then my will ys and soe I devise and bequeath the saied Hundred and ffyftie poundes to be sett out by my executors and overseers for the best benefit of her and her issue and the stock not to be paied unto her soe long as she shalbe marryed and Covert Baron ~~by my executors and overseers~~ but my will ys that she shall have the consideracion yearelie paied unto her during her lief and after her deceas the saied stock and condieracion to bee paid to her children if she have Anie and if not to her executors or Assignes she lyving the saied terme after my deceas provided that if such husbond as she shall att the end of the saied three yeares by marryed unto or attain after doe sufficiently Assure unto her and the issue of her bodie landes answereable to the portion gyven unto her and to be adjudged soe by my executors and overseers then my will ys that the saied CL li [£150] shal be paied to such husbond as shall make such assurance to his owne use.

Item. I gyve and bequeath unto my saied sister Jone XX li [£20] and all my wearing Apprell to be paied and delivered within one yeare after my deceas. And I doe will and devise unto her the house with the appurtenances in Stratford where in she dwelleth for her naturall lief under the yearelie Rent of xiid [12 pence]

Item. I gyve and bequeath unto her three sonnes William Hart—Hart and Michaell Harte ffyve pounds A peece to be payed within one yeare after my decease ~~to be sett out for her within one yeare after my deceas by my executors with thadvise and direccons of my overseers for her best proffitt untill her marriage and then the same with the increase thereof to be paied unto her.~~

Item. I gyve and bequath unto her the said Elizabeth Hall All my Plate (except my brod silver and gilt bole) that I now have att the date of this my will.

Item. I gyve and bequeath unto the Poore of Stratford aforesaied tenn poundes; to Mr Thomas Combe my Sword; to Thomas Russell Esquier ffyve poundes and to ffrauncis collins of the Borough of Warr' in the countie of Warr' gent. thriteene poundes Sixe shillinges and Eight pence to be paied within one yeare after my deceas.

Item. I gyve and bequeath to ~~mr richard~~ Hamlett Sadler ~~Tyler thelder~~ XXVIs VIIId [26 shillings and 8 pence] to buy him A Ringe; to William Raynoldes gent XXVIs VIIId [26 shillings and 8 pence] to buy him a Ringe; to my godson William Walker XXVIs VIIId [26 shillings and 8 pence] ~~in gold~~ and to my ffellowes John Hemynges, Richard Burbage and Heny Cundell XXVIs VIIId [26 shillings and 8 pence] A peece to buy them Ringes.

Item. I Gyve Will Bequeth and Devise unto my Daughter Susanna Hall for better enabling of her to performe this my will and towardes the performans thereof All that Capitall Messuage or tenemente with thappertenaces in Stratford aforesaid called the newe plase wherein I now Dwell and two messuags or tenementes with thappurtenances scituat lyeing and being in Henley Streete within the borough of Stratford aforesaied. And all my barnes, stables, Orchardes, gardens, landes, tenementes and herediaments whatsoever scituat lyeing and being or to be had receyved, perceyved or taken within the townes and Hamletts, villages, ffieldes and groundes of Stratford-upon-Avon, Oldstratford, Bushopton and Welcombe or in anie of them in the saied countie of warr And alsoe All that Messuage or tenemente with thappurtenances wherein one John Robinson dwelleth, scituat, lyeing and being in the blackfriers in London nere the Wardrobe and all other my landes tenementes and hereditamentes whatsoever. To Have and to hold All and singular the saied premisses with their Appurtenances unto the saied Susanna Hall for and during the terme of her naturall lief and after her deceas to the first sonne of her bodie lawfullie yssueing and to the heiries Males of the bodie of the saied Second Sonne lawfullie yssyeinge and for defalt of such heires Males of the bodie of the saied third sonne lawfullie yssye ing And for defalt of such issue the same soe to be Reamine to the ffourth sonne, ffythe, sixte and seaventh sonnes of her bodie lawfullie issueing one after Another and and to the heires Males of the bodies of the saied ffourth, ffythe, Sixte and Seaventh sonnes lawfullie yssueing in such mamer as yt ys before Lymitted to be and remaine to the first, second and third Sonns of her bodie and to their heires males. And for defalt of such issue the saied premisses to be and Remaine to my sayed Neede Hall and the heires Males of her bodie Lawfully yssueing for default of… such issue to my daughter Judith and the heires of me the saied William Sahckspere for ever.

Item. I gyve unto my wief my second best bed with the furniture; Item I gyve and bequeath to my saied daughter Judith my broad silver gilt bole.

All the rest of my goodes Chattels, Leases, plate, jewles and Household stuffe whatsoever after my dettes and Legasies paied and my funerall expences discharged, I gyve devise and bequeath to my Sonne in Lawe John Hall gent and my daughter Susanna his wief whom I ordaine and make executors of this my Last will and testament. And I doe intreat and Appoint the saied Thomas Russell Esquier and ffrauncis Collins gent to be overseers herof And doe Revoke All former wills and publishe this to be my last will and testament. In witnes whereof I have hereunto put my Seale hand the Daie and Yeare first above Written.

Witness to the publishing hereof: Fra: Collyns, Juilyus Shawe, John Robinson, Hamnet Sadler, Robert Whattcott.

By me William Shakespeare

411

Probatum coram Magistro Williamo Byrde legum doctore Commissario etc xxiido [twenty-second] die mensis Junii Anno domini 1616 Juramento Jahannis Hall unius executorum etc. Cui etc de bene etc Jurati Reservata potestate etc Sussane Hall alteri executorum etc cum venerit etc petitur.

Inventarium exhibitum.

APPENDIX D
TAX CERTIFICATES FROM ST ELLEN'S PARISH

Transcript of an extract from a certificate by London tax commissioners, ated 1597 (E 179/146/354). In the references below, each line names the person, then the first monetary amount is the value of their belongings, the second amount is what they had to pay on this in tax. Thus in the example on the second line below, Shakespeare had £5 (v li) worth of goods and owed five shilling (v s).

St Ellens parishe.

Peter Dallila	l li	l s
William Shackspeare	v li	v s
Thomas Smythe gent	xxx li	xxx s
William Boyele	xxx li	xxx s

.... dyd saye and affirme that the persons hereunder named are all other dead departed and gone out of the sayd warde or their goodes so eloigned or conveyed out of the same or in suche pryvate or coverte manner kepte whereby the severall Sommes of money on them severally taxed and assessed towardes the sayde second payment of the sayde laste subsydye nether might nor coulde by anye meanes by them the sayde Petty collectors or ether of them be leveyed of them or anye of them to her majestie's use.

The usual defaulters were noted the following year.

Tax Assessment

Extract from an indenture by London tax commissioners, 1598:

St Hellens parishe

Sir John Spencer knight a commissioner   ccc li   xl li
William Reade in landes cl li   xxx li
John Scymme   iii li   viii s
Affid William Shakespeare   v li   xiii s iiii d
George Axon   iii li   viii s
Edward Jackson   iii li   viii s

...said that the people named on this list are either dead or have left this area or have taken their belongings out of the area or have secretly hidden them so that the tax collectors cannot charge them the correct amount of tax for the second payment which will be sent to Her Majesty (Queen Elizabeth).

(Fuller information is available at the National Archives in Kew, Richmond, Surrey TW9 4DU.)

APPENDIX E
SHAKESPEARE'S EXPRESSIONS

William Shakespeare coined many expressions that today we take for granted.

📖 'As mad as a March hare' (*Two Noble Kinsmen*, Act 3, Sc 5).

📖 'All that glisters is not gold' (Prince of Morocco: *The Merchant of Venice*).

📖 'Bated breath' (Shylock: *The Merchant of Venice*).

📖 'Love is blind' (Jessica: *The Merchant of Venice*).

📖 'Pound of flesh' (Shylock: *The Merchant of Venice*).

📖 'Truth will out' (Launcelot: *The Merchant of Venice*).

📖 'The world's my oyster' (Pistol: *The Merry Wives of Windsor*).

📖 'The short and the long of it' (Mistress Quickly: *The Merry Wives of Windsor*).

📖 'Come full circle' (Edmund: *King Lear*).

📖 'Foul play' (Gloucester: *King Lear*).

📖 'Knock, knock. Who's there?' (Porter: *Macbeth*).

'Be cruel to be kind' (Hamlet: *Hamlet*).

'Each dog will have its day' (Hamlet: *Hamlet*).

'In my heart of hearts' (Hamlet: *Hamlet*).

'The lady doth protest too much, methinks' (Gertrude: *Hamlet*).

'To the manner born' (Hamlet: *Hamlet*).

'Though this be madness yet there's method in it (Polonius: *Hamlet*). Over time this has been corrupted to 'There's method in his madness'.

'To be-all and end-all' (Macbeth: *Macbeth*).

'The milk of human kindness' (Lady Macbeth: *Macbeth*).

'A sorry sight' (Macbeth: *Macbeth*).

'Brave new world' (Miranda: *The Tempest*).

'Into thin air' (Prospero: *The Tempest*).

'Strange bed-fellows' (Trinculo: *The Tempest*).

'Such stuff as dreams are made on' (Prospero: *The Tempest*).

'Wild goose chase' (Mercutio: *Romeo and Juliet*).

'Green-eyed monster' (Iago: *Othello*).

'I will wear my heart upon my sleeve' (Iago: *Othello*).

'Pomp and circumstance' (Othello: *Othello*).

'Foregone conclusion' (Othello: *Othello*).

'I have not slept one wink' (Pisanio: *Cymbeline*).

'Eaten me out of house and home' (Mistress Quickly: *Henry IV*, *Part 2*).

'Heart's content' (Henry VI: *Henry VI, Part 2*).

'Seal up your lips and give no words but mum' (Hume: *Henry VI*, *Part 2*). Over time this has corrupted to 'Keep mum'.

'Send him packing' (Falstaff: *Henry IV, Part 1*).

'Run the wild-goose chase' (Mercutio: *Romeo & Juliet*).

APPENDIX F
TEA, COFFEE AND CHOCOLATE

Tea, coffee and chocolate were unknown to Shakespeare.

1650: Peter Stuyvesant brought tea to the colonists inhabiting New York, or 'New Amsterdam' as it was known then.

1652: Pasqua Rosée opened the first London coffee house, situated in St Michael's Alley, Cornhill.

1657: Thomas Garway owned a coffee house in Exchange Alley, London and introduced tea at £10 per pound.

1689: Sir Hans Sloane brought back a cocoa (cacao) tree from Jamaica, crushed the seeds, added sugar and called the result chocolate.

APPENDIX G
THE 1603 QUARTO EDITION OF *HAMLET*

In 1832, an early quarto edition of *Hamlet* was discovered. It was printed in 1603 and it radically departs from the other versions printed in 1604 and 1623. For example, here is the famous soliloquy from the 1603 edition:

> To be, or not to be, aye there's the point,
> To Die, to sleep, to dream, aye marry there it goes,
> For in that dream of death, when we awake,
> And borne before an everlasting Judge,
> From whence no passenger ever return'd,
> The undiscovered country, at whose fight
> The happy smile, and the accursed damn'd,
> But for this, the joyful hope of this,
> Who'd bear the scorn and flattery of the world,
> Scorned by the right rich, the rich cursed of the poor?
> The widow being oppressed, the orphan wrong'd,
> The taste of hunger, or a tyrant's reign,

And thousand more calamities besides,

To grunt and sweat under this weary life,

When that he may his full quietus make

With a bare bodkin, who would this endure,

But for a hope of something after death?

Which puzzles the brain, and doth confound the sense

Which makes us rather bare those evils we have

Than fly to other that we know not of.

Aye that, O this conscience makes cowards of us all,

Lady in thy orizons, be all my sins remembered.

APPENDIX H

A magazine called *Curtain Up* is occasionally printed by the Theatre Royal, Windsor. In 1966, to commemorate the 350th anniversary of William Shakespeare's death, your chronicler wrote the following mock obituary.

All Swans Are White (except the black ones)

Three hundred and fifty years ago – to the very year – the Swan if Avon died. Unfortunately, like a television performer too frequently seen, he has been over-exposed.

Saints are all very well (and definitely good), but they don't lend themselves much to variety. All *Complete Works* and no understanding of the individual play makes Will a dull boy. Go up to a man in the street and mention Shakespeare and his face falls. Shakespeare's sacrosanct. To most people this means very dead, God rest his soul.

In fact, he was regarded in his own lifetime as a sort of hotch-potch combination of Brian Rix, Charlie Clore, Ned Sherrin and John Betjeman. He was patronised by royalty nearly as much as John Counsell!

It has been said that a man only exists in the light of his achievements. Shakespeare helps to back up this idea. For apart from what he is alleged to have actually written down on paper, practically nothing is known about him. Yet not even 'the Works' are wholly his. Of thirty-seven plays extant and attributed to Shakespeare, no fewer than twenty-one of them are merely straight adaptations from plays and novels that had existed and were actually enjoying popularity before Shakespeare got his unblottable pen on them.

The only reason that scholars seem to concede that Shakespeare might have written anything original at all is because his are the only versions extant, whereas the plays from which they were more than likely plagiarised have been lost. However, it is generally acknowledged that his rewrites are a vast improvement on the originals – except by those who claim that 'William Shakespeare' was a kind of nom-de-stool-pigeon for Sir Francis Bacon (and/or the seventeenth Earl of Oxford/Sir Edward Dyer/the fifth Earl of Rutland/the sixth Earl of Derby/the Countess of Pembroke, etc. etc. . . .).

Surely the only important thing is that they were written, that they do exist, and that they are pretty damn good. It doesn't matter that little is known about Shakespeare the man (though a lot more is known about him than most of his contemporaries). It's the poet that counts.

The fact is, we have enough information to write the kind of obituary that might have appeared in the *Stratford Gazette*, had such a newspaper existed at the time. It states all we know about

Shakespeare for sure, together with all that we can credibly accept from the reams of conjecture that have been conjured up about him. Let us re-bury our dead and accept our inheritance. Poor old Shakespeare – rich old us.

Obituary Notice

SHAKESPEARE, WILLIAM. Actor, comedian, poet, dramatist, property speculator. Died on Tuesday, 23 April 1616 at the age of fity-three at his home, 'New Place', Stratford-upon-Avon, of suspected alcoholic poisoning. His father was *the* John Shakespeare – one-time Chief Alderman of the town. William, or 'Will', as he was affectionately called, left Stratford for London exactly thirty years ago. He started as an actor but had early aspirations as a poet. He slowly gained recognition with his sonnets and his epic poems, particularly *The Rape of Lucrece* and *Venus and Adonis*. He retired at the age of forty-six and came back to Stratford to concentrate on his booming property investments. He was the landlord of some tenement buildings in Blackfriars and had financial interests in a London theatre group which included both the Globe and the Blackfriars Theatres. He controlled a considerable amount of real estate in the country, including at least 150 acres of land in Stratford. He also dabbled with play-writing, which brought him some financial success. He was especially gifted in the portraiture of comedy. Unfortunately, he was prone to the actor's occupational disease. It was brought on during the night of 22 April whilst celebrating his birthday in the company of Michael Drayton and Ben Jonson – fellow writers. He leaves a wife, Agnes, from whom he has been separated for many years, and two daughters, Judith and

Suzanne. The funeral will take place on Thursday, 25 April 1616 at two of the afternoon at the Church of the Holy Trinity in Stratford-upon-Avon. Flowers gratefully accepted.

Bibliography
and Notes

BIBLIOGRAPHY

Ackroyd, Peter, *Shakespeare: The Biography*, Chatto & Windus (London, 2005)

Ackroyd, Peter, *London: The Biography*, Vintage (London, 2001)

Anonymous, *The London Prodigal*, pub. Nathanial Butter (London, 1605)

Anonymous, *The Return from Parnassus; or, the scourge of simony*, pub. John Wright (London, 1611)

Anonymous, *The Troublesome Reigne of John King of England*, pub. John Helme (London, 1611)

Aubrey, John, *Brief Lives*, ed. Richard Barber, Boydell Press (Suffolk, 2009)

Bandello, Matteo Belleforest, *Histoires Tragiques*, (trans.) François de Belleforest, 7 volumes (1566-1583)

Bate, Jonathan; Thornton, Dora, *Shakespeare Staging the World*, The British Museum Press (London, 2012)

Bate, Jonathan, *Soul of the Age*, Penguin (London, 2009)

Bevington, David, *Shakespeare's Histories*, Pearson Longman (New York, 2007)

Boswell, James, *Boswell's Life of Johnson*, vol. 2, Forgotten Books, (London, 2015)

Bowdler, Thomas (ed.), *The Family Shakespeare*, pub. J. Hatchard (London, 1807)

Bowsher, Julian, *Shakespeare's London Theatreland: Archaeology, History and Drama*, Museum of London Archaeology (London, 2012)

Brinkworth, E.R.C., *Shakespeare & the bawdy court of Stratford*, Phillimore (London, 1972)

Brown, Ivor, *How Shakespeare Spent the Day*, Bodley Head (London, 1963)

Bryson, Bill, *Shakespeare*, HarperPress (London, 2009)

Camden, William, *Remaines of a greater worke, concerning Britaine, the inhabitants thereof, their languages, names, surnames, empreses, wise speeches, poesies, and epitaphs*, pub. Simon Waterson (London, 1605)

Cervantes, Miguel de, *Don Quixote*, Penguin Classics (London, 2003)

Chambers, E. K., *William Shakespeare: A Study of Facts and Problems*, vol. 1, Forgotten Books (2012, Oxford)

Chaucer, Geoffrey, 'The Knight's Tale' in *The Canterbury Tales*, Oxford University Press (Oxford, 2011)

Cheshire Archives (for National Archives), The Aldersey Collection (deeds and estate papers, family papers and correspondence, and Bunbury parish papers, 1534–1938): http://discovery.nationalarchives.gov.uk/details/rd/c8160be7-041a-4531-bde0-110539e2be7f

Chester, Robert, *Love's Martyr; or, Rosalin's Complaint: With its supplement, 'Diverse Poeticall Essaies on the Turtle and Phoenix'*, Cambridge University Press (Cambridge, 2014)

Chute, Marchette, *Shakespeare and his Stage*, University of London Press (London, 1953)

Chute, Marchette, *Shakespeare of London*, Souvenir Press (London, 1977)

Collier, John Payne, *Collier's History of English Dramatic Poetry*, John Murray (London, 1831)

Collier, John Payne, *Collier's New Facts Regarding the Life of Shakespeare*, Rodd (London, 1835)

Cook, Judith, *Golden Age of the English Theatre*, Simon & Schuster (London, 1995)

Coryat, Thomas, *Coryat's Crudities Hastily Gobled up in Five Moneths Travells in France, Savoy, Italy, Rhetia commonly called the Grisons country, Heluetia alias Switzerland, some parts of high Germany, and the Netherlands: newly digested in the hungry aire of Odcombe in the county of Somerset, & now dispersed to the nourishment of the trauelling members of this kingdome*, pub. Thomas Coryat (London, 1611)

Crystal, David; Crystal, Ben, *The Shakespeare Miscellany*, Penguin (London, 2005)

Darwin, Charles, *The Autobiography of Charles Darwin*, Watts & Co (London, 1929)

Deghy, Guy; Waterhouse, Keith, *Café Royal: Ninety Years of Bohemia*, Hutchinson (London, 1955)

Doran, Gregory, *The Shakespeare Almanac*, Hutchinson (London, 2009)

Drayton, Michael, *England's Heroical Epistles*, pub. Nicholas Ling (London, 1597)

Dugdale, Sir William, *The Antiquities of Warwickshire illustrated; from* records, leiger-books, manuscripts, charters, evidences, tombes, and armes: beautified with maps, prospects and portraictures (London, 1656)

Eccles, Christine, The Rose Theatre, Hern (London, 1990)

Eliot, T.S., Classics and the Man of Letters, Oxford University Press (London, 1942)

Fiorentino, Giovanni, Il Pecorone, trans. W.G Waters, privately printed (Boston, 1897)

Ward, John, Diary of Reverend John Ward, H. Colburn (London, 1839)

Folger Shakespeare Library in association with George Washington University, Shakespeare Quarterly, various volumes, Johns Hopkins University Press (Baltimore, MD, 1950–)

Folio, First: Shakespeare, William, The First Folio of Shakespeare: The Norton Facsimile, ed. Charlton Hinman, W.W Norton (New York, 1996)

Fowler, Gene, Goodnight, Sweet Prince, Viking Press (New York, 1944)

Fuller, Thomas, The History of the Worthies of England, who for parts and learning have been eminent in the several counties. Together with an historical narrative of the native commodities and rarities in each county. Endeavoured by Thomas Fuller, pub. Thomas Williams (London, 1662)

Garrick, David, High Life Below Stairs (London, 1815)

Greene, Robert, A Groatsworth of Witte, bought with a million of repentance, pub. William Wright (London, 1592)

Hall, Edward, The Union of the Two Noble and Illustrious Families of Lancaster and York (London, 1548)

Halliwell-Phillips, J.O., Outlines of the life of Shakespeare, vol. 2, Longmans, Green & Co. (Brighton, 1883)

Halliwell-Phillips, J.O, *A Life of William Shakespeare*, J.R Smith (London, 1848)

Hartnoll, Phyllis (ed.), *The Oxford Companion to the Theatre*, Oxford University Press (Oxford, 1995)

Hartnoll, Phyllis, *A Concise History of the Theatre*, Thames & Hudson (London, 1978)

Harwood, Ronald, *All the World's a Stage*, Methuen (London, 1984)

Holinshed, Raphael, *The firste volume of the chronicles of England, Scotlande, and Irelande*, pub. Lucas Harrison (London, 1577)

Holinshed, Raphael, *The first and second volumes of Chronicles*, pub. John Harison, George Bishop, Rafe Newberie, Henrie Denham, Thomas Woodcocke (London, 1587)

Holland, Peter, 'Shakespeare, William (1564–1616)', *Oxford Dictionary of National Biography*, Oxford University Press (Oxford, 2004); online edn. Jan 2013 [http://www.oxforddnb.com/view/article/25200, accessed 13 Jan 2016]

Honan, Park, *Shakespeare: A life*, Oxford University Press (Oxford, 1998)

Honigmann, E.A.J., *Shakespeare: The 'Lost Years'*, Manchester University Press (Manchester, 1985)

Honigmann, E.A.J., *Shakespeare's Impact on His Contemporaries*, Macmillan (London, 1982)

Ireland, Samuel (ed.), *Miscellaneous Papers and Legal Instruments under the Hand and Seal of William Shakespeare, including the tragedy of 'King Lear' and a small fragment of 'Hamlet' from the original MSS in the possession of Samuel Ireland* (London, 1796)

Irving, Laurence, *Henry Irving: The Actor and his World*, Columbus Books (London, 1989)

Jourdain, Silvester, *A Discovery of the Barmudas, Otherwise called the Ile of Devils,* pub. Roger Barnes (London, 1610)

Keightley, Thomas (ed.), *The Complete Works of Shakespeare*, Bell & Daldy (London, 1865)

Kermode, Frank, *Shakespeare's Language*, Farrar, Straus, and Giroux (New York, 2000)

LaMar, Virginia A., *Travel & Roads in England,* The Folger Shakespeare Library (Washington D.C, 1960)

Lambarde, William (trans.), *Archaionomia, sive de priscis anglorum legibus libri* (London, 1568)

Lane, Peter, *The Theatre*, Batsford (London, 1975)

Lanier, Emilia, *Salve Deus Rex Judaeorum*, pub. Richard Bonian (London, 1611)

Lawrence, Herbert, *The Life and Adventures of Common Sense: An Historical Allegory,* pub. Montagu Lawrence (London, 1769)

Lee, Sir Sidney, *A life of William Shakespeare,* Smith, Elder, & Co. (London, 1899)

Lelyveld, Toby, *Shylock on the Stage*, Routledge & Kegan Paul (London, 1961)

Lodge, Thomas, *Rosalynde, Euphues Golden Legacie,* pub. Thomas Gubbin; John Busbie (London, 1590)

Looney, Thomas, *Shakespeare Identified*, Cecil Palmer (London, 1920)

Lyly, John, *Euphues: The Anatomy of Wit,* pub. Gabriel Cawood (London, 1578)

Lyly, John, *Euphues and His England,* pub. Gabriel Cawood (London, 1580)

MacGregor, Neil, *Shakespeare's Restless World*, Allen Lane (London, 2012)

Marriott, J.W., *The Theatre*, G.G. Harrap & Co. (London, 1931)

Marston, John, *Histriomastix*, pub. Thomas Thorpe (London, 1599)

Masefield, John, *William Shakespeare*, Williams & Norgate (London, 1925)

Meres, Francis, *Palladis Tamia, Wit's Treasury*, pub. Cuthbert Burbie (London, 1598)

Montague, Bruce, *Wedding Bells and Chimney Sweeps*, Metro (London, 2014)

Munday, Anthony, *Fidele and Fortunia,* pub. Thomas Hacket (London, 1585)

Niven, David, *The Moon's a Balloon*, Penguin (London, 1994)

North, Sir Thomas (trans.), *Plutarch's Lives of the Noble Greeks and Romans*, pub. John Wright (London, 1579)

O'Connor, Garry, *Ralph Richardson: an Actor's Life*, Coronet (Sevenoaks, 1983)

Olivier, Laurence, *Confessions of an Actor*, Orion (London, 1994)

Olivier, Laurence, *On Acting,* Weidenfield and Nicolson (London, 1986)

Painter, William, *Palace of Pleasure. Vol. 2*, pub. Nicholas England (London, 1567)

Pickering, David (ed.), *Dictionary of Theatre*, Sphere (London, 1988)

Quennell, Peter; Johnson, Hamish, *Who's Who in Shakespeare*, Routledge (London, 2013)

Robertson, Geoffrey, *The Tyrannicide Brief*, Chatto & Windus, (London, 2005)

Rowse, A.L., *William Shakespeare; A Biography*, Macmillan & Co. (London, 1963)

Rowse, A.L., *Shakespeare the Man*, Macmillan (London, 1973)

Rubinstein, Frankie, *A Dictionary of Shakespeare's Sexual Puns and their Significance*, Macmillan (London, 1984)

Schelegal, August W.; Tieckin, Ludwig, *Shakespeares Dramatische Werke*, pub. G. Reimer (Berlin, 1867)

Shaw, George Bernard, *Overruled, and The Dark Lady of the Sonnets*, Constable and Co. (London, 1921)

Shaw, George Bernard, *Dramatic Opinions and Essays,* vol. 2. Brentanos (New York, 1922)

Sidney, Philip, *Countess of Pembroke's Arcadia*, ed. Katherine Duncan-Jones, Oxford University Press (Oxford, 2008)

Stow, John, *Survey of London*, pub. John Wolfe (London, 1598)

Stubbes, Phillip, *Second part of Anatomy of Abuses*, pub. William Wright (London, 1583)

Tarlton, Richard, *Tarlton's Jests*, pub. John Budge (London, 1613)

Twain, Mark, *1601 and Is Shakespeare Dead?*, Oxford University Press (Oxford, 1996)

Webster, Margaret, *Shakespeare Without Tears*, McGraw-Hill Book Co. (New York; London, 1942)

Weldon, Sir Anthony, *Court and Character of King James I*, pub. John Wright (London, 1650)

Wells, Stanley, *Shakespeare & Co,* Allen Lane (London, 2006)

Wells, Stanley, *Shakespeare, Sex & Love*, Oxford University Press (Oxford, 2010)

Williams Hugh, *50 Things You Need to Know About British History*, Collins (London, 2008)

Wiseman, Richard, *Severall Chirurgicall Treatises*, pub. R. Royston (London, 1676)

Wood, Anthony, *Historia, et Antiquitates Universitatis Oxoniensis*, Sheldonian Theatre (Oxford, 1674)

Wood, Michael, *In Search of Shakespeare*, BBC (London, 2003)

PLAYS BY OTHER WRITERS
MENTIONED IN THE TEXT

Christopher Marlowe:

Edward the Second

Tamburlaine the Great

The Jew of Malta

Ben Jonson:

The Poetaster

Cynthia's Revels

Bartholomew Fair

The Isle of Dogs

Epicœne, or the Silent Woman

Every Man in His Humour

Every Man out of His Humour

Sejanus His Fall

John Fletcher and Francis Beaumont:

Cupid's Revenge

Philaster, or Love Lies Bleeding

Robert Greene:

Pandosto: The Triumph of Time (also later published as *Dorastus and Fawnia*)

Greene's Groatsworth of Wit

Greene's Vision, Written at the Instant of His Death

Nathan Field and Philip Massinger:
Amends for Ladies
The Fatal Dowry

Robert Armin:
Foole Upon Foole
Quips Upon Questions

Other authors:
D'Avenant, William: *Love and Honour*
——: *The Siege of Rhodes*
Davies, John: *The Scourge of Folly*
Dekker, Thomas: *Satiro-Mastix*
Henslowe, Philip, with Jonson, Ben: *Eastward Ho!*
Kyd, Thomas: *The Spanish Tragedy*
Marston, John: *What You Will*
Middleton, Thomas and Dekker, Thomas: *The Roaring Girl*
Shakespeare, William and Fletcher, John: *The History of Cardenio*
Theobald, Lewis, Shakespeare, William and Fletcher, John: *Double Falsehood, or The Distrest Lovers*

NOTES

A.L. Rowse was prone to disparage much of the work of earlier researchers. He said of E.K. Chambers: 'He was a civil servant, humanly imperceptive.' He said of Dove Wilson: 'Another "educationist" by origin, enthusiastic, rather a dear, but notoriously erratic.' On the other hand, he placed great credence on Dr Simon Forman's casebooks. Though he was a contemporary of Shakespeare,

Forman is treated warily by later researchers. He was a fortune-teller, an astrologer, a self-styled doctor, an alchemist and a dabbler in the darker arts.

Frankie Rubinstein's *Dictionary of Shakespeare's Sexual Puns and their Significance* seems to me to be somewhat over the top. I came away from this book reeling in disbelief. Surely Shakespeare could not have intended so many innocent words as double-entendres? Or was language more coded in his day?